First World War
and Army of Occupation
War Diary
France, Belgium and Germany

17 DIVISION
Headquarters, Branches and Services
Commander Royal Engineers
1 January 1915 - 1 May 1919

WO95/1990/1

The Naval & Military Press Ltd
www.nmarchive.com
Published in association with The National Archives

Published by

The Naval & Military Press Ltd

Unit 10 Ridgewood Industrial Park,

Uckfield, East Sussex,

TN22 5QE England

Tel: +44 (0) 1825 749494

www.naval-military-press.com

www.nmarchive.com

This diary has been reprinted in facsimile from the original. Any imperfections are inevitably reproduced and the quality may fall short of modern type and cartographic standards.

Contents

Document type	Place/Title	Date From	Date To
Heading	WO95/1990/1		
Heading	17th Division C.R.E. Jly 1915-May 1919		
Heading	17th Division H.Q. 17th Div. C.R.E. Vol I July To Oct 15		
War Diary	Havre	13/07/1915	15/07/1915
War Diary	Lumbres	16/07/1915	16/07/1915
War Diary	Renescure	18/07/1915	18/07/1915
War Diary	Steenvoorde	19/07/1915	24/07/1915
War Diary	Reninghelst	24/07/1915	21/10/1915
War Diary	Steenvoorde	22/10/1915	25/10/1915
War Diary	Reninghelst.	26/10/1915	31/10/1915
Heading	H.Q. 17th Div. C.R.E. Vol. 2 Nov 15		
War Diary	Reninghelst.	01/11/1915	30/11/1915
Heading	C.R.E. 17th Div. Vol. 3		
War Diary	Reninghelst	01/12/1915	31/12/1915
War Diary	Reninghelst.	01/01/1915	07/01/1915
War Diary	Salperwick	08/01/1916	31/01/1916
Heading	C.R.E. 17th Div. Vol. 5		
War Diary	Salperwick nr St Omer.	01/02/1916	06/02/1916
War Diary	Reninghelst	07/02/1916	10/03/1916
War Diary	Merris	11/03/1916	19/03/1916
War Diary	Armentieres Sheet 36	20/03/1916	31/03/1916
Heading	War Diaries 11 Div. A.E. Headquarters Period. April 1916		
War Diary	Armentieres	01/04/1916	30/04/1916
War Diary	Armentieres	01/05/1916	16/05/1916
War Diary	Tilques	17/05/1916	08/06/1916
War Diary	Allonville	09/06/1916	09/06/1916
War Diary	Morlancourt	10/06/1916	13/06/1916
War Diary	Allonville	14/06/1916	28/06/1916
War Diary	Mericourt	29/06/1916	30/06/1916
Operation(al) Order(s)	Extracts from 17th Division Operation Order No. 57 dated 28th June 1916 App 1		
War Diary	Treux	01/07/1916	01/07/1916
War Diary	Ribemont	02/07/1916	04/07/1916
War Diary	Near Meaulte	05/07/1916	12/07/1916
War Diary	Fourdrinoy	13/07/1916	13/07/1916
War Diary	Fourdrinoy Pont Remy	23/07/1916	23/07/1916
War Diary	Ribemont	24/07/1916	31/07/1916
Miscellaneous	O.C. 77th Coy R.E. App I	02/07/1916	02/07/1916
Miscellaneous	O.C. 77th Coy R.E. App. II	03/07/1916	03/07/1916
Miscellaneous	O.C. 78th Coy R.E. App. III	03/07/1916	03/07/1916
Miscellaneous	O.C. 93rd Coy R.E. App IV	04/07/1916	04/07/1916
Miscellaneous	A Form. Messages And Signals App. V		
Miscellaneous	O.C. 78th Coy. R.E. App. VI	05/07/1916	05/07/1916
Miscellaneous	O.C. 77th (Field) Coy R.E. App. VII		
Miscellaneous	A Form. Messages And Signals. App VIII		
Miscellaneous	A Form. Messages And Signals. App IX		
Miscellaneous	A Form. Messages And Signals. App X		
Miscellaneous	A Form. Messages And Signals. App XI		

Miscellaneous	A Form. Messages And Signals. App XII		
Miscellaneous	A Form. Messages And Signals. App XIII		
Miscellaneous	O.C. 77th Coy R.E. App. XIV	08/07/1916	08/07/1916
Miscellaneous	O.C. 78th Coy R.E. App. XV	08/07/1916	08/07/1916
Miscellaneous	O.C. 77th Coy R.E. App XVI	09/07/1916	09/07/1916
Miscellaneous	O.C. 78th Coy R.E. App XVII	09/07/1916	09/07/1916
Miscellaneous	A Form. Messages And Signals. App XVIII		
Miscellaneous	Handing Over Notes on Consolidation, Etc. App. XIX	10/07/1916	10/07/1916
Miscellaneous	Report On Work Of R.E. & Pioneers, 17th Division. App XX		
Miscellaneous	17th. Division G. 611 App XXI	25/07/1916	25/07/1916
Heading	17th Divisional Engineers C.R.E. 17th Divisional Engineers August 1916		
War Diary	Ribemont	01/08/1916	02/08/1916
War Diary	Bellevue Farm.	03/08/1916	16/08/1916
War Diary	Doullens	17/08/1916	21/08/1916
War Diary	Henu	22/08/1916	31/08/1916
Operation(al) Order(s)	Extract from 17th. Division Operation Order No. 70, dated 31st, July 1916 App I	31/07/1916	31/07/1916
Miscellaneous	A Form. Messages And Signals. App II		
Miscellaneous	17th Div. G. 870 App III	06/08/1916	06/08/1916
Miscellaneous	Working Parties. App. III		
Miscellaneous	17th. Division Engineers. App IV		
Miscellaneous	A Form. Messages And Signals. App V		
War Diary	Henu	01/09/1916	22/09/1916
War Diary	St. Ricquier	23/09/1916	30/09/1916
Heading	War Diaries Of C.R.E. 17 Division 77 Field To. RE 78 Field To. RE 93 Field To. RE October 1916 Vol 13		
War Diary	St Ricquier	02/10/1916	06/10/1916
War Diary	Pas	07/10/1916	22/10/1916
War Diary	Treux	23/10/1916	26/10/1916
War Diary	Citadel	27/10/1916	30/10/1916
War Diary	Bernafay Wood	31/10/1916	31/10/1916
Heading	War Diaries Of C.R.E. 17th Division. 77th Field Coy. R.E. 78th Field Coy. R.E. 93rd Field Coy. R.E. From 1/11/1916 to 30/11/16		
War Diary	Bernafay Wood	01/11/1916	14/11/1916
War Diary	Picquigny	15/11/1916	29/11/1916
Heading	War Diaries of H.Q. R.E. 17th Division. 77th Field Company, R.E. 78th Field Company, R.E. 93rd Field Company, R.E. From 1st December 1916 to 31st. December 1916. Vol 15		
War Diary	Picquigny	01/12/1916	13/12/1916
War Diary	Corbie	14/12/1916	25/12/1916
War Diary	Sheet 62 C N.W. A4d.5.2	26/12/1916	31/12/1916
Heading	War Diaries Of C.R.E. 17th Division 77th Field Company RE 78th Field Company RE 93rd Field Company RE From 1/1/1917 to 31/1/1917 Vol 16		
War Diary	A.4.d.5.2	01/01/1917	18/01/1917
War Diary	Corbie	19/01/1917	28/01/1917
War Diary	Arrow Head Copse.	29/01/1917	31/01/1917
Heading	War Diary Of CRE-17th Division 77th Field Co. RE 78th Field Co. RE 93rd Field Co. RE For February 1917 Vol 17		
War Diary	Arrow Head Copse	01/02/1917	21/02/1917
War Diary	Heilly	22/02/1917	02/03/1917

War Diary	Contay	03/03/1917	04/03/1917
War Diary	Vadencourt	05/03/1917	15/03/1917
War Diary	Willeman	16/03/1917	23/03/1917
War Diary	Le Cauroy	24/03/1917	06/04/1917
War Diary	Haut Avesnes	08/04/1917	09/04/1917
War Diary	Arras	10/04/1917	25/04/1917
War Diary	Le Cauroy.	26/04/1917	02/05/1917
War Diary	Hermaville	03/05/1917	10/05/1917
War Diary	St Nicholas	11/05/1917	31/05/1917
War Diary	Couterelle	01/06/1917	21/07/1917
War Diary	Arras	22/07/1917	24/09/1917
War Diary	Le. Cauroy	25/09/1917	30/09/1917
Miscellaneous	A Form. Messages And Signals.		
Miscellaneous	17th. Division.	25/09/1917	25/09/1917
Miscellaneous	17th. Division.	24/09/1917	24/09/1917
War Diary	Le Cauroy	01/10/1917	03/10/1917
War Diary	Proven	04/10/1917	10/10/1917
War Diary	Elverdinghe	11/10/1917	17/10/1917
War Diary	Proven	18/10/1917	20/10/1917
War Diary	Wolphus	21/10/1917	31/10/1917
War Diary	Le Cauroy	01/10/1917	03/10/1917
War Diary	Proven	04/10/1917	11/10/1917
War Diary	Elverdinghe	12/10/1917	17/10/1917
War Diary	Proven	18/10/1917	20/10/1917
War Diary	Wolphus	21/10/1917	31/10/1917
Miscellaneous	A Form. Messages And Signals.		
Operation(al) Order(s)	Operation Order No. 14. by Lieut. Colonel. C.M. Carpenter. D.S.O. R.E.	08/10/1917	08/10/1917
Operation(al) Order(s)	Operation Order No. 15. by Lieut. Colonel. C.M. Carpenter., D.S.O., R.E.	15/10/1917	15/10/1917
War Diary	Wolphus	01/11/1917	06/11/1917
War Diary	Proven	07/11/1917	07/11/1917
War Diary	Canal Bank	08/11/1917	12/11/1917
War Diary	Welsh Farm Elverdinghe	13/11/1917	30/11/1917
Operation(al) Order(s)	Operation Order No. 16. by Lieut. Colonel. C.M. Carpenter., D.S.O., R.E.	06/11/1917	06/11/1917
War Diary	Welsh Farm Elverdinghe	01/12/1917	06/12/1917
War Diary	Wolphus	07/12/1917	12/12/1917
War Diary	Eperlecques	13/12/1917	13/12/1917
War Diary	Achiet-Le-Petit.	14/12/1917	21/12/1917
War Diary	Ytres	22/12/1917	31/12/1917
Operation(al) Order(s)	Operation Order No. 17. by Lieut. Colonel. C.M. Carpenter., D.S.O., R.E.	04/12/1917	04/12/1917
Miscellaneous	77th Field Co., R.E.		
Operation(al) Order(s)	All recipients of O.O. 18		
Operation(al) Order(s)	Operation Order No. 18 by Lieut. Colonel. C.M. Carpenter., D.S.O., R.E.	19/12/1917	19/12/1917
War Diary	Ytres	01/01/1918	31/01/1918
Operation(al) Order(s)	Operation Order No. 19. by Lieut. Colonel. C.M. Carpenter., D.S.O., R.E.	01/01/1918	01/01/1918
Operation(al) Order(s)	Operation Order No. 20. by Lieut. Colonel. C.M. Carpenter., D.S.O., R.E.	05/11/1918	05/11/1918
Operation(al) Order(s)	Operation Order No 21 by Major. R.C. Lundie., D.S.O., R.E.	30/01/1918	30/01/1918
War Diary	Ytres	01/02/1918	23/02/1918
War Diary	Bertincourt	24/02/1918	28/02/1918

Heading	Headquarters, Royal Engineers, 17th Division. March 1918		
War Diary	Bertincourt	01/03/1918	24/03/1918
War Diary	Courcelette	24/03/1918	24/03/1918
War Diary	Meaulte	24/03/1918	24/03/1918
War Diary	Meaulte	25/03/1918	25/03/1918
War Diary	Henencourt	26/03/1918	26/03/1918
War Diary	Senlis	26/03/1918	26/03/1918
War Diary	Contay	27/03/1918	31/03/1918
Operation(al) Order(s)	Amendment No 1 to 17th Divisional Engineers Operation Order No 21	09/03/1918	09/03/1918
Miscellaneous	To all Recipients of C.R.E. O.O. 21 dated 7th March, 1918	07/03/1918	07/03/1918
Heading	War Diary C.R.E. 17th Division April 1918		
War Diary	Contay	01/04/1918	04/04/1918
War Diary	Flesselles	05/04/1918	10/04/1918
War Diary	Puchevillers	11/04/1918	15/04/1918
War Diary	Lealvillers	16/04/1918	30/04/1918
Operation(al) Order(s)	Operation Order No. 24. by Lieut. Colonel. C.M. Carpenter., D.S.O., R.E.	01/04/1918	01/04/1918
Operation(al) Order(s)	Operation Order No. 1. By Lieut. Colonel., F. Ferguson., R.E.	13/04/1918	13/04/1918
Miscellaneous	17th Divisional Engineers.	24/04/1918	24/04/1918
War Diary	Lealvillers	01/05/1918	08/05/1918
War Diary	Toutencourt	09/05/1918	26/05/1918
War Diary	Reincheval	27/05/1918	31/05/1918
Operation(al) Order(s)	Operation Order No. 2. By Lieut. Colonel., F.A. Ferguson., R.E. C.R.E., 17th Division.	01/05/1918	01/05/1918
Operation(al) Order(s)	Operation Order No. 3. By Lieut. Colonel., F.A. Ferguson., R.E. C.R.E., 17th Division.	06/05/1918	06/05/1918
Miscellaneous	To all recipients of C.R.E's. Operation Order No. 4	24/05/1918	24/05/1918
Operation(al) Order(s)	Operation Order No. 4. By Lieut. Colonel. F.A. Ferguson., R.E. C.R.E., 17th Division.	21/05/1918	21/05/1918
Miscellaneous	17th Divisional Engineers. & Pioneers.	01/05/1918	01/05/1918
Miscellaneous	17th Divisional Royal Engineers And Pioneers.	07/05/1918	07/05/1918
War Diary	Reincheval	01/06/1918	23/06/1918
War Diary	Herissart	24/06/1918	30/06/1918
Operation(al) Order(s)	Operation Order No. 5. By Lieut-Colonel F.A. Ferguson D.S.O., R.E. C.R.E. 17th Division.	20/06/1918	20/06/1918
Miscellaneous	To all recipients of C.R.E's. Operation Order No. 5 dated 20th June, 1918	20/06/1918	20/06/1918
Miscellaneous	O.C. 77th Field Coy. R.E.	20/06/1918	20/06/1918
War Diary	Herissart	01/07/1918	10/07/1918
War Diary	Toutencourt	11/07/1918	31/07/1918
Operation(al) Order(s)	Operation Order No. 7 by Major R.C. D.S.O., R.E. A/C.R.E. 17th Division.	17/07/1918	17/07/1918
Heading	17th Divl. Engineers C.R.E. 17th Division. August 1918		
War Diary	Toutencourt	01/08/1918	07/08/1918
War Diary	Allonville	08/08/1918	11/08/1918
War Diary	Hamelet	12/08/1918	16/08/1918
War Diary	Allonville	17/08/1918	17/08/1918
War Diary	Toutencourt	18/08/1918	22/08/1918
War Diary	Beaussart	23/08/1918	23/08/1918
War Diary	Hamel	24/08/1918	26/08/1918
War Diary	Courcelette	27/08/1918	29/08/1918

War Diary	Martinpuich	30/08/1918	31/08/1918
Operation(al) Order(s)	Operation Order No. 9. By Lieut. Colonel., F.A. Ferguson., D.S.O., R.E. C.R.E., 17th Division.	12/08/1918	12/08/1918
Operation(al) Order(s)	Operation Order No. 10. By Lieut. Colonel., F.A. Ferguson., D.S.O., R.E. C.R.E., 17th Division.	15/08/1918	15/08/1918
Miscellaneous			
War Diary	Martinpuich	01/09/1918	02/09/1918
War Diary	Le Transloy	03/09/1918	06/09/1918
War Diary	Lechelle	07/09/1918	30/09/1918
Operation(al) Order(s)	Warning Order No. 11. by Lieut. Colonel F.A. Ferguson, D.S.O., R.E. C.R.E., 17th Division.	10/09/1918	10/09/1918
Operation(al) Order(s)	Operation Order No. 12 by Lieut. Col. F.A. Ferguson, D.S.O., R.E. C.R.E., 17th Division.	10/09/1918	10/09/1918
Operation(al) Order(s)	Operation Order No. 13 by Lieut. Col. F.A. Ferguson, D.S.O., R.E. C.R.E., 17th Division.	16/09/1918	16/09/1918
Operation(al) Order(s)	Operation Order No. 14 by Lieut. Col. F.A. Ferguson, D.S.O., R.E. C.R.E., 17th Division.	22/09/1918	22/09/1918
Operation(al) Order(s)	Operation Order No. 15 by Lieut. Col. F.A. Ferguson, D.S.O., R.E. C.R.E., 17th Division.	24/09/1918	24/09/1918
Operation(al) Order(s)	Operation Order No. 16 by Lieut. Col. F.A. Ferguson, D.S.O., R.E. C.R.E., 17th Division.	29/09/1918	29/09/1918
Miscellaneous	Table 'A'		
Operation(al) Order(s)	Operation Order No. 17. by Lieut. Col. F.A. Ferguson, D.S.O., R.E. C.R.E., 17th Division	30/09/1918	30/09/1918
War Diary	Lechelle	01/10/1918	04/10/1918
War Diary	Heudecourt	05/10/1918	08/10/1918
War Diary	Guillemin 57 b N17.a 2.4	09/10/1918	09/10/1918
War Diary	Montigny	10/10/1918	22/10/1918
War Diary	Inchy	23/10/1918	25/10/1918
War Diary	Ovillers	26/10/1918	31/10/1918
Operation(al) Order(s)	Operation Order No. 18. by Lieut. Col. F.A. Ferguson, D.S.O., R.E. C.R.E., 17th Division.	05/10/1918	05/10/1918
Operation(al) Order(s)	Operation Order No. 19. by Lieut. Col. F.A. Ferguson, D.S.O., R.E. C.R.E., 17th Division.	08/10/1918	08/10/1918
Operation(al) Order(s)	Operation Order No. 20. by Lieut. Col. F.A. Ferguson, D.S.O., R.E. C.R.E., 17th Division.	08/10/1918	08/10/1918
Operation(al) Order(s)	Operation Order No. 21. by Lieut. Col. F.A. Ferguson, D.S.O., R.E. C.R.E., 17th Division.	14/10/1918	14/10/1918
Operation(al) Order(s)	Operation Order No. 22. by Lieut. Col. F.A. Ferguson, D.S.O., R.E. C.R.E., 17th Division.	22/10/1918	22/10/1918
Operation(al) Order(s)	Operation Order No. 23. by Lieut. Col. F.A. Ferguson, D.S.O., R.E. C.R.E., 17th Division.	23/10/1918	23/10/1918
Operation(al) Order(s)	Operation Order No. 24. by Lieut. Col. F.A. Ferguson, D.S.O., R.E. C.R.E., 17th Division.	24/10/1918	24/10/1918
Operation(al) Order(s)	Warning Order No. 25 by Lieut. Col., F.A. Ferguson, D.S.O., R.E. C.R.E., 17th Division.	25/10/1918	25/10/1918
Operation(al) Order(s)	Operation Order No. 26. by Lieut. Col., F.A. Ferguson, D.S.O., R.E. C.R.E., 17th Division.	26/10/1918	26/10/1918
Miscellaneous	Table To Accompany C.R.E's Operation Order No. 26		
Operation(al) Order(s)	Warning Order No. 27. by Lieut. Col. F.A. Ferguson, D.S.O., R.E. C.R.E., 17th Division.	28/10/1918	28/10/1918
Operation(al) Order(s)	Operation Order No. 28. by Lieut. Col. F.A. Ferguson, D.S.O., R.E. C.R.E., 17th Division.	25/10/1916	25/10/1916
Miscellaneous	Defence Instructions No. 3. by Lieut. Col. F.A. Ferguson, D.S.O., R.E. C.R.E., 17th Division.	26/10/1918	26/10/1918
Miscellaneous	Table To Accompany C.R.E. O.O. No. 28		

Operation(al) Order(s)	Operation Order No. 29. by Lieut. Col. F.A. Ferguson, D.S.O., R.E. C.R.E., 17th Division.	01/11/1918	01/11/1918
Operation(al) Order(s)	Operation Order No. 30	03/11/1918	03/11/1918
Operation(al) Order(s)	Amendments To Operation Order No. 29 by Lieut. Col. F.A. Ferguson, D.S.O., R.E. C.R.E., 17th Division.	02/11/1918	02/11/1918
War Diary	Inchy	01/11/1918	01/11/1918
War Diary	Ovillers	02/11/1918	04/11/1918
War Diary	Poix Du Nord	05/11/1918	05/11/1918
War Diary	Locquignol	06/11/1918	07/11/1918
War Diary	Aulnoye	08/11/1918	13/11/1918
War Diary	Inchy	14/11/1918	30/11/1918
Operation(al) Order(s)	C.R.E's Operation Order No. 31	06/11/1918	06/11/1918
Operation(al) Order(s)	C.R.E's Operation Order No. 32	09/11/1918	09/11/1918
Operation(al) Order(s)	C.R.E's Operation Order No. 33	11/11/1918	11/11/1918
Operation(al) Order(s)	C.R.E's Operation Order No. 34	13/11/1918	13/11/1918
Operation(al) Order(s)	C.R.E's Operation Order No. 35	14/11/1918	14/11/1918
War Diary	Inchy	01/12/1918	05/12/1918
War Diary	Hallencourt	06/12/1918	31/12/1918
Miscellaneous	77th Field Co. R.E.	04/12/1918	04/12/1918
Miscellaneous	O.C. 77th Field Coy. R.E.	02/12/1918	02/12/1918
Operation(al) Order(s)	C.R.E's Operation Order No. 36	02/12/1918	02/12/1918
Miscellaneous	March Route.		
War Diary	Hallencourt	01/01/1919	31/01/1919
War Diary	Hallencourt	01/02/1919	28/02/1919
War Diary	Hallencourt	01/03/1919	31/03/1919
War Diary	Hallencourt	01/04/1919	14/04/1919
War Diary	Longpre	15/04/1919	30/04/1919
War Diary	Longpre	01/05/1919	01/05/1919

17TH DIVISION

C. R. E.

JLY 1915 - MAY 1919

17th Division

121
7517

H.Q. 17th Div: CRE.

Vol I

July to Oct 15

to

May 19

K

3rd
Cu

HQ
17
Div
CRE
270

July 1915 WAR DIARY C.R.E. 17th Division I

Place-Time-hour	Summary of Events	Remarks
Havre 13-7-15	17th Div. R.E. Hd Qrs proceeded from Southampton to HAVRE.	
HAVRE 15-7-15	Left HAVRE by train.	
Lumbres 16-7-15	Arrived LUMBRES.	
RENESCURE 18-7-15	Marched by road LUMBRES to RENESCURE.	
STEENVOORDE 19-7-15	Marched by road RENESCURE to ~~[illegible]~~ STEENVOORDE.	

II

Place & Date	Summary of Events	Remarks
STEENVOORDE 20-7-15 - 24-7-15	In billets at STEENVOORDE	
RENINGHELST 24-7-15	Marched STEENVOORDE to RENINGHELST.	
24-7-15 to 27-7-15	Taking over line from trench M, to trench 27	
27-7-15 to 31-7-15	Holding line from M, to 27.	

[illegible] Col.
Cmd. 17th Div.

August 1915

War Diary C.R.E. 17th DIVISION.

Place + Date		
RENINGHELST 1-8-15 to 31-8-15	Work on line from M, to trench 27. including .I. Improvement of communication trenches. .2. Work on supporting points .3. Roads to forward dumps. .4. Trench Tramways.- laying wooden & iron rails .5. Water supply - laying pipe line .6. Supply of material.	

J.M. Gall Col.
CRE

WAR DIARY

C.R.E. 17th Division September 1915

Place + date	Summary of Events	Remarks
RENINGHELST	Work on line M, to trench 27	
1-9-15 to 30-9-15	work including. 1. Improvement of Communication trenches 2. Work on Supporting points 3. Roads to forward dumps - corduroy + brick. 4. Trench tramways - laying ~~wood~~ + steel rails 5. Water supply - laying pipe line - erecting tanks + engine 6. Drainage generally.	[signature] CRE

WAR DIARY

C.R.E. 17th Division. OCTOBER 1915.

Place · Date · hour	Summary of Events	Remarks
RENINGHELST.	Work on Line M. to Trench 27	
1-10-15 to 5-10-15	~~Reop~~ Handing over to 9th 14th 24th and Canadian Divisions.	
	Handing over completed morning Wednesday 6-10-15.	

29

Date. Hour - Place	Summary of Events	Remarks.
Tuesday 5-10-15	78th Coy moved to billets at STEENVOORDE. 93rd Coy moved to billets at GODESWAERSVELDE.	
Wednesday 6-10-15	C.R.E. & HQ.R.E. moved to Billets at STEENVOORDE. 77th Coy R.E. moved to billets at EECKE.	
afternoon.	C.R.E. visited 93rd Coy RE to discuss duties of R.E. in [redacted] attacks.	
Thursday 7.10.15	Visited 77th Coy RE. Visited 78th Coy RE. } to discuss placing & numbers of R.E. in attacks.	

11

Date. Hour Place	Summary of Events	Remarks.
Friday 8-10-15 to Wednesday 20-10-15	In rest billets at STEENVOORDE - EECKE - GODESWAERSVELDE - Companies experimenting in I Bridging trenches, (for guns) II Stepping trenches. III Grenades - use of & makes of. IV 'Crates' of wire netting	
Tuesday night 19.10.15	Orders received to relieve 3rd Division.	
Wednesday 20.10.15	~~Orders received to relieve 3rd Division.~~ 77th Coy RE. marched with 51st Bde to 3rd Division Rest area	
Thursday 21.10.15	78th Coy RE marched with 50th Bde to 3rd Div rest area. 77th Coy proceeded to billets at H28 a. 68 C.R.E & adjutant motored to RENINGHELST to commence taking over from 3rd Division.	

13

Date + Place	Summary of Events.	Remarks
St[illegible]voorde.		
Friday. 22-10-15	C.R.E. proceeded to RENINGHELST to go round 3rd Division works. 93rd Coy R.E. marched with 52nd Bde to rest area 78th Coy R.E. took over billets of Cheshire field company at H.22.d.6.3 93rd Coy R.E. detailed for Col[illegible] to take over R.E. dump. H16.d.[illegible]	
Saturday 23-10-15	Completed taking over from 3rd Division. Headquarters R.E. marched to 93rd Coy R.E. took over billets at H.29.b.6.2 from 56th Coy R.E.	
Sunday 24-10-15	C.R.E. went round works with O.C. 77th Coy	
Monday 25-10-15	C.R.E. went round company billets. & Kruistraat.	

14

Date & Place	Summary of Events	Remarks
RENINGHELST Tuesday 26.10.15	C.R.E. visited works.	
Wednesday 27/10/15.	C.R.E visited No 2 Coy R.A.R.E and 2nd Entrenching Battalion. Also works near KRUISTRAAT and Dugouts in RAMPARTS at YPRES.	
Thursday 28/10/15.	[redacted]. H.M. The King inspected troops at RENINGHELST. C.R.E. attended parade.	

Reference to Sheet 28 $\frac{1}{40,000}$

Day & Place	Summary of Events	Remarks
RENINGHELST. Friday 29.10.15	C.R.E. visited ~~[illegible]~~. Dugouts under construction at BELGIAN FARM.	
Saturday 30.10.15	C.R.E. visited ZILLEBEKE dugouts MAPLE COPSE & SANCTUARY WOOD also Trench Tramway from KRUISTRAAT.	
Sunday 31.10.15	C.R.E. attended Water Board 10 a.m. afternoon visited DICKEBUSCH BEEK. to see what drainage is required between H17a8.2. and YPRES.	H.W. Gale Col. CRE

16

H.Q. 17th Div:
C.R.E.
Vol: 2

121
7678

Nov 15

WAR DIARY C.R.E. 17th Division - November 1915

Place - Date - Hour	Summary of Events	Remarks
RENINGHELST Monday 1.11.15	C.R.E. visited works at ZILLEBEKE ETANG and trenches as far a C3.	
Tuesday 2.11.15	C.R.E. visited Hutting Sites.	
Wednesday 3.11.15	CRE visited work.	
Thursday 4.11.15	CRE visited work.	
Friday 5.11.15	C.R.E. visits Canal Bank Dugouts - Rampart Dugouts & trench tramway.	

Hour - Date - Place	Summary of Events	Remarks.
Saturday 6.11.15	C.R.E. visited C.R.E. 6th Division re. Taking over.	
Sunday 7.11.15	C.R.E. visited C.R.E. 6th Division.	
Monday 8.11.15	C.R.E. visited work. C.R.E. 33rd Division arrived 6pm for 3 days attachment.	
Tuesday 9.11.15	C.R.E. took C.R.E. 33rd round trenches leading to HOOGE.	
Wednesday 10.11.15	C.R.E. ~~goes~~ went to trenches to arrange work for Cavalry attached for work.	
Thursday 11.11.15	C.R.E. visited work at Belgian Farm and Billets of 77th Coy R.E. in YPRES.	
Friday 12.11.15	~~[illegible]~~ — C.R.E. handed over to Major Hogg 93rd Coy R.E. prior to proceeding on Leave.	

32

Time Date	Place	Summary of Events	Remarks.
Saturday 13-11-15		C.R.E. went on leave -	
Sunday 14-11-15		Water Board at 9th Division H.Qrs - visited Bickchurch Beek to see how drainage was going.	Fine.
Monday 15-11-15		acting C.R.E. went to inspect drainage of VIJLE BEEK & dugouts BELGIAN CHATEAU.	Fine - Frosty -
Tuesday 16.11.15		Obtained 3rd blade for circular saw at GROENEN JAEGER.	
Wednesday 17.11.15		Visited 2nd Army workshops HAZEBROUCK Discussion in evening with Water Patrol officers as to drainage of our area.	

— WAR DIARY C.R.E. 17th Division —

Thursday 18/11/15	Visited ASYLUM at YPRES with a view to billeting one section 93rd Fd Company R.E.
Friday 19/11/15	Visited Chateaux Dugouts and DICKEBUSCH BEEK.
Saturday 20/11/15	– Office –
Sunday 21/11/15	Visited CRE 14th Division obtained information ~~Re~~ re Northern Sector 17th Divisional Front.
Monday 22/11/15	Visited Shelling Dump & Huts – Capt Oakes came in to take over duties of Adjutant during absence Capt Heath.

WAR DIARY C.R.E. 17th Division

Time Date Place	Summary of Information	Remarks
Tuesday 23/12/15	Visited O.C. 77th Coy RE in YPRES to discuss work.	
Wednesday 24/12/15	Adjutant proceeds on leave till 2/12/15.	
Thursday 25/12/15	Nothing of importance to record.	
Friday 26/12/15		
Saturday 27/12/15		
Sunday 28/12/15		
Monday 29/12/15		
Tuesday 30/12/15	C.R.E. returns from leave & takes over from Major Hogg	J.P. Heath Captain for C.R.E. 17th Division

I

Reference BELGIUM Sheet 28 $\frac{1}{40,000}$

Instructions regarding War Diaries and Intelligence Summaries are contained in F. S. Regs., Part II. and the Staff Manual respectively. Title Pages will be prepared in manuscript.

WAR DIARY
or
~~INTELLIGENCE SUMMARY~~
(Erase heading not required.)

Army Form C. 2118

1915 – C.R.E. 17th Division – DECEMBER

Place	Date	Hour	Summary of Events and Information	Remarks and references to Appendices
RENINGHELST	1/12/15		CRE visits works. – wet.	
– do –	2/12/15		CRE visits works – wet	
– do –	3/12/15		CRE visits works – wet	
– do –	4/12/15		Adjt R.E. returned from leave, – wet	
– do –	5/12/15		CRE visited works near KRUISTRAAT. – wet.	
– do –	6/12/15		CRE visited RE Park ABEELE – wet.	
– do –	7/12/15		CRE visited works of 77th Coy RE – wet	
– do –	8/12/15		CRE visited Dump and works near KRUISTRAAT. – fine –	
– do –	9/12/15		CRE visited Dump at H16d1.1 and BELGIAN CHATEAU Dugouts. – Day wet	
– do –	10/12/15		CRE. visited O.C. 78th Coy RE at ZILLEBEKE. – Day wet	
– do –	11/12/15		C.R.E. visited YPRES & 77th Coy RE. – Day wet	
– do –	12/12/15		Water board 9th Division HQrs. CRE attends. Day wet.	
– do –	13/12/15		CRE visits HQrs 78th Coy RE at ZILLEBEKE and has conference with OCs 78th Coy RE & 93rd Coy RE as to works in progress.	
– do –	14/12/15		CRE visits 77th Coy RE in YPRES.	
– do –	15/12/15		C.R.E. visits RE Dump and Hutting dump to decide (a) whether steam engine can be run by day (b) whether it shall be moved to Hutting Dump.	
– do –	16/12/15		Battle HQrs commenced at 4.22 a.m. – C.R.E. visits trenches at [illegible] & inspects site of proposed night work – night work 1000 men in two reliefs – 6 G.11 & 11 G.5 put up 40 yds parapet – 7 feet thick at 2'6" to 4' high –	
– do –	17/12/15		C.R.E. visits 93rd Coy RE to discuss work done on night 16/17th – Battle HQrs dugouts progressing favourably though delayed through lack of bolts.	
– do –	18/12/15		C.R.E. visits YPRES to go round work night of 18th/19th & stays in YPRES for night. Fine [illegible]	

1875 Wt. W593/826 1,000,000 4/15 J.B.C. & A. A.D.S.S./Forms/C. 2118.

2

Instructions regarding War Diaries and Intelligence Summaries are contained in F. S. Regs., Part II. and the Staff Manual respectively. Title Pages will be prepared in manuscript.

WAR DIARY
or
~~INTELLIGENCE SUMMARY~~
(Erase heading not required.)

Army Form C. 2118

C R E 17th Division

DECEMBER 1915

Place	Date	Hour	Summary of Events and Information	Remarks and references to Appendices
Reninghelst	19.12.15	8.35am	Gas attack reported N.E. of YPRES – Communication with companies cut till midday – CRE returned from YPRES at about 9.30 am. Companies stood to awaiting orders – 77th company repaired X1a. damaged by bombardment during day.	
			C.R.E. visits 93rd Coy RE + goes out to supervise working party near GORDON HOUSE (Hooge trench map)	
Reninghelst	20.12.15			
			Work as usual in front works – working party from Princes not available	
"	21.12.15			
"	22.12.15		The Nothing to report – work as usual.	
"	23.12.15			
"	24.12.15			
"	25.12.15			
"	26.12.15			
"	27.12.15			
"	28.12.15			
			C.R.E. 24th Division comes over from restaurant to talk over arrangements for handing over –	
"	29.12.15			
			~~Colonel~~ CRE 24th Division taken up to front line by CRE to see trenches prior to taking over	
"	30.12.15			
"	31.12.15		Preparing movement orders for move to rest area.	

9/1/16

F P Heath Capt RE
for CRE 17th Division

Instructions regarding War Diaries and Intelligence Summaries are contained in F. S. Regs., Part II. and the Staff Manual respectively. Title Pages will be prepared in manuscript.

1916

WAR DIARY
or
INTELLIGENCE SUMMARY
(Erase heading not required.)

C.R.E. 17th Division

Army Form C. 2118

Place	Date	Hour	Summary of Events and Information	Remarks and references to Appendices
REN[illegible]HEAST	1.1.15		Preparing [illegible] for movement to Rest area.	
	2.1.15		Advance party sent on to Rest Area. C.R.E. visits YPRES and company Billets.	
	3.1.15		C.R.E. left to join [illegible]. R.E. [illegible] 24th Division came up to take over.	
			Dismounted portions of 24th Division companies taking over from Rear Parties.	
	4.1.15		Dismounted portion of Field Companies left for Rest area by Bus at 11 a.m.	
	5.1.15		Mounted portions Field Companies marched to rest area. Changing billets	
	6.1.15		Mounted portions Field Companies at halfway billets. Headquarters R.E. moved to Rest Area.	
	7.1.15		Mounted portions complete march to going Billets. 77th Company at TILQUES. 78th Company at NORBECOURT. 93rd Company at MONECOVE. [illegible]	
SALPERWICK	8.1.16 to 27.1.16		In rest area. Companies refitting. Drilling. Pontooning & musketry.	
	20.1.16		Colonel Carpenter [illegible] C.R.E.	
	28.1.16 to 31.1.16		Musketry. Drill. [illegible] [illegible]	

Copy 3/3/16

[illegible] Heath [illegible]

[illegible] C.R.E. 17th Division

4/2/16

1875 Wt. W593/826 1,000,000 4/15 J.B.C. & A. A.D.S.S./Forms/C. 2118.

CRE. 17th Div:
Vol: 5

Reference to BELGIUM Sheet 28 $\frac{1}{40,000}$

Instructions regarding War Diaries and Intelligence Summaries are contained in F. S. Regs., Part II. and the Staff Manual respectively. Title Pages will be prepared in manuscript.

WAR DIARY
or
~~INTELLIGENCE SUMMARY~~

(Erase heading not required.)

Army Form C. 2118

C.R.E. 17th Division

February 1916

Place	Date	Hour	Summary of Events and Information	Remarks and references to Appendices
SAPERWICK nr ST OMER.	1/2/16	–	In rest area – companies training –	
– do –	2/2/16	–	– do –	
– do –	3/2/16	–	Information received that Division is to relieve 3rd Division – in line from Trench P1 to Trench 38.	VOORMEZEELE $\frac{1}{10,000}$ ~~[illegible]~~ 28 O 7 b 7.9; HOLLEBEKE $\frac{1}{10,000}$ I 34 b 3.1
		6 pm.	Experiments carried out at Technical School ~~[illegible]~~ TILQUES with rockets, flares etc for signalling –	
– do –	4/2/16		Orders received from staff for move to forward area. (O.O. 35) – C.R.E.'s orders for move issued to Companies.	
		7 p.m.	Wire received from 93rd Field Company R.E. stating Major P.G. HOGG thrown from his horse and injured.	
– do –	5/2/16		C.R.E. visits C.R.E. 3rd Division at RENINGHELST for preliminary taking over.	
		10 pm.	Advanced portions of 1 officer and 6 sappers per company left WATTEN for forward area.	
– do –	6/2/16		Mounted portions Field Companies left for forward area.	
RENINGHELST	7/2/16		2 Sections per company left Rest Area by bus going straight into forward billets. C.R.E. took over finally from C.R.E. 3rd Division.	
– do –	8/2/16		C.R.E. visited right sector with 2nd Lt Wood (93rd Field Company) front line P1 – R1.	
			Remaining parties of R.E. arrived from Rest area.	

1875 Wt. W593/826 1,000,000 4/15 J.B.C. & A. A.D.S.S./Forms/C. 2118.

References to BELGIUM Sheet 28 1/40,000

Instructions regarding War Diaries and Intelligence Summaries are contained in F. S. Regs., Part II. and the Staff Manual respectively. Title Pages will be prepared in manuscript.

WAR DIARY
or
~~INTELLIGENCE SUMMARY~~
(Erase heading not required.)

II

Army Form C. 2118

C.R.E. 17th Division

Place	Date	Hour	Summary of Events and Information	Remarks and references to Appendices
~~[illegible]~~ RENINGHELST	9/2/16		C.R.E. visits left sector with O.C. 77th Field Company. Front line 29 - 36	
-do-	10/2/16		C.R.E. visits left centre sector with O.C. 78th Field company. " " T1 - 28b	
-do-	11/2/16		C.R.E. visits left Sector with ~~G.S.O.~~ I. " " " " 24 - R8	
-do-	12/2/16		C.R.E. visits right sector with G.S.O.I. " " P1 - R1	
-do-	13/2/16		C.R.E. visits left centre sector with G.S.O.I. " " T1 - 28b	
-do-	14/2/16	6.40pm.	German attack reported in left Sector. Trenches 33 & 34 reported occupied.	
		10pm.	Trench 34 and part of 33 reported recaptured. - Loss of front trenches from BLUFF to 32 reported with doubt as to situation on the BLUFF. Weather - dull - with gale from S.W.	
RENINGHELST	15/2/16	9.30am	Wire received from Lt Lundie (O.C. 77th Field Company) asking for 1 officer and 30 men from back section to be sent forward to assist in consolidating - orders issued for Lt ~~[illegible]~~ BENT and 30 sappers to proceed to 51st Bde HQ as & report ~~[illegible] Field Company sent~~	Weather wet - from 7pm gale from S.W.
		5pm.	Operation Order No 88 received at 5pm. giving details of counter attack.	
		6pm.	78th Field Company sends 2 sections to work in NORFOLK ROAD. - 2 sections to [illegible]	
		7.5pm.	Wire received from 51st Bde addressed O.C. 77th Company RE. asking Lt LUNDIE or other officer to report at 51st Bde HQ to arrange co-operation in consolidating - answer sent ~~do~~ to 51st Bde stating O.C. 77th Company in advanced billets.	

REFERENCES to BELGIUM
Sheet 28
1/40000

Instructions regarding War Diaries and Intelligence Summaries are contained in F. S. Regs., Part II. and the Staff Manual respectively. Title Pages will be prepared in manuscript.

WAR DIARY
or
~~INTELLIGENCE SUMMARY~~
(Erase heading not required.)

111

Army Form C. 2118

C.R.E. 17th Division

Place	Date	Hour	Summary of Events and Information	Remarks and references to Appendices
RENINGHELST	15/2/16	11pm.	Order received from staff that remaining Three section of R.E. in Divisional Reserve should be sent to 52nd Bde Hd Qrs to Bomb store to assist in fixing detonators in bombs. – Orders issued at once.	
		11.45pm.	Three sections R.E. (2 section 93rd Company 1 section 77th company) moved from point G 29 a 8.2. by bus to Bomb store.	
		11.25pm.	Wire received from 78th Company that Major BELL OC. 78th Company RE was slightly wounded and 2 Sappers wounded.	
RENINGHELST.	16.2.16	9.30am.	Message received stating Lt LUNDIE and 12 Sappers wounded.	
			Ordered [illegible] army asking for return of Capt Carter from 50th Division.	
		5pm.	Wire received from Capt. Carter stating he had rejoined.	
	17/2/16		C.R.E. visit left sector trenches & 77th Company advanced Billets	
		2pm.	93rd Field Company RE ordered to relieve 77th Company RE in forward area (left sector).	
		6pm.	Wire received that 1/East Riding Field company RE was arriving at 11.00pm. – Order to 93rd Company cancelled.	
	18/2/16	18th/19th	1/1 East Riding Field Company R.E. arrive from rest area for temporary attachment from IIIrd Division	

Reference to BELGIUM Sheet 28 $\frac{1}{40,000}$

Instructions regarding War Diaries and Intelligence Summaries are contained in F. S. Regs., Part II. and the Staff Manual respectively. Title Pages will be prepared in manuscript.

WAR DIARY
or
~~INTELLIGENCE SUMMARY~~
(Erase heading not required.)

Army Form C. 2118

C.R.E. 17th Division

Place	Date	Hour	Summary of Events and Information	Remarks and references to Appendices
			C.R.E. visits right sector.	
RENINGHELST	19/2/16		East Riding Field Company relieved 77th Field Company in left sector moving in at night 19th/20th	
	20/2/16		C.E. V th Corps visit C.R.E. to discuss defences of ST. ELOI.	
	21/2/16		C.R.E. visits trenches in right sector. 56th Company R.E. arrives from rest area for temporary attachment.	
	22/2/16		CRE visits Bde HQ 76 Bde, & forward sections of Fd Cos. & pioneers - Co-ordinators on Bde HQ.	
	23/2/16		C.R.E. visited trenches at (front line) at ST ELOI with O.C. 77th Company. 56th Company at present forward billets at Bridge 17th Canal Bank for work in left sector.	
	24/2/16		Controller of Mines visited C.R.E. — C.R.E. visited ST. ELOI and supervised distribution of working parties at SCOTTISH WOOD	
	25/2/16		C.R.E. went round front line trenches P1 to ST ELOI with C.E. IInd Army & CE Vth Corps also supervised distribution working parties at SCOTTISH WOOD.	
	26/2/16		CRE visits front line trenches left sector with G.S.O. 1 & 2.	

Instructions regarding War Diaries and Intelligence Summaries are contained in F. S. Regs., Part II. and the Staff Manual respectively. Title Pages will be prepared in manuscript.

WAR DIARY
or
INTELLIGENCE SUMMARY
(Erase heading not required.)

Army Form C. 2118

CRE, 17th Div
February 1916

Place	Date	Hour	Summary of Events and Information	Remarks and references to Appendices
	27		CRE visits left half right sector front line trenches with GSO 3 & GOC 50th Bde. Lorries with stores went nightly to WOODCOTE HOUSE 26 27 28 29.	
	28		" " CHQ 2nd line & arranged to put entrenching Bn to work.	
	29		" " Right sector front & support lines.	

C.H. Carpenter
Lieut Col
CRE 17th Div
1.3.16

1875 Wt. W593/826 1,000,000 4/15 J.B.C. & A. A.D.S.S./Forms/C. 2118.

Reference: Trench Maps
VERBRANDEN MOLEN } 1/10,000
VOORMEZEELE }

Instructions regarding War Diaries and Intelligence Summaries are contained in F. S. Regs., Part II. and the Staff Manual respectively. Title Pages will be prepared in manuscript.

WAR DIARY
or
~~INTELLIGENCE SUMMARY~~
(Erase heading not required.)

Army Form C. 2118

Vols 5-6 7

C.R.E. 17th Division
MARCH 1916

Place	Date	Hour	Summary of Events and Information	Remarks and references to Appendices
RENINGHELST	1-3-16	–	Field Companies temporarily withdrawn from advanced BILLETS to make room for Infantry ~~Brigade~~ reserves with the exception of 56th Company RE and 1/1 EAST RIDING Company RE. 1 lorry load trench "crates" 1 lorry load "trenchboards" sent up to WOODCOTE HOUSE at 10.30 pm.	
	2/3/16		One lorry load sandbags sent to LANGHOF CHATEAU at 1.4 pm.	
	3/3/16		C.R.E. visits ST ELOI defences. EAST RIDING Field Company and 56th Field Company withdrawn to rest. 93rd Company RE goes into advanced billets in CANAL BANK for work on left sector.	
	4/3/16		C.R.E. visits trenches 24 - 25 - 26 - 27	
	5/3/16		C.R.E. visits St ELOI defences.	
	6/3/16		C.R.E. 3rd Division arrives to take over. 77th Company RE marches to LA CRECHE to rest Billets. 105 Company RE, 106 Company RE, 6th Battalion SOUTH WALES BORDERERS (pioneer battalion) } from 25th Division arrive to assist in work in area. C.R.E. goes round ST. ELOI defences with C.R.E. 3rd Division and O.C. 105th Company RE. Lt Col. KENDALL	
	7/3/16		1/1 East RIDING Company RE goes round trenches in left sector with O.C. 106th Company RE.	
	8/3/16		C.R.E. goes round left sector trenches with C.R.E. 3rd Division - C.R.E.'s office moves to STEENVOORDE	
	9/3/16		C.R.E. remains to hand over work to C.R.E. 3rd Division.	
	10/3/16		C.R.E. + CRE's office move to MERRIS in rest area.	

1875 Wt. W593/826 1,000,000 4/15 J.B.C. & A. A.D.S.S./Forms/C. 2118.

Instructions regarding War Diaries and Intelligence Summaries are contained in F. S. Regs., Part II. and the Staff Manual respectively. Title Pages will be prepared in manuscript.

WAR DIARY
or
~~INTELLIGENCE SUMMARY~~
(Erase heading not required.)

Army Form C. 2118

CRE 17th Div.
MARCH 1916

Place	Date	Hour	Summary of Events and Information	Remarks and references to Appendices
MERRIS	11.3.16		C.R.E. visits C.E. II Corps	
	12.3.16		C.R.E. visits C.E. II Corps & 77th Coy. R.E.	
	13.3.16		C.R.E. visits 93rd Coy R.E.	
	14.3.16		C.R.E. visits ARMENTIERES to confer with CRE 21st Div.	
	15.3.16		C.R.E. visits Right Sector of trenches held by 21st Div.	
	16.3.16		CRE visits Left Sector " " "	
	17.3.16		C.R.E. visits ARMENTIERES & billets of the Field Companys of ~~RE~~ 21st (RCP) Div.	
	18.3.16		C.R.E. goes round Centre Sector with C.R.E. 21st Div.	
	19.3.16		C.R.E. visits METEREN baths.	
ARMENTIERES	20.3.16		CRE moves into ARMENTIERES and goes round Right Sector.	
Sheet 36.	21.3.16		C.R.E. goes round Centre Sector.	
	22.3.16		Adjutant, Office etc. move into ARMENTIERES – C.R.E. goes round ~~Right Sector~~. (RCP) Waterworks & Coy. Shops.	
	23.3.16		C.R.E. 17th Div. took over from C.R.E. 21st Div & went round ARMENTIERES Defences Field Companies moved into ARMENTIERES between 18.3.16 & 23.3.16.	
	24.3.16		C.R.E. goes round Town Works.	
	25.3.16		C.R.E. goes round Left Sector	
	26.3.16		Field Company Commanders arrange programme of work in consultation with CRE & Gen Staff.	
	27.3.16		CRE goes round Right Sector	
	28.3.16		C.R.E. goes round Centre Sector	
	29.3.16		CRE goes round Left Sector	
	30.3.16		CRE goes round Bridges & visits II Corps Workshops	
	31.3.16		C.R.E. goes round Subsidiary Line.	

C.W. Carpenter Lt. Col.
CRE 17 Div.

1875 Wt. W593/826 1,000,000 4/15 J.B.C. & A. A.D.S.S./Forms/C. 2118.

Army Form W.3091.

Cover for Documents.

Nature of Enclosures.

War Diaries

17. Div. R.E. Headquarters

Period. April 1916

17th Div.

Notes, or Letters written.

Map Ref Sheet 36

Instructions regarding War Diaries and Intelligence Summaries are contained in F. S. Regs., Part II. and the Staff Manual respectively. Title Pages will be prepared in manuscript.

WAR DIARY
or
~~INTELLIGENCE SUMMARY~~

(Erase heading not required.)

CRE 17th Div.
April 1916.

Army Form C. 2118

Place	Date April	Hour	Summary of Events and Information	Remarks and references to Appendices
ARMENTIERES	1st		CRE visited Bridges. Companies. Pioneers etc.	
$	2nd		" went on leave. Major Hogg acted.	
	5th		Capt. Heath, adjutant, transferred to 103rd Fd. Co. Lieut. R.C. LUNDIE appointed adjt.	
$	9th			
	10th		CRE returned.	
	11th		" visited front line & support trenches Right section. with OC 77th Fd Co.	
	12		" " 2nd Army shops, 2nd Army mine controller, & 2nd Corps CE.	
	13		" " Right centre with OC Pioneers & OC 78th RE.	
	14		" " Right section. Right centre with CE 2nd Corps.	
	15th		" " Left " with OC 93rd RE.	
$	16		" " 11 Corps Dump & 9th Div. RE.	
	17		" " Armentieres defences with CE 2nd Corps.	
	18		" " Right section front line etc with OC 77th RE	
	19		" " Left " " " " 93rd -	
	20		" " " " support. " GS2.	
	21		" " Right. front. GS2	
	22		" " Pioneers & Companies etc	

1875 Wt. W593/826 1,000,000 4/15 J.B.C. & A. A.D.S.S./Forms/C. 2118.

Army Form C. 2118

Instructions regarding War Diaries and Intelligence Summaries are contained in F. S. Regs., Part II. and the Staff Manual respectively. Title Pages will be prepared in manuscript.

WAR DIARY
or
~~INTELLIGENCE SUMMARY~~
(Erase heading not required.)

CRE 17th Divn
April 1916

Place	Date	Hour	Summary of Events and Information	Remarks and references to Appendices
	April			
Armentieres	23		CRE visited Centre sector - supports with G S 2	
	24		" " Bridges, dumps etc	
	25		" " Right sector and centre sector, GS, front and support.	
	26		" " Centre " with G S 2	
	27		" " " G S 1	
	28		" " Right & centre support, front -	
	29		" " Left with G S 1, " "	
	30		" " Bridges & dumps.	

C M Carpenter
Lieut Col
CRE 17th Divn

1875 Wt. W593/826 1,000,000 4/15 J.B.C. & A. A.D.S.S./Forms/C. 2118.

Instructions regarding War Diaries and Intelligence Summaries are contained in F. S. Regs., Part II. and the Staff Manual respectively. Title Pages will be prepared in manuscript.

WAR DIARY
or
INTELLIGENCE SUMMARY
(Erase heading not required.)

CRE 17th Div

April 1916

Army Form C. 2118.

185

Place	Date April	Hour	Summary of Events and Information
ARMENTIERES	1st		CRE visits Bridges, Companies, Pioneers etc.
&	2nd		" went on leave. Major Hogg acts.
	5th		Capt. Heath, adjutant, transferred to 103rd Fd Co. Lieut. R.C. LUNDIE appointed adjt.
&	9th		
	10.		CRE returns.
	11th.		" visits front line, support trenches Right sector, with OC 77th Fd Co.
	12.		" " 2nd Army Chief, 2nd Army mine controller, 2nd Corps CE.
	13		" " Right centre with OC Pioneers & OC 78th RE.
	14		" " Right sector. Right centre with CE 2nd Corps.
	15th		" " Left " with OC 93rd RE.
&	16		" " 11 Corps Dump & 9th Div: RE.
	17		" " Armentieres defences with CE 2nd Corps.
	18		" " Right sector front line etc with OC 77th RE
	19		" " Left " " " " 93rd "
	20		" " " " support " 652.
	21		" " Right " front " 652
	22		" " Pioneers, Companies etc.

Instructions regarding War Diaries and Intelligence Summaries are contained in F. S. Regs., Part II. and the Staff Manual respectively. Title Pages will be prepared in manuscript.

WAR DIARY
or
~~INTELLIGENCE SUMMARY~~
(Erase heading not required.)

CRE 17 Divn
April 1916

Army Form C. 21

186

Place	Date	Hour	Summary of Events and Information	Remarks and references to Appendices
	April			
Armentieres	23		CRE visited Centre section - support with G.S.2.	
	24		" " Bridges, dumps etc	
	25		" " Right sector and centre sector, G.S., front and support.	
	26		" " Centre " with G.S.2	
	27		" " " G.S.1.	
	28		" " Right - centre support, front.	
	29		" " Left with G.S.1. " "	
	30		" " Bridges - dumps.	

[signature] Lieut. Col.
CRE. 17 Divn.

1875 Wt. W593/826 1,000,000 4/15 J.B.C. & A. A.D.S.S./Forms/C. 2118

Instructions regarding War Diaries and Intelligence Summaries are contained in F. S. Regs., Part II. and the Staff Manual respectively. Title Pages will be prepared in manuscript.

WAR DIARY
or
INTELLIGENCE SUMMARY

(*Erase heading not required.*)

CRE. 17th Div MAY 1916

Army Form C. 2118

Vol 8

Place	Date MAY	Hour	Summary of Events and Information	Remarks and references to Appendices
Armentières	1		CRE visited Subsidiary line with GS 2nd Corps	
	2		" " Left sector	
	3		" " Centre " & bridges over canal	
	4		" " Right "	
	5		" " Right Centre - Epinette	
	6		" " Right sector	
	8 7		" " 3rd Companies	
	8		" " Right centre Epinette	
	9		" made preparations for handing over to CRE N.Z. Div	
	10		" visited Subsidiary line with GS1	
	11		" " Right sector " CRE NZ	
	12		" " Left " " "	
	13		" " Centre " " "	

1875 Wt. W593/826 1,000,000 4/15 J.B.C. & A. A.D.S.S./Forms/C. 2118.

Instructions regarding War Diaries and Intelligence Summaries are contained in F. S. Regs., Part II. and the Staff Manual respectively. Title Pages will be prepared in manuscript.

WAR DIARY

or

INTELLIGENCE SUMMARY

(Erase heading not required.)

Army Form C. 2118

CRE. 17th Div.
MAY. 1916

Place	Date	Hour	Summary of Events and Information	Remarks and references to Appendices
ARMENTIERES.	14/5/16		CRE showed CRE. N.Z. Div. round Bridges	
"	15th		CRE. visited Subsidiary Line with CRE. N.Z. Div.	
"	16th		CRE. Adjutant & Office Staff moved to TILQUES.	
TILQUES	17th		CRE. visited 78th Field Coy at POLINCOVE.	
	18th		CRE. visited 77th Field Coy at MORINGHEM & reconnoitred Training Area	
	19th		CRE. reconnoitred Training Area & visited 93rd Field Coy. at LEULINGHEM.	
	20th		Adjutant visited 78th Fd. Coy doing schemes in 50th Bgde Area	
	21st		Adjutant reconnoitred Training Area of 52nd Bgde & visited 93rd Coy R.E.	
	22nd		CRE worked out Training schemes.	
	23rd		Reconnaissance of 52nd Bgde Area by CRE. with view to Training Schemes for 93rd Field Coy.	
	24th		C.R.E. went over schemes done by 78th Fd. Coy on 20.5.16 on the actual ground. At night visited 77th Field Coy on night scheme.	
	25th		CRE. visited 77th Coy RE. and attended G.O.C's Conference.	
	26th		CRE. worked out schemes for strong points & working party tables. Adjutant visited Forest Control Officer at CLAIRMARAIS re materials for Div. Training.	
	27th		CRE. visits 93rd Fd. Co. & Pioneers.	
	28		Div: Staff ride.	
	29		CRE. adjt. preparation for Div. scheme.	
	30		Div: scheme. 2 Bdes. assaulting 2 Fd. Cos. allotted to work on strong points	
	31		CRE visits 93rd Co practising crossing trenches & demolition. GOC's conference.	

C. W. Carpenter
Lieut. Col. CRE 17 Div.

1875 Wt. W593/826 1,000,000 4/15 J.B.C. & A. A.D.S.S./Forms/C. 2118.

Instructions regarding War Diaries and Intelligence Summaries are contained in F. S. Regs., Part II. and the Staff Manual respectively. Title Pages will be prepared in manuscript.

WAR DIARY
or
INTELLIGENCE SUMMARY
(Erase heading not required.)

C.R.E.
17th Div.

Army Form C. 2118

Vol 9

JUNE 1916

Place	Date	Hour	Summary of Events and Information	Remarks and references to Appendices
TILQUES	1st June	-	C.R.E. inspects Field Coys taking part in Div. Route March. Visited 77th Coy practising consolidation of Mine Crater.	
"	2nd		Preparations for Final Div. Scheme. Conference of Field Coy Commanders.	
	3rd		CRE. took part in final Div. Scheme. Visited 77th Coy.	
	4th		CRE. attends G.O.C's Conference & prepares pamphlet on various types of Strong Points for Div. "G" Staff	
	5th		CRE. visits 93rd Coy RE.	
	6th		Adjutant visits 78th Coy RE at POLINCOVE.	
	7th		Orders received for move to IV Army Area. Adjutant visits 77th Coy.	
	8th		CRE. and Adjutant move to ALLONVILLE.	
ALLONVILLE	9th		CRE. visits C.E. XV Corps and 77th & 78th Coys at BUSSY-LES-DAOURS. Ordered to MORLANCOURT	
MORLANCOURT	10th		CRE & H.Q. move to MORLANCOURT. G.S.O.1. 17th Div visits CRE.	
	11th		CRE. & Adjutant visit CE XV & No 6 RE Park	
	12th		CRE goes round left sector of XV Corps intermediate line with O.C. 77th Coy RE & visits CE XV Corps.	
	13th		CRE. visits trenches with G.S.O.1. 17th Div and studies front-views of enemy positions. H.Q. return to ALLONVILLE	
ALLONVILLE	14th, 15th		CRE. reconnoitres sites for advanced dumps of RE material for use in event of operations with G.S.O.3 17th Div.	
	16th		CRE. visits trenches with Adjutant & studies enemy positions from different points of vantage.	
	17th		CRE. started 93rd Field Coy making "Concertina" Wire Entanglement Frames.	
	18th		CRE. made arrangements for transport & disposal of "Concertina" Frames.	
	19th		CRE. visited 77th & 78th Companies.	
	20th		CRE. visits C.E. XV Corps.	
	21st		Advanced Dumps finally completed.	

1875 Wt. W593/826 1,000,000 4/15 J.B.C. & A. A.D.S.S./Forms/C. 2118.

Army Form C. 2118

Instructions regarding War Diaries and Intelligence Summaries are contained in F. S. Regs., Part II. and the Staff Manual respectively. Title Pages will be prepared in manuscript.

WAR DIARY
or
INTELLIGENCE SUMMARY
(Erase heading not required.)

C.R.E. 17th Div.
JUNE 1916

Place	Date	Hour	Summary of Events and Information	Remarks and references to Appendices
ALLONVILLE	22nd June		C.R.E. visited Advanced Dumps also C.E. XV Corps	
	23rd		C.R.E. makes arrangements for drawing & transporting to site Div Reserve Dump of RE stores.	
	24th		C.R.E. visits CE XV Corps & night-sees trenches of Corps Front with G.S.O.3 17th Div.	
	25th		CRE attends G.O.C.'s conference	
	26th		C.R.E. gets out plans of lines of approach for carrying parties from Advanced Brigade Dump	
	27th		C.R.E. completes arrangements for loading & transport of a mobile reserve of Stores on G.S. wagons.	
	28th	6 A.M.	Field Coys ordered to move into Assembly Areas under arrangements made by G.S. in consultation with C.R.E.	APP. I
			All Operations postponed 48 hours on account of wet weather, including above move.	
			Hd. Qrs RE move to MERICOURT.	
			C.R.E. visits 77th & 78th Coys & C.E. XV Corps at HEILLY	
MERICOURT	29th		Visited Advanced Battle H.Q. 21st Div to arrange work. CRE visits C.E. XV Corps	
	30th		Hd Qrs RE. move to Treux.	
			C.R.E. visits Coys.	
			C.E. IV Army visits C.R.E.	

[illegible] Lt. Col RE.
C.R.E. 17th Div

1875 Wt. W593/826 1,000,000 4/15 J.B.C. & A. A.D.S.S./Forms/C. 2118.

SECRET App ① h.1

Extracts from 17th Division Operation Order No. 57 dated 28th June 1916.

Ref. map 1/40.000.

1. The Division will move to assembly areas as follows:-

× × × ×

93rd Fd. Coy. } to BOIS DES TAILLES.

× × × ×

× × × ×

44th Fd Coy } to MORLANCOURT.

× × × ×

× × × ×

42th Fd Coy. } to VILLE.
(less 1 section) }

2. Field Companies & Field Ambulances will be under the command of the G. Os. C. of the Brigades to which they are affiliated during the march and while in the assembly areas.

3. × × × × × ×

4. × × × × × ×

5. × × × × × ×

APP. (1)

p.2

-2-

6. 51st. and 52nd. Brigades, O.C. 7th Yorks and Lancaster Regt. and O.C. 78th Field Coy. will report their arrival at their respective destinations by wire.

7. x x x x x x

8. x x x x x x

(Sd.) R. J. COLLINS,

Lt. Col., G.S.,

17th Division.

Issued at 6am.

SHEET (1)

Army Form C. 2118

C.R.E. 17th Div.
JULY. 1916
Vol 10

Instructions regarding War Diaries and Intelligence Summaries are contained in F. S. Regs., Part II. and the Staff Manual respectively. Title Pages will be prepared in manuscript.

WAR DIARY
or
~~INTELLIGENCE SUMMARY~~
(Erase heading not required.)

Place	Date	Hour	Summary of Events and Information	Remarks and references to Appendices
TREUX.	1.7.16		Division standing by for orders. Mobile reserve stores (20 Wagons G.S.) reported loaded & ready to move.	
		9.30pm.	C.R.E's H.Q. move to RIBEMONT	RCL
RIBEMONT.	2.7.16		C.R.E. & Adjutant proceed to Advanced Div. H.Q. near MEAULTE. Visit 77th Coy at MEAULTE & O.C. 77th Coy at 51st Bgde Battle H.Q. Visit Advanced Div. Dump (App I) — 93rd Coy at MORLANCOURT — 78th Coy at VILLE. 77th Coy RE ordered to work on FRICOURT System of Strong Points, with one Coy Pioneers (7th Battn. York & Lancaster Regt.) RCL.	app I
	~~[illegible]~~ 3.7.16		C.R.E visits Advanced Div H.Q. visits O.C. 77th Coy at 51st Bgde H.Q. "Concertina" Frames collected from 51st & 52nd Bgde Advanced Dumps. Visits 78th Coy & 7th Y & L. 93rd Coy turned back to MORLANCOURT. Orders to 77th & 78th Coys. RCL.	app II app III
	4.7.16		CRE and Adjt. join Advanced Div. H.Q. at E.28.a.5.7. CRE visits 52nd Bgde H.Q. with O.C. 93rd Coy to arrange work. visits 7th Y & L. visits 77th Coy at MEAULTE. Orders to 93rd Coy. Orders to 1 Coy 7th Y & L to work on road for RGA under 17th Div. arrangements. Direct orders from CRE for two Coys Pioneers to work, one on FRICOURT System of Strong Points & the other on line of hedge between BOTTOM WOOD & SHELTER WOOD. RCL.	app IV app V
near MEAULTE	5.7.16		CRE visits 178th (Tunnelling) Coy RE: (at his disposal for this day only) & orders them to dredge? all bridges on BECORDEL - FRICOURT Road. Visits 78th Coy, 7th Y & L & 52nd Bgde H.Q. to arrange work. Visits FRICOURT System of Strong Points. 2 Sections 93rd Coy RE at disposal of 52nd Bgde. Pioneers – 1 Coy on CRUCIFIX TRENCH – 1 Coy on FRICOURT System – 1 Coy on road for R.G.A. Orders to 78th Coy. Major J. G. H. Clogg? RE O.C. 93rd Coy injured his knee & went to Hospital. RCL	app VI
	6.7.16		CRE reconnoitres S. side of FRICOURT WOOD with Pioneer Coy. Commander & starts him on constructing track along it. Visits BOTTOM WOOD, & QUADRANGLE TRENCH & RAILWAY COPSE. Visits 78th & 93rd Coy. Extract from 17th Div O.O. No 60 sent to all three Companies. Pioneers informed by Div. direct. New RE Dump	app VII

1875 Wt. W593/826 1,000,000 4/15 J.B.C. & A. A.D.S.S./Forms/C. 2118.

SHEET (2)

Instructions regarding War Diaries and Intelligence Summaries are contained in F. S. Regs., Part II. and the Staff Manual respectively. Title Pages will be prepared in manuscript.

WAR DIARY

or

~~INTELLIGENCE SUMMARY~~

(Erase heading not required.)

Army Form C. 2118

C.R.E. 17th Div.
July. 1916

Place	Date	Hour	Summary of Events and Information	Remarks and references to Appendices
near MEAULTE	6/7/16		of wire pickets & tools also cutting tools for use in woods formed at X28.d.3.2. by 15 G.S. wagons from Mobile Reserve.	RCL
	7.7.16	10 A.M. 10.30 A.M.	Orders to 93rd Coy & 7th Y & L.	App VIII & IX
			Orders to 78th Coy & 7th Y & L.	App X & XI
			Orders to 77th Coy & 7th Y & L.	App XII
			A very wet day which greatly interfered with work & operations.	
			C.R.E. visited FRICOURT and arranged repair of 60 cm. Tramway up WILLOW AVENUE with C.E. XV Corps & O.C. 149th (Army Troops) Coy. R.E.	RCL
	8.7.16	10 A.M.	Orders to 77th Coy to relieve 93rd Coy	App XIII
			New RE Dump selected & commenced at F4.c. central. (End of Tramway, 60 cm.)	
			Orders to 77th Coy.	App XIV
			Orders to 78th Coy. RCL	App XV
	9.7.16		C.R.E. visited H.Q. 33rd Div. re trolleys. Visited 77th, 78th Coys & 7th Y & L. Arranged for mule haulage of tramways	
			Orders to 77th Coy.	App XVI
			Orders to 78th Coy. RCL	App XVII
	10.7.16	9 A.M.	Orders to 93rd Coy. Other units resting	App XVIII
	11.7.16		Division relieved by 21st Div. Handing over notes. RCL	App XIX
	12.7.16		C.R.E.'s H.Q. arrive at FOURDRINOY. RCL	
FOURDRINOY.	13.7.16		C.E. II Corps visits C.R.E. & makes notes of work of 17th Div R.E. during Operations. RCL	App XX

SHEET (3)

Army Form C. 2118

Instructions regarding War Diaries and Intelligence Summaries are contained in F. S. Regs., Part II. and the Staff Manual respectively. Title Pages will be prepared in manuscript.

WAR DIARY
or
~~INTELLIGENCE SUMMARY~~
(Erase heading not required.)

CRE: 17th Div.
JULY. 1916.

Place	Date	Hour	Summary of Events and Information	Remarks and references to Appendices
FOURDRINOY			C.R.E. & his H.Q. move to PONT REMY.	RCL
PONT REMY			Division resting & refitting.	
	23.7.16		C.R.E.'s H.Q. move to RIBEMONT	RCL
RIBEMONT	24.7.16		C.R.E. visited by C.E. XV Corps. CRE & Adj. visit FRICOURT. Visits all Companies	
	25.7.16		C.R.E. visits "Corps Line" with C.E. XV Corps. Visits all Companies. 77th 78th Field Coys & Pioneer Battn ordered to move to MAMETZ to start "Corps Line"	RCL App XXI
	26.7.16		C.R.E. goes round proposed "Corps Line" with O.C.s 77th & 78th Coys. Visits C.R.E. 5th Div at FRICOURT & O.C. 2nd Indian Field Squadron at DERNANCOURT.	RCL
	27.7.16		C.R.E. visits 77th & 78th Coys at MAMETZ. O.C. 2nd Ind. Field Squad. at DERNANCOURT & CE XV Corps at HEILLY. No work done on new line owing to attacks in front.	RCL
	28.7.16		C.R.E. visits MAMETZ. Orders to 77th & 78th Coys to withdraw. visits CE. XV Corps & O.C. 2nd Indian Fd. Squadron.	App. XXII RCL
	29.7.16		C.R.E. visits 2nd Div H.Q. takes CRE 33rd Div. round Corps "Check" Line. visits CE XV Corps & O.C. 2nd Indian Field Squadron.	RCL
	30.7.16		C.R.E. visits H.Q. 5th Div. & O.C. Indian Fd. Squadron	RCL
	31.7.16		C.R.E. visits new Div H.Q. at BELLEVUE FARM visits H.Q. 2nd Indian Field Squadron visits H.Q. 33rd Div & hands over work on Corps "Check" line to Adj RE. 33rd Div. in absence of CRE.	
		6.0pm	CRE visits CRE 33rd Div. re XV Corps "Check" Line.	RCL

C. W. Carpenter
Lt Col. RE
CRE 17th Div.

1875 Wt. W593/826 1,000,000 4/15 J.B.C. & A. A.D.S.S./Forms/C. 2118.

App I

(Copy)

O.C. 77th Coy R.E.

1. Your Company will proceed to make Strong Points at or near the following places tonight.

FRICOURT FARM.
X 28. c. 9. 1.
X 23. d. 7. 3.
F 4. a. 8. 5

Ground is to be reconnoitred before dusk.

2. 1 Coy Pioneers will be at your disposal, under arrangements to be made direct with O.C. Pioneer Battn by you.

3. 6 G.S. Wagons from Div Mobile Reserve are at your disposal

2.7.16
2 p.m.

(Signed) E. M. Carpenter
Lt Col RE CRE 17th Div.

REF. MAP. MONTAUBAN 1/20,000

Copy to 7th Y. & L.

App. II
(Copy.)

O.C. 77th Coy RE.

1.) Work for your unit tonight as follows
Strong Point in CRUCIFIX TRENCH X.28.a.4.2.
Clearing & Reversing CRUCIFIX TRENCH
East from this point in direction of
RAILWAY COPSE turning back a flank
towards X.28. Central.
Construction of a line of points on line
of hedge between BOTTOM & SHELTER WOODS.

2.) Two Coys 7th York and Lancasters will
meet your guides at BECORDEL Cross
Roads (F7c.8.2.) at 9 p.m.

3.) Carrying Party (200 men from 7th Dorsets)
has been arranged & will be at BECORDEL
Cross Roads at 9 p.m.

4.) Six G.S. Wagons from Mobile Reserve
Dump are at your disposal for Stores.

3.7.16 (Signed) C. M. Carpenter
4.0 p.m. Lt-Col RE. CRE 17th Div.

Ref Map 1/20,000

App. III

O.C. 78th Coy R.E. (Copy)

1.) Work for your Coy tonight as follows—
Strong Points at—
X.28.d.6.3.
X.28.d.8.2.
Complete Strong Points at—
X.28 c.9.1.
F.4.a.8.5.

2.) One Coy Pioneers will meet your guides at BECORDEL Cross Roads (F.7 c.3.2.) at 9 p.m.

3.) Carrying Party (200 men from 7th Bn Dorsets) will meet your guides at BECORDEL Cross Roads at 9.p.m.

4.) 6. G.S. Wagons from Mobile Reserve Dump are at your disposal for Stores.

3.7.16 (Signed) C.M. Carpenter
4 p.m. Lt Bd RE CRE. 17th Div.

Ref Map 1/20,000

App IV

O.C. 93rd Coy RE (Copy)

1) Two of your Sections are placed at disposal of 52nd Bgde tonight for use in operations.

2.) Two Sections will complete strong points as follows

X.27.b.5.6.

X.21.d.7.1.

X 27 d 4.6.

and will also improve CRUCIFIX TRENCH and wire in front of it.

3.) One Coy 7th Y.& L. will assist under arrangements to be made by you direct with O.C. of that Battn.

4.) Carrying party of 50 men will be provided by 7th Bn. Dorset Regt.

4.7.16 (Signed) C.M. Carpenter
5.15 p.m. Lt Col RE. CRE. 17th Div.

REF MAP MONTAUBAN 1/20,000

"A" Form. Army Form C. 2121

MESSAGES AND SIGNALS. No. of Message..........

Prefix.......... Code..........m. | Words | Charge | This message is on a/c of: ....Service. (Signature of "Franking Officer.") | Recd. at..........m Date.......... From.......... By..........

Office of Origin and Service Instructions.

Sent At..........m. To.......... By..........

TO 7th York & Lancs Regt

app. V (Copy)

* Sender's Number	Day of Month	In reply to Number	AAA
R.L. 42	4		

Please detail one company to work on road for heavy gun and tractor from SUNKEN ROAD at F.3.b.2.10 near LONELY COPSE to a point about F3.b central aaa Filling & levelling only required aaa Representative R.G.A. will meet your coy commander at first named point near LONELY COPSE at 8AM tomorrow to arrange details aaa G.O.C. wishes you to ensure completion of this road by tomorrow night aaa Report completion to 17th Div G aaa Acknowledge

From
Place CRE. 17th Div
Time

The above may be forwarded as now corrected. (Z)

Censor. Signature of Addressor or person authorised to telegraph in his name.

* This line should be erased if not required.

(A1) O. Ltd., London— W.14042/M.44. 150,000 Pads. 12/15. Form C.2121.

App. VI
(Copy)

O.C. 78th Coy RE.

1.) Work for your Coy tonight as follows:—
Strong Points
X 27. b. 5. 6.
X 28. a. 4. 2.
M.G. Emplacement near
X. 28. b. 2. 1.

2.) No Pioneers available.

5.7.16
2. p.m.

(Signed) G. M. Carpenter
Lt. Col. RE. CRE 17th Div

Ref. Map. MONTAUBAN 1/20,000

app. VII
(Copy)

O.C. 77th (Field) Coy RE
78th " " "
93rd " " "

Extract from 17th Div. Operation Order No 69 dated 6.7.16

9. Reserve — The 51st Bgde, 7th York & Lancs and all three Field Cos. (less one section each placed at disposal of affiliated Infy Bgdes.) will be in reserve & will be ready to move forward from present positions at half hours notice from 6 A.M. on July 7th

"A" Form. Army Form C. 2121

MESSAGES AND SIGNALS.

No. of Message...........

Prefix........... Code............m. Words Charge

Office of Origin and Service Instructions.

Sent At..........m. To.......... By..........

This message is on a/c of: .... *Service.*

(Signature of "Franking Officer.")

Recd. at..........m Date.......... From.......... By..........

TO { 93rd Field Coy. RE.
4th. Yorks & Lancs Regt. }

(app VIII)

Sender's Number	Day of Month	In reply to Number	AAA
* R.L. 47.	7th.		

Remaining 3 sections 93rd Fd Coy and 1 Coy. 7th. Yorks & Lancs Regt will proceed at once to consolidate QUADRANGLE trench from its junction with BOTTOM ALLEY inclusive to its junction with SHELTER ALLEY X.22.b.54 aaa Special attention to be paid to these points and one about X.22.d.8.7 aaa These points should be wired aaa Remainder of trench to be prepared for fire aaa Details of work to be arranged between 93rd Fd Coy. and 7th Yorks & Lancs direct aaa Addressed 93rd Coy. RE and 7th York & Lancs aaa Repeated 52nd. Bde.

From
Place CRE 17th Div. 10 A.M.
Time

The above may be forwarded as now corrected. (Z)

Censor. Signature of Addressor or person authorised to telegraph in his name.

* This line should be erased if not required.

(A1) O. Ltd., London— W.14042/M.44. 150,000 Pads. 12/15. Form C.2121.

"A" Form. Army Form C. 2121

MESSAGES AND SIGNALS. No. of Message..........

Prefix.......... Code..........m. Office of Origin and Service Instructions.	Words	Charge	This message is on a/c of: .... Service. (Signature of "Franking Officer.")	Recd. at..........m Date.......... From.......... By..........
	Sent At..........m. To.......... By..........			

TO { 93rd. Fd. Coy. RE.
7th. York & Lancs. Regt. } (App IX)

* Sender's Number	Day of Month	In reply to Number	AAA
R.L. 48	7		

Ref. my R.L 47 of today aaa Enquiries should be made ~~at~~ en route at 52nd Bde HQ. as to the situation in QUADRANGLE TRENCH aaa 52nd Bde should be able to say when you may go forward to work aaa Added 93rd Fd Co. and 7th York & Lancs aaa Repeated 52nd Bde

From
Place CRE 17th Div.
Time 10.30 A.M.

The above may be forwarded as now corrected. (Z)

.... Censor. Signature of Addressor or person authorised to telegraph in his name.

* This line should be erased if not required.

(A1) O. Ltd., London— W.14042/M.44. 150,000 Pads. 12/15. Form C.2121.

"A" Form. Army Form C. 2121

ME... SSAGES AND SIGNALS. No. of Message...........

.... Code.............m. Origin and Service Instructions.	Words / Charge — Sent at..........m. To........ By........	*This message is on a/c of:* .... *Service.* .... (Signature of "Franking Officer.")	Recd. at........m Date........ From........ By........

TO: 78th Fd Co RE (App X)

Sender's Number	Day of Month	In reply to Number	AAA
RL49	7		

1 Section 78th Fd Coy will at once reconnoitre & commence repair of tramway running N.E. up WILLOW AVENUE from FRICOURT aaa Wooden rails may have to be substituted for broken portions aaa Reference should first be made to Corps Troops believed to be working on this line WEST of FRICOURT

FROM: CRE 17th Div

The above may be forwarded as now correcte... (Z)

Cen... ...sor. Signature of Addressor or person authorised to telegraph in his name.

* This li...ne should be erased if not required.

...o. Ltd., London— W.14042/M.44. 150,000 Pads. 12/15. Form C.2121.

"A" Form. Army Form C. 2121

MESSAGES AND SIGNALS.

No. of Message...........

Prefix........... Code...........m. | Words | Charge | This message is on a/c of: .... Service. | Recd. at..........m

Office of Origin and Service Instructions.

Sent
At..........m.
To..........
By..........

(Signature of "Franking Officer.")

Date..........
From..........
By..........

TO { 78th. Fd. Co. RE.
7th. Yorks & Lancs Regt.

App XI

Sender's Number	Day of Month	In reply to Number	AAA
* R.L. 50	7th.		

Two sections 78th Fd. Co. and 1 Coy. Pioneers will be prepared to go forward as soon as situation permits, to consolidate QUADRANGLE TRENCH from its junction with BOTTOM ALLEY exclusive on the left along WOOD TRENCH & STRIP TRENCH aaa Right boundary will depend on situation aaa Special attention should be paid to points at junction of QUADRANGLE TRENCH & QUADRANGLE ALLEY one about X.23.d.5.6. and one at junction of WOOD TRENCH & STRIP TRENCH aaa These should be wired aaa Send representative to 50th. Bde HQ. to find out when this work can go on aaa Added 78th. Fd. Co. & 7th Yorks Lancs Regt. aaa Repted 50 Bde

From
Place
Time

CRE. 17th. Div.

The above may be forwarded as now corrected. (Z)

Censor. Signature of Addressor or person authorised to telegraph in his name.

* This line should be erased if not required.

(A1) O. Ltd., London— W.14042/M.44. 150,000 Pads. 12/15. Form C.2121.

"A" Form. Army Form C. 2121

MESSAGES AND SIGNALS.

No. of Message...........

Prefix........... Code...........m. Office of Origin and Service Instructions.	Words	Charge	This message is on a/c of:	Recd. at..........m
	Sent		..........Service.	Date..........
	At..........m.			From..........
	To..........			
	By..........		(Signature of "Franking Officer.")	By..........

TO 44th. Fd.Co. RE
7th. York & Lancs Regt.

(App. XII)

* Sender's Number	Day of Month	In reply to Number	AAA
RL 51	7th.		

Three sections 44th Fd.Co RE and two coys. 7th York & Lancs Regt. now in Div. Reserve will stand by to move at two hours notice aaa Added 44th Fd.Co. and 7th. York & Lancs Regt. aaa Reptd. 17th Div.

From
Place CRE. 17th. Div.
Time

The above may be forwarded as now corrected.

(Z)

Censor. Signature of Addressor or person authorised to telegraph in his name.

* This line should be erased if not required.

(A1) O. Ltd., London— W.14042/M.44. 150,000 Pads. 12/15. Form C.2121.

"A" Form. Army Form C. 2121

MESSAGES AND SIGNALS

No. of Message..........

Prefix.......... Code..........m. | Words | Charge | This message is on a/c of: .... Service. (Signature of "Franking Officer.") | Recd. at..........m Date.......... From.......... By..........

Office of Origin and Service Instructions.

Sent At..........m. To.......... By..........

TO { 44th. Fd.Co RE / 93rd. Fd.Co RE } App XIII

Sender's Number	Day of Month	In reply to Number	AAA
* Rh. 55	8		

44th. Fd.Co RE. and 93rd. Fd.Co RE will interchange billets today aaa Arrangements to be made direct between units concerned aaa move must be completed by 4 pm. aaa Added 44th Fd.Co RE and 93rd Fd.Co RE

From
Place CRE 17th Div
Time 10 A.M.

The above may be forwarded as now corrected. (Z)

Censor. Signature of Addressor or person authorised to telegraph in his name.

* This line should be erased if not required.

(A1) O. Ltd., London— W.14042/M.44. 150,000 Pads. 12/15. Form C.2121.

App. XIV
(Copy)

O.C. 77th Coy R.E.

1. Your unit (less the section with 51st Bgde) will proceed tonight to consolidate RAILWAY COPSE, CRUCIFIX TRENCH and that portion of RAILWAY ALLEY in 51st Bgde Area.

2. You will also arrange for repair of Railway N of RAILWAY COPSE.

3. One Coy 7th York & Lancaster Regt will be at your disposal.

3.7.16
2.30 p.m.

(Signed) R.G. [illegible] Lt RE
for CRE 17th Div.

REF MAP MONTAUBAN 1/20,000

App. XV
(Copy.)

O.C. 78th Coy RE

1.) Your unit will proceed tonight to consolidate BOTTOM WOOD and the part of RAILWAY ALLEY in 50th Bgde Area and make one strong point at East End of RAILWAY ALLEY.

2.) You will arrange for repair of light railway in 50th Bgde Area.

3.) Two Companies 7th Y. & L. at your disposal

3.7.16 (Signed) R.E. Lund (Lt RE)
(2.30 pm.) for CRE 17th Div.

REF MAP MONTAUBAN 1/20,000

App. XVI

(Copy)

O.C. 77th Coy RE.

1.) Your unit (less one section with 51st Bgde will proceed tonight to repair light railway as far as possible in the direction of BOTTOM WOOD.

2.) You will arrange work on Strong point at X.23. d. 3.7. in RAILWAY ALLEY clearing revetting & wiring.

3.) Road from FRICOURT to FRICOURT FARM must also be repaired by you

4.) Half Coy of 7th Y. & L. at your disposal

9.7.16
3.45 p.m.

(Signed) G. M. Carpenter Lt Col RE
CRE 17th Div.

App XVII
(Copy)

O.C. 78th Coy R.E.

1.) Your unit will proceed tonight to reverse, clear & wire RAILWAY ALLEY and carry on with Strong point at East End of RAILWAY ALLEY & Strong Points at X 29. c. 2. 8. & X 28. b. 9. 4.

2) Half a Coy 7th Y & L at your disposal

3.7.16
3.45 p.m.

Signed G. H. Carpenter
Lt Col R.E. CRE 17th Div.

"A" Form. Army Form C. 2121.

MESSAGES AND SIGNALS. No. of Message...........

Prefix........... Code...........m. | Words | Charge | This message is on a/c of: Copy Service. | Recd. at.........m.

Office of Origin and Service Instructions.

Sent At.........m. To......... By.........

(Signature of "Franking Officer.") Date......... From......... By.........

TO { 93rd Coy R.E. / 7th York & Lancs } app XVIII

Sender's Number	Day of Month	In reply to Number	AAA
* L.25	10		

93rd Company R.E. and one Company 7th Battn York & Lancs will proceed at once to WILLOW TRENCH F4a8.5 prepared to work in forward area aaa Representatives to be sent at once to 50th Brigade H.Q. for further instructions aaa Add 93rd Field Co R.E. 7th York & Lancs aaa repeated 50th Brigade.

From C.R.E.

Place 17th Division

Time

The above may be forwarded as now corrected. (Z)

Censor. Signature of Addressor or person authorised to telegraph in his name.

* This line should be erased if not required.

(A1) C. Ltd., London— W.14042/M.44. 150,000 Pads. 12/15. Form C.2121.

App. XIX (1)

Handing over notes on Consolidation, etc.

FRICOURT WOOD.

S.P. (3) F.4.a.8.4 – 3 sides 100x each. traversed firebays sandbagged & wired (mostly concertina frames) – wire nearly to (6).

(6) X.28.c.9.1. – Small point – firestepped & sandbagged – wired single apron fence.

(12) X.28.d.73. – 2 points at corners of wood, connected by straight, and stepped, sandbagged, wire in edge of wood.

(1) X.28.b.1.8. – Square point – 5 bays side wired.

RAILWAY ALLEY — CRUCIFIX.

S.P. East end of alley, X.29.c.9.8. – to connect with Division on right at QUEENS NULLAH circular point – M.Gs.

300x of RAILWAY ALLEY reversed – wired as per sketch at A.

S.P. at small copse X.29.c.3.8. – M.G.s & traversed, as per sketch, at B.

S.P. consisting of portion of trench with flanks

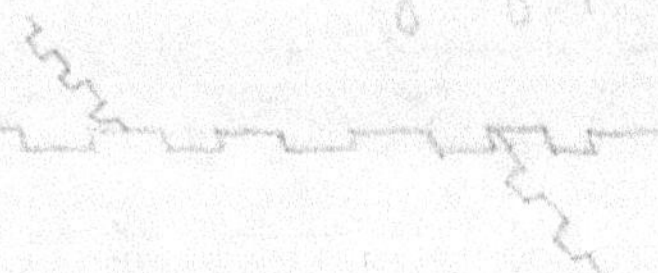

& wired – X.28.d.3.5.

Trench cleared and reversed.

S.P. – RAILWAY COPSE – X.28.d.3.9. made island traversed point – & M.G. emplacement.

CRUCIFIX trench has been reversed and prepared for defence. This has been badly shelled.

BOTTOM WOOD.

Front edge dug for firebays in places and about 150x wired; BOTTOM ALLEY partly prepared for fire towards east.

S.P. at S.W. corner of wood X.28.b.9.4. good circular point – at sketch C.

Hedge from BOTTOM WOOD to SHELTER WOOD - with posts in front, and about 350 of trench behind hedge dug 4'6" deep - no wire was put, in case of advance.

Bombing post - PEARL ALLEY - QUAD. TRENCH.

BOTTOM WOOD.

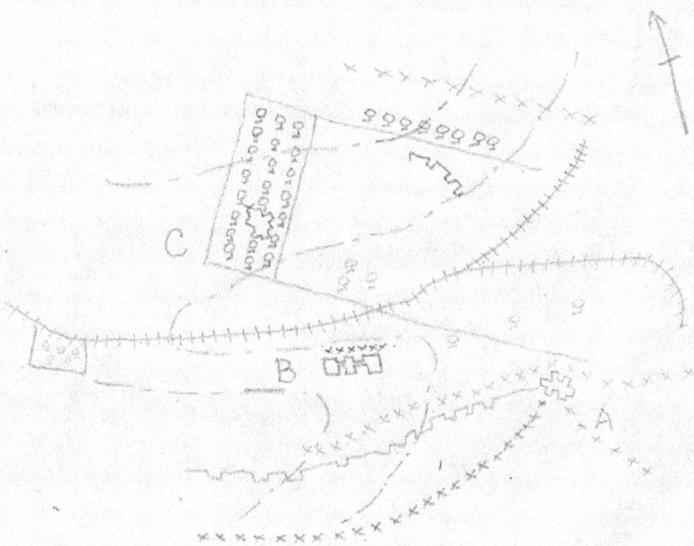

10/7/16.

COPY. App XX

REPORT ON WORK OF R.E. & PIONEERS, 17th DIVISION.

C.R.E., Lieut. Col. C.M. Carpenter, DSO, RE
77th. Field Co. R.E., Major J.G. Fleming, DSO, RE
78th. Field Co. R.E.; Captain C.F. Carson, RE.
93rd. Field Co. R.E., Major P.G.H. Hogg, DSO, RE
7th. York & Lancs. Pioneers., Colonel H.W. Byass.

Each Brigade in front line had OC. and 1 section, R.E. at Brigade Headquarters, remaining 3 sections and Pioneers were in Divisional Reserve and practically under orders of C.R.E.

---

2 Brigades were in front line and 1 in reserve.

2/7/16. OBJECTIVES.

First: FRICOURT VILLAGE.

Second: Road from FRICOURT CHURCH to FRICOURT FARM and to POODLES.

Third: RAILWAY ALLEY and to join with 7th. Division about X.29.d.0.6.

ORDERS.

(1) 77th. Field Co. R.E. proceed to-night and make strong points at FRICOURT FARM: X.28.c.9.1: X.28.d.7.3: F.4.a.8.5.

Arrangements will be made to reconnoitre before dusk.

(2) 1 Coy. Pioneers were placed at disposal of OC. 77th. Field Co. R.E.

(3) 6 wagons from 1st. line transport were allotted for stores. 78th. & 93rd. Coys R.E. will remain in reserve.

3/7/16.

7th. Division took over BOTTOM WOOD from 17th. Division and 17th. Division took over from 21st. Division up to a line 200 yards East of and parallel to the straight FRICOURT — CONTALMAISON Road.

Orders for R.E.

(1) 77th. Co. R.E. will make a strong point

in

in CRUCIFIX trench about X. 28. a. 4. 2.

(2) Clear and reverse CRUCIFIX trench East of X. 28. a. 4. 2. in direction of RAILWAY COPSE turning back a flank towards X. 28 Central.

(3) 2 Coys Pioneers were told off to work under direction of O.C. 77th. Co. R.E. to construct a line of points on line of hedge between BOTTOM and SHELTER WOODS.

Carrying party of 200 strong from 6th. Dorset Regt, who were in Reserve, was provided and 6 G.S. wagons from 1st. line transport carried stores.

78th. Co. R.E. will

(1) Construct strong points at X.28. d.6.3: X.28. d. 8.2.
(2) Complete strong points at X. 28. c. 9.1: F. 4. a. 8.5

1 Coy. Pioneers assisted, and stores were brought up by 6 G.S. Wagons from 1st. line transport and by 200 men of 6th. Dorset Regt.

93rd. Field Co. R.E., and 1 Coy. Pioneers remained in Division Reserve.

4/7/16:

77th. & 78th. Coys in Reserve moving & resting.

93rd. Co. R.E.

2 Sections at disposal of 52nd. Bde, who did not use them. 2 sections to complete strong points X. 27. b. 5. 6: X. 21. d. 7.1: X. 27. d. 4.6, commenced by 21st. Division, also to improve CRUCIFIX trench, and wire in front (350 yards).

1 Coy. Pioneers helped, and 50 Dorsets carried wire and sandbags.

R.E. Wagons which previously had been loaded ready to advance were now brought up close and unloaded, and became available, so that wagons from the 1st line transport were no longer detailed.

2 Coys. of Pioneers worked under the direct orders of C. R. E; 1 Coy. on FRICOURT System Supporting points, viz:- FRICOURT FARM; X. 28. c. 9.1; X. 28. d. 7.3; F. 4. a. 8.5, the 2nd Coy. on line of hedge between BOTTOM and

/SHELTER

WOODS.

110 men of Dorset Regt. were detailed as carriers.

---

1 Coy. of Pioneers remained in Reserve.

5/7/16.

77th. Co. R.E. & 2 sections 93rd. Field Co. R.E. remained in reserve.

78th. Co. R.E. worked on strong points X.27.b.5.6: X.28.a.4.2; and prepared a M.G. Emplacement near X.28.b.2.1.

93rd Co. R.E. 2 sections were placed at the disposal of 52nd. Brigade to form bombing stops in PEARL ALLEY and QUADRANGLE ALLEY, near junction with QUADRANGLE SUPPORT.

Pioneers were employed:—

1 Coy. making road from LONELY COPSE to FRICOURT WOOD for 8" guns.

1 Coy. cleaning, deepening, and firestepping CRUCIFIX trench.

1 Coy. in FRICOURT WOOD, working on supporting points.

1 Coy. in Division Reserve.

178th. Tunnelling Co. R.E., at the disposal of the Division for this day only, doubled bridges on BECORDEL—FRICOURT Road.

6/7/16.

An attack took place, but it did not succeed, as the 3 Field Coys R.E. and 3 Coys. Pioneers in reserve, were not employed.

---

1 Coy. Pioneers worked on road ROSE COTTAGE to N.E. corner of FRICOURT WOOD (X.28.d.3.2).

15 wagons formed dumps of wire, pickets, and tools, and cutting tools to this corner. The cutting tools were in great demand for use in MAMETZ WOOD.

7/7/16.

7/7/16.

A very wet day, which interfered very much with work.

77th. Co. R.E. and 2 Coys. Pioneers were held in Divisional Reserve.

78th. Co. R.E. & 1 Coy. Pioneers worked in trenches in BOTTOM WOOD and in BOTTOM ALLEY.

93rd. Co. R.E. and 1 Coy. Pioneers were ordered to consolidate QUADRANGLE trench, but owing to troops intended for attack of QUADRANGLE SUPPORT not getting forward, this could not be carried out.

8/7/16.

77th. Co. R.E., less 1 section (with Brigade), and 1 Coy. Pioneers, were ordered to consolidate RAILWAY COPSE, CRUCIFIX trench, and part RAILWAY ALLEY in 51st. Brigade area (left), and to repair 60 cm. railway N. of RAILWAY COPSE. The section with the Brigade consolidated part QUADRANGLE trench and PEARL ALLEY 1st line; they were able to do useful work.

78th. Co. R.E. & 2 Coys Pioneers consolidated BOTTOM WOOD and part RAILWAY ALLEY in 50th. Brigade area (right) and 1 strong point at East end of RAILWAY ALLEY, and repaired the light railway. The section with the Brigade working with the Coy.

93rd. Co. R.E. & 1 Coy. Pioneers were kept in Reserve. A Dump was formed at F.4.c.6.4.

9/7/16.

77th. Co. R.E. less 1 section and ½ Co. Pioneers, repaired railway to within 50 yards of BOTTOM WOOD and also worked on strong point X.28.d.3.5. in RAILWAY ALLEY, cleared, reversed and wired part of RAILWAY ALLEY; and repaired road from FRICOURT to FRICOURT FARM.

/The

the section with Brigade, formed Bombing post at junction of PEARL ALLEY and QUADRANGLE SUPPORT.

<u>78th Co. RE.</u> & ½ Co. Pioneers manned and wired 300 yards RAILWAY ALLEY and strong point east end of RAILWAY ALLEY— Strong point X. 29. c. 2. 8. (Sketch B) and X. 29. b. 9.4. (S.W of BOTTOM WOOD).

<u>93rd Co. RE.</u> & 1 Coy. Pioneers were in Reserve.

<u>10/7/16.</u>

no particular work done. men resting.

<u>11/7/16.</u>

Division was taken out of line.

App XXI

Copy.

SECRET.

CRE.
7th. York & Lancs.
77th. Fd Co. RE.
78th. Fd Co. RE.
5th Div (for info).

17th. Division
G. 611
25th. July, 1916.

1. The 7th. York & Lancs. Regt., 77th. and 78th. Fd Cos. will move tomorrow to an area between MAMETZ and POMMIER REDOUBT for work on the Corps 2nd line of defence under instructions which will be issued to them direct by CRE. 17th. Division.

2. Route DERNANCOURT – VIVIER MILL – MEAULTE – cross roads F.9.a. – cross roads F.10.b. – MAMETZ.
Starting point cross roads E.20.b.2.6.

3. 77th. & 78th. Fd Cos. under command of senior officer to pass starting point at 12.45 pm. 7th. York & Lancs. Regt. will pass starting point at 1.10 pm.
The march will be timed so that head of Fld. Cos. passes cross roads in F.9.a. at 2.30 pm and head of 7th. York & Lancs same point at 3 pm.

4. Only such vehicles & animals as are absolutely necessary will accompany units and as far as possible all vehicles & animals will be sent back after arrival to wagon lines which will be established in the present bivouac area.

5. An officer from each Fd Co. and from 7th. York & Lancs. will report at 12 noon to 5th. Division 'Q' near ROSE COTTAGE, FRICOURT for instructions as to the area available for bivouacs and for watering facilities. All three units will be rationed by the 17th. Division as at present.

6. The medical officer of RE will accompany the two Fld. Companies. The A.D.M.S. will communicate to the medical officers concerned the whereabouts of advanced dressing stations of the 5th. & 51st. Divns.

7. The CRE. and O.C. 7th. York & Lancs will report to Div. H.Q. the location of units near MAMETZ.

Acknowledge.

(sd) R.J. COLLINS, Lt. Col. G.S.
17th. Division

17th Divisional Engineers

C. R. E.

17th DIVISIONAL ENGINEERS

AUGUST 1 9 1 6

Vol 11 (1.)

Army Form C. 2118

Instructions regarding War Diaries and Intelligence Summaries are contained in F. S. Regs., Part II. and the Staff Manual respectively. Title Pages will be prepared in manuscript.

WAR DIARY
or
INTELLIGENCE SUMMARY
(Erase heading not required.)

CRE. 17th Div.
AUGUST 1916

Place	Date	Hour	Summary of Events and Information	Remarks and references to Appendices
RIBEMONT.	1.8.16		C.R.E. takes over from CRE 5th Div. Visits CRE 5th Div., H.Q. 51st Div., H.Q. 51st Bde. Adjutant visits all Fd. Coys re move. In evening all three Coys & Pioneers moved up to forward billets near MAMETZ. 17th Div O.O. No 70 (extract)	RCL. APP. I
	2.8.16		CRE visits H.Q. 52nd Bde to arrange work in their area. Visits all Fd. Coys. & Pioneers. H.Q. RE move to BELLEVUE FARM.	RCL.
BELLEVUE FARM.	3.8.16		CRE visits CRE 2nd Div. - all Fd. Coys - RE. ALLEY - Y.&L. ALLEY - 51st & 52nd Bde H.Q. Orders to 51st & 50th Bdes re work on R.E. ALLEY.	RCL. App II
	4.8.16		CRE visits all Coys & Pioneers on their jobs & 52nd Bde H.Q.	RCL.
	5.8.16		CRE visits all works in progress with G.S.O. 1 with a view to establishing a second line of defence through or behind LONGUEVAL.	RCL.
	6.8.16		CRE. visits 51st Bde H.Q. 93rd & 77th Coys & Pioneers. G. 870. of 6.8.16 (extract)	RCL. App III
	7.8.16		CRE. visits all work in progress - 2 Bn H.Q. in old German Second Line - 50th Bde H.Q. all Field Coys & Pioneers.	RCL
	8.8.16		CRE. goes round ~~all~~ trenches with G.S.O. 1.	RCL.
	9.8.16		CRE. visits forward works - 2 Bns in German Second Line - 50th Bde H.Q. & all Field Coys. Visits Pioneers & orders Coy in Div Reserve to work on WEST YORKS ALLEY.	RCL.
	10.8.16		CRE. takes CRE 14th Div round Dump & Field Coy Billets	RCL.
	11.8.16		CRE. 14th Div visits CRE. CRE visits all Coys. & Pioneers. Adjutant takes Adj. 14th Div round forward works.	RCL.

1875 Wt. W593/826 1,000,000 4/15 J.B.C. & A. A.D.S.S./Forms/C. 2118.

(2)

Army Form C. 2118

Instructions regarding War Diaries and Intelligence Summaries are contained in F. S. Regs., Part II. and the Staff Manual respectively. Title Pages will be prepared in manuscript.

WAR DIARY
or
INTELLIGENCE SUMMARY
(Erase heading not required.)

C.R.E. 17th Div.
AUGUST 1916

Place	Date	Hour	Summary of Events and Information	Remarks and references to Appendices
BELLEVUE FARM	12/8/16		CRE 14th Div visits CRE. CRE. & Adjutant compile Works Reports (Copy attached) CRE. visits CRE 14th Div.	App. IV RCL.
"	13/8/16		H.Q.RE. move to BUIRE. C.R.E. visits all Companies	RCL.
	14/8/16 – 15/8/16		H.Q.RE. on the march	RCL.
	16/8/16		H.Q.RE. arrive at DOULLENS	RCL.
DOULLENS	17/8/16		C.R.E. visits H.Q. 56th Div with G.S.O.1. – visits right Bde Sector with CRE 56th Div	RCL.
"	18.8.16		C.R.E. visits Centre & left Bde Sectors with CRE 56th Div. Orders to Coys.	RCL App V
"	19.8.16 – 20.8.16		CRE visits CRE 56th Div.	RCL.
"	21.8.16		H.Q.RE move to HENU	RCL.
HENU	22.8.16		C.R.E. goes round Left Sector with O.C. 77th Coy. RE	RCL.
"	23.8.16		C.R.E. goes round Centre Sector with Lt Travers RE.	RCL
	24.8.16		CRE goes round Right Sector with O.C. 78th Coy RE.	RCL
	25.8.16 to 31.8.16		C.R.E. goes round trenches – arranges schemes for water supply of front line trenches and defence schemes for villages & localities in line in conjunction with G.S. 17th Div.	RCL.

C.W. Carpenter Lt. Col. RE
CRE 17th Div.

1875 Wt. W593/826 1,000,000 4/15 J.B.C. & A. A.D.S.S./Forms/C. 2118.

App I

Extract from 17th. Division Operation Order No 70, dated 31st July, 1916.

2 (e).- The three Fd. Cos. will move tomorrow evening under arrangements to be made by the C.R.E. to relieve the Fd. Cos. of the 5th. Division as follows:-

77th. Fd. Co. - 59th. Fd. Co.
93rd. Fd. Co. - The Durham Fd. Co.
78th. Fd. Co. - The Home Counties Fd. Co.

"A" Form. Army Form C. 2121.

MESSAGES AND SIGNALS. No. of Message..........

Prefix.......... Code..........m. | Words | Charge | This message is on a/c of: | Recd. at..........m.

Office of Origin and Service Instructions.

Sent At..........m. To.......... By..........

..........Service.

Copy.

(Signature of "Franking Officer.")

Date..........

From.......... Appx II

By..........

TO { 51 Bde / 50 Bde } 78 Fld. Co.

* Sender's Number	Day of Month	In reply to Number	AAA
G.764	3rd		

51st Bde will find working party on C.T. running through S.22 central on 4th and 5th aaa Two reliefs of 150 men each under O.C. 78th Fd. Co. RE. who will notify Bde time and place of rendezvous aaa On 6th 50th Bde will take up this work finding same parties under O.C. 78th Fd. Co. RE. who will arrange with Bde direct. aaa Acknowledge aaa added 50 Bde 51st Bde 78th Fd. Co. RE

From 17th Div

Place

Time 7.30 pm.

The above may be forwarded as now corrected. (Z)

Censor. Signature of Addressor or person authorised to telegraph in his name.

* This line should be erased if not required.

(A1) C. Ltd., London.— W.14042/M.44. 150,000 Pads. 12/15. Form C.2121.

App III

EXTRACT

17th Div. G. 870
6th Aug 1916

(1) The Div. Commander is not satisfied that consolidation of the various lines of defence occupied by the Inf. is being vigorously carried out. - - - - - - - .

(2) - - - - - Work will be commenced at once by all Bdes on narrowing the trenches & putting in traverses by means of sandbag revetments.

Those portions actually occupied by Inf. will be narrowed first. All available men will be put on to work and not less than 4 hours work per man will be done daily.

(3) For advice as to such works and for indenting for RE material Field Coys. will be affiliated temporarily as follows—

50th Bde — 93rd Field Coy RE
51st Bde — 77th Field Coy RE
52nd Bde — 78th Field Coy RE

(5) For the present work other than that mentioned above will be allotted as shown on attached table

(6) O.C.'s Field Coys will report as before to CRE

(Sd) R.J. COLLINS Lt Col.
G.S. 17th Div.

17th. Divn. G.878.

WORKING PARTIES.

APP. III

LOCALITY.	R.E.	INF.	PIONEERS	OFFICER IN CHARGE	TASK.
Y.L. ALLEY.	Nil	1 Coy. 52nd. Bde	1 Coy.	O.C. 7th. York & Lancs.	(a) Connect left fork through to depth from about GREEN DUMP to German 2nd. line about S.16.a.6.0. (b) Connect right fork through to depth along track to German 2nd line about S.16.b.6.1. (c) Widen trench throughout to take stretchers.
R.E. ALLEY and Support trenches in 50th. Bde. area	78th. Fd. Co	1 Coy. 52nd Bde	1 Coy.	O.C. 78th Fd. Co	(a) Work through to depth to Bn. Hd. Qrs. about S.17.d.1.6. (b) Widen trench throughout to take stretchers. (c) Construct support trench simultaneously
CRUCIFIX ALLEY & support trenches in 51st. Bde. area.	77th. Fd. Co.	1 Coy. 52nd. Bde	1 Coy.	O.C. 77th. Fd. Co.	(a) Work through to depth to junction with support trench at CRUCIFIX. (b) Construct support trench simultaneously.

(1) App IV

17th. Division Engineers.

Works Diary.

2nd.Aug.1916.

77th. Coy. Working on completion of dugouts for Gunners. Also working on dugouts in Camp.

78th. Coy. Working in dugout dressing station. Also working on dugouts in camp.

93rd. Coy. 2 Sections at Div. H.Q. Camp. 1 Section told off to 52nd. Bde. Exploiting Longueval Water Supply. 1 Section working in Camp.

Pioneers. 3 Companies working on C.T. MONTAUBAN.ALLEY to German 2nd. line - called Y.L.ALLEY. Trench was left by 5th. Div. 1' to 2' deep.

3rd. August.

77th. Coy. Working on a new C.T. in R.E. ALLEY from MONTAUBAN ALLEY toward LONGUEVAL with 2 Coys. Infantry.

78th. Coy. Working on Aid Post and Signal Dugout at FRICOURT.

93rd. Coy. 2 Sections on R.A. Dugouts in neighbourhood of MARLBORO' WOOD.
1 Section at disposal of Bde., as above, working on Battn. H.Q. for 10th. Lancashire Fus.
1 Section working at Div.H.Q.

Pioneers 3 Coys. working in Y.L. ALLEY.

4th. August.

77th. Coy. Working on R.E. ALLEY - 240 yds. dug to 3' x 3'

78th. Coy. Completed dugout for Signal Coy.
Completed Aid Post and 500 yds. C.T. (R.E.ALLEY) 6' deep.

93rd. Coy. 2 Sections on Bomb Posts for 52nd. Inf. Bde. and 80th. Bde. R.F.A., Shelters for Manchesters H.Q. and trench improved on German Second Line - S.16.d.
1 Section on Shelters for 52nd. Bde. H.Q. and Lancashire Fus.

Pioneers 3 Coys. on Y.L ALLEY. Deepened to 5'6", with exception of new piece near Rly.
1 Coy. ~~carrying~~ laying cable for Signals.

5th. August.

77th. Coy. 200 yds. more of R.E. ALLEY 3' x 3'.
New support trench commenced called YORK TRENCH - S.16.d. - S.23.a. - marked out.

78th. Coy. Worked on R.E. ALLEY.

93rd. Coy. 1 Section German 2nd. Line and O.P. for R.A.
1 Section Dugouts for R.F.A.
1 Section Shelters for Bde. & Bn. H.Q.
1 Section working in Camp.

Pioneers 3 Coys. - Y.L. ALLEY.

6th. August.

77th. Coy.

With 1 Coy. Infantry deepened C.T. BERNAFAY WOOD - SHRINE, called CRUCIFIX ALLEY to 3'6", left by 5th. Div. 2' deep.

3 Sections working YORK TRENCH, dug 2' with party of Manchesters.

1 Section marking out support trench S.23.a towards N. corner TRONES WOOD.

78th. Coy.

With 2 Coys. Infantry on R.E. ALLEY and YORK TRENCH S.16.d. - S.16.c.

93rd. Coy.

2 Sections R.F.A. Shelters.
1 Section Bde. & Bn. H.Q.
1 Section Camp.

Pioneers

3 Coys. Y.L ALLEY widening and deepening.

7th. August.

77th. Coy.

2 Sections working YORK TRENCH with one Coy. Infantry.

78th. Coy.

R.E. ALLEY with 1 Coy. Infantry. & 1 Coy.Pioneers

1 Section with 1 Coy. Infantry widening and deepening.

1 Section on Dugouts for 27th. Bde. R.F.A.

Work commenced on dugout for 52nd. Bde. at BEETLE ALLEY - A.1.b.4.8

93rd. Coy.

1 Section Dugouts for R.F.A.

1 Section clearing wells in LONGUEVAL and improving second line.

1 Section on repairs to MONTAUBAN ALLEY - splinterproofs.

Pioneers

1 Coy. laying cable.

Night 6/7th. 1 Coy. working with 78th. Coy. 1 Coy. working Y.L ALLEY from Green Dump S.16.d. to 2nd. Line S.16.a. - to 4'6" deep, with 1 Coy. Infantry.

8th. August.

77th. Coy.

On CRUCIFIX ALLEY with 1 Coy. Infantry 250 yds. dug 4'9".

Night 7/8th. with 1 Coy. Pioneers worked on YORK TRENCH from SHRINE towards TRONES WOOD.

78th. Coy.

On R.E. ALLEY with 1 Coy. Infantry.

1 Coy. Pioneers widened & deepened to 5'6" YORK TRENCH between R.E. ALLEY & Y.L ALLEY, digging down to 4'6" forming firestep.

Worked on BEETLE ALLEY.

93rd. Coy.

Dugouts for R.F.A. sandbagged and German 2nd. Line improved.

1 Section preparing road near MONTAUBAN.

Pioneers

1 Coy. working Y.L. ALLEY, widening and deepening with 1 Coy. Infantry.

Night 8/9th.

1 Coy. Pioneers under 77th. Coy. continuation of YORK TRENCH, SHRINE to TRONES WOOD.

9th. August

77th. Coy. 2 Sections widening and deepening CRUCIFIX with 1 Coy. of Infantry.
Night 9/10th. 1 Coy. Pioneers put out 700 yds. double apron wire from S.23.a. to S.22.b.

78th. Coy. Same as 8th.

93rd. Coy. Improvements to German 2nd. line. C.T. S.16.b. to S.10.b.
1 Coy. West Yorks dug through to 2'6"
1 Coy. Pioneers 160 yds. trenches in S.17.a.

Pioneers. 1 Coy. worked with one Coy. Inf. widening and deepening Y.L ALLEY.

10th. August

77th. Coy. With one Coy. Inf. widening YORK TRENCH and deepening - 4'6"
Night 10/11th. 1 Section 77th. R.E. and 2 Coys Pioneers dug trench from YORK TRENCH to German 2nd. line, South of DELVILLE WOOD (700 yds.) 3 ft. deep.

78th. Coy. Worked on R.E. ALLEY with 1 Coy. Inf. ALLEY now suitable for stretchers to within 50 yds. of WILLOW AVENUE. From AVENUE to Check Line - down to 5'6" requires widening.
YORK TRENCH - worked with 1 Coy. Pioneers.
Bde. H.Q. BEETLE ALLEY.
1 platoon Inf. worked continuously.
Dugout for Signals is being done.
Dugout for 27th. Bde. R.F.A. completed.
R.E. ALLEY now suitable for laying cable.

93rd. Coy. Improving German 2nd Line and German support trench.
Night 10th. 2 Coys. Inf. worked on communication of WEST YORK ALLEY - S.16.a. to S.10.d. and a Coy. of Inf. worked on German support S.17.a. towards PONT SREET.

Pioneers Same as 9th.

11th. August (Night)

77th. Coy. 2 Sections with 2 Coys. Inf. worked on continuation of YORK TRENCH up to DELVILLE WOOD commenced night before.
1 Coy. Pioneers on Eastern portion of YORK TRENCH and clearing old trench to N end of TRONES WOOD.
1 platoon Pioneers on continuation of YORK TRENCH to DELVILLE WOOD.

78th. Coy. 1 Section and 1 Coy. Inf. on R.E ALLEY. Trench now averages 5'6" deep and is passable for stretchers throughout. YORK TRENCH between R.E. ALLEY & Y.L ALLEY completed. Average depth 6'6" with fire step.
Signal dugout at Green Dump completed.
Worked on new Bde. H.Q.

93rd. Coy. Trench between SEAFORTH & DORSET trenches deepened and converted into fire trench.
C.T. along PONT STREET deepened & widened.
Part of Northern end of YORK ALLEY deepened.
New C.T. from German 2nd. line to PONT STREET partly dug right through.

Pioneers

"A" Form. Army Form C. 2121.

MESSAGES AND SIGNALS. No. of Message............

Prefix.......... Code..........m. Office of Origin and Service Instructions.	Words	Charge	This message is on a/c of: ....Service.	Recd. at..........m.
	Sent At..........m. To.......... By..........		Copy (Signature of "Franking Officer.")	Date.......... From.......... By.......... App V

TO		
44th Fd Co. RE	CRE 56th Div.	
48th Fd Co. RE		
93rd Fd Co. RE		

* Sender's Number	Day of Month	In reply to Number	AAA
E. 1319	18th		

Field Coys will relieve Field Coys of 56th Division as follows aaa 44th Fd Co. will relieve 2/2nd London Fd Co at SOUASTRE on 19th inst aaa 48th Fd Co. will relieve 2/1st London Fd Co. at SAILLY-AU-BOIS on 19th inst aaa 93rd Field Co. will relieve 1st Edinburgh Field Co at BAYENCOURT on 20th inst aaa Details will be arranged direct between OsC. incoming and outgoing Fd Coys aaa Addsd. 44th 48th and 93rd Fd Coys aaa Repeated CRE. 56th Div. for information.

From CRE. 17th. Div.
Place
Time

The above may be forwarded as now corrected. (Z)

Censor. Signature of Addressor or person authorised to telegraph in his name.

* This line should be erased if not required.

(A1) O. Ltd., London — W.14012/M.44. 150,000 Pads. 12/15. Form C.2121.

(1)

Army Form C. 2118

WAR DIARY
or
~~INTELLIGENCE SUMMARY~~
(Erase heading not required.)

Instructions regarding War Diaries and Intelligence Summaries are contained in F. S. Regs., Part II. and the Staff Manual respectively. Title Pages will be prepared in manuscript.

CRE. 17th Div.
SEPT. 1916
Vol 12

Place	Date	Hour	Summary of Events and Information	Remarks and references to Appendices
HENU	1.9.16 – 2 – 3 – 4 – 5 – 6 – 7 – 8 – 9.9.16		C.R.E. visits trenches in all sectors & arranges defence schemes for the forward villages.	R.C.L.
	9.9.16		C.R.E. 33rd Div. visits C.R.E.	RCL.
	10.9.16		C.R.E. takes C.R.E. 33rd Div round northern & centre sectors.	
	11.9.16		C.R.E. hands over office & back work relative to northern & centre sectors to CRE. 33rd Div	RCL.
	12.9.16		C.R.E. visits HEBUTERNE	RCL
	13.9.16		C.R.E. visits HEBUTERNE	RCL
	14.9.16		CRE goes round HEBUTERNE trenches with G.S.O.1	RCL.
	15.9.16 – 16 – 17.9.16		CRE goes round HEBUTERNE trenches	RCL.
	18.9.16		CRE. takes C.E. VIIth Corps round HEBUTERNE trenches	RCL.
	19.9.16		CRE. 33rd Div. visits HEBUTERNE trenches with CRE. and commences taking over.	RCL.
	20.9.16		Handing over to CRE 33rd Div. completed.	RCL.
	21.9.16 – 22.9.16		H.Q. RE. 17th Div on the march	RCL.
ST. RICQUIER	23.9.16		a/CRE. makes out & submits Training Scheme	RCL
	24.9.16		a/CRE. visits ~~33rd~~ 93rd & 78th Coys & explores training area	RCL.
	25.9.16		a/CRE. visits 77th Coy and explores training area. Attends Demonstration of "TANKS".	RCL.
	26.9.16		a/CRE visits 93rd Coy RE.	RCL.

C.N. Carpenter Lt. Col. RE.
C.R.E. 17th Div.

(2)

WAR DIARY

~~or~~

~~INTELLIGENCE SUMMARY~~

(Erase heading not required.)

Army Form C. 2118

Instructions regarding War Diaries and Intelligence Summaries are contained in F. S. Regs., Part II. and the Staff Manual respectively. Title Pages will be prepared in manuscript.

C.R.E. 17th Div
SEPT. 1916

Place	Date	Hour	Summary of Events and Information	Remarks and references to Appendices
ST. RICQUIER	27.9.16		a/CRE. visits 78th Coy R.E.	RCL.
	28.9.16		a/CRE. lectures to Officers of 52nd Bde on "Consolidation"	RCL.
	29.9.16		a/CRE. prepares schemes for 77th & 93rd Coys.	RCL.
	30.9.16		a/CRE visits 77th & 93rd Coys doing their schemes on the Training Area & lectures to Officers of 50th Bde on Consolidation.	RCL.

C.M. Carpenter
Lt. Col R.E.
C.R.E. 17th Div.

1875 Wt. W593/826 1,000,000 4/15 J.B.C. & A. A.D.S.S./Forms/C. 2118.

CONFIDENTIAL

Vol 13

WAR DIARIES

OF

CRE 17 Division

77 Field Co. R E

78 - do -

93 - do -

OCTOBER 1916.

Instructions regarding War Diaries and Intelligence Summaries are contained in F. S. Regs., Part II. and the Staff Manual respectively. Title Pages will be prepared in manuscript.

Army Form C. 2118

WAR DIARY
or
~~INTELLIGENCE SUMMARY~~
(Erase heading not required.)

Place	Date	Hour	Summary of Events and Information	Remarks and references to Appendices
ST RICQUIER	2.10.16		C.R.E. visits trenches in HEBUTERNE sector	
	3.10.16		C.R.E. visits C.E. VIIth Corps.	
	4.10.16		C.R.E. rides over training area. attends Conference at the Division.	
	5.10.16		C.R.E. visits trenches in HEBUTERNE sector and 77th Field Coy. RE.	
	6.10.16		H.Q. RE. 17th on the march. C.R.E. visits HEBUTERNE	
PAS.	7.10.16		C.R.E visits HEBUTERNE. Conference at Div. H.Q.	
	8.10.16		CRE visits HEBUTERNE and 93rd Field Coy at HALLOY	
	9.10.16		CRE visits Trenches at HEBUTERNE	
	10.10.16		CRE visits 93rd Field Coy, watched experiments with Ammonal tubes.	
	11.10.16		CRE visits HEBUTERNE and Trenches.	
	12.10.16		CRE visits 93rd Field Coy for demonstration [illegible] CRE visits HEBUTERNE	
	13.10.16		CRE. visits 77th Field Coy in HEBUTERNE.	
	14.10.16		CRE visits HEBUTERNE.	
	15.10.16		CRE visits 93rd Field Coy RE for demonstration with Ammonal tubes.	
	16.10.16		CRE visits 77th + 78th Field Coy RE	
	17.10.16		CRE visits SAILLY. Took over from CRE. 33rd Division.	
	18.10.16		CRE visits SOUASTRE for Demonstration of ammonal Tubes. Visits CRE 40th Div.	
	20-10-16		CRE visits 77th Coy RE at MILLY and 78th Coy RE at HALLOY.	
	22-10-16		CRE. H.Q. on the march.	
TREUX.	23-10-16		CRE visits 14th Corps H.Q and 77th Coy R.E. attends Div. Conference	
	24-10-16		CRE visits Trenches in XIV Corps sector,	
	25-10-16		CRE visits 77th Coy. and 78th Coy RE.	
	26-10-16			
CITADEL	27-10-16		HQ RE on the march.	
	28-10-16		Visits Trenches	
	29-10-16		Visits trenches	
	30-10-16		Visits Trenches	
BERNAFAY WOOD	31-10-16		HQ RE on the march.	

K Travers [illegible] for
Lieut Col RE
CRE 17th Div.

Vol 14

– CONFIDENTIAL –

WAR DIARIES OF

C.R.E. 17th. Division.

77th. Field Coy. R.E.

78th. -do-

93rd. -do-

From 1/11/1916 to 30/11/16.

Army Form C. 2118

Instructions regarding War Diaries and Intelligence Summaries are contained in F. S. Regs., Part II. and the Staff Manual respectively. Title Pages will be prepared in manuscript.

WAR DIARY
or
INTELLIGENCE SUMMARY
(Erase heading not required.)

Place	Date	Hour	Summary of Events and Information	Remarks and references to Appendices
BERNAFAY WOOD	1.11.16		C.R.E visits GINCHY in the morning to site new Bde. H.Q.	
	2.11.16		C.R.E visits trenches with O.C. 93rd Field Coy RE.	
	3.11.16		C.R.E. visits trenches.	
	4.11.16		C.R.E. visits the three Field Coys. H.Q. RE move from MINDEN POST to BERNAFAY WOOD	
	5.11.16		C.R.E. visits the three Field Coys and Pioneers	
	6.11.16		C.R.E. visits the trenches and three Field Coys. C.R.E. 29th Division visits C.R.E.	
	7.11.16		C.R.E visits the trenches and 78th and 93rd Field Coys.	
	8.11.16		C.R.E. visits the trenches with G.S.O. 1. C.R.E. Guards Division visits C.R.E.	
	9.11.16		C.R.E visits 78th and 93rd Field Coys in morning, 77th Field Coy in afternoon	
	10.11.16		C.R.E. visits trenches with G.S.O. 1.	
	11.11.16		C.R.E visits trenches with C.R.E Guards Division and also 78th + 93rd Field Coys.	
	12.11.16		C.R.E. visits Field Coys.	
	13.11.16		Handing over to C.R.E Guards Division. H.Q. RE moves to TREUX.	
	14.11.16		H.Q. RE on the move.	
PICQUIGNY	15.11.16		H.Q. RE arrive	
	16.11.16		a/C.R.E visits D.H.Q at CAVILLON.	
	17.11.16		a/C.R.E visits 77th Field Coy RE at ST PIERRE EN GROUY	
	18.11.16		a/C.R.E rides round the Divnl Area	
	19.11.16		a/C.R.E. visits 77th Field Coy at FOUDRINOY and D.H.Q.	
	20.11.16		a/C.R.E visits D.H.Q. and 50th Bde at MOLLIENS-VIDAME.	
	21.11.16		a/C.R.E. visits Divnl School DAOURS	
	22.11.16		a/C.R.E visits 51st Bde at SOUES and D.H.Q.	
	23.11.16		a/C.R.E visits D.H.Q and rides round the area	
	24.11.16		a/C.R.E visits D.H.Q. and 77th Coy and 52nd Bde at PICQUIGNY	
	25.11.16		a/C.R.E visits D.H.Q and 52nd Bde.	
	26.11.16		a/C.R.E visits D.H.Q. Two trucks of timber arrived from ABANCOURT (30 days on the way)	
	27.11.16		visits 50th Bde and Det. 77 Field Coy at MOLLIENS-VIDAME.	
	28.11.16		a/C.R.E visits AMIENS to purchase stores	
	29.11.16		a/C.R.E visits D.H.Q.	

[signature] Lieut RE /W.
Lieut. Col. R.E.
CRE 17th Div.

1875 Wt. W593/826 1,000,000 4/15 J.B.C. & A. A.D.S.S./Forms/C. 2118.

Vol 15

— CONFIDENTIAL —

War Diaries

of.

H.Q. R.E. 17th. Division.

77th. Field Company, R.E.

78th. " " "

93rd. " " "

From 1st. December 1916 to 31st. December. 1916.

Instructions regarding War Diaries and Intelligence Summaries are contained in F. S. Regs., Part II. and the Staff Manual respectively. Title Pages will be prepared in manuscript.

WAR DIARY
or
~~INTELLIGENCE SUMMARY~~
(Erase heading not required.)

Army Form C. 2118

Place	Date	Hour	Summary of Events and Information	Remarks and references to Appendices
PICQUIGNY	1/12/16 2-12-16 3-12-16 4-12-16 5-12-16		CRE visits D HQ daily and also 77th Field Coy, rides over the training area.	LLT
	6-12-16		CRE lectures at Divisional school DAOURS	LLT
	7-12-16 8-12-16 9-12-16 10-12-16 11-12-16		CRE visits 77th Field Coy and inspects rifle ranges etc in the training area.	LLT
	12-12-16		CRE lectures at Divisional school DAOURS	LLT
	13-12-16		H.Q. RE on the move	LLT
CORBIE	14-12-16		CRE visits XIV Corps C.E., 20th and Guards Div as CRE Back area	LLT
	15-12-16 16-12-16 17-12-16 18-12-16 19-12-16 20-12-16 21-12-16 22-12-16		CRE Back area visits camps, 20th Div and XIV Corps, supervising all work being done in the back area. Visits also 77th Field Coy at MEAULTE, 78th at TREUX and 93rd at CORBIE daily	LLT
	23-12-16		CRE visits CE XIV Corps & 77th & 78 Field Coys RE.	LLT
	24.12.16			
	25.12.16		H.Q. RE on the move.	LLT
Sheet 62 C N.W. A 4 d 5.2	26.12.16 27.12.16		CRE visits the trenches and field Coys.	LLT
	28.12.16 29.12.16		CRE visits the field Coys and the forward area.	LLT
	30.12.16		CRE visits the trenches.	LLT
	31.12.16		CRE visits the trenches ~~with~~ visits field Coy commanders and O.C. 7th Y & L (Pioneers)	LLT

L L Travers Lieut RE
for Lieut Col RE.
C.R.E. 17th Div.

1875 Wt. W593/826 1,000,000 4/15 J.B.C. & A. A.D.S.S./Forms/C. 2118.

Vol 16

WAR DIARIES

OF

C.R.E. 17th Division

~~77th Field Company~~ R.E.

78th Field Company. R.E.

93rd Field Company. R.E.

From 1/1/1917 to 31/1/1917.

Instructions regarding War Diaries and Intelligence Summaries are contained in F. S. Regs., Part II. and the Staff Manual respectively. Title Pages will be prepared in manuscript.

WAR DIARY

or

~~INTELLIGENCE SUMMARY~~

(Erase heading not required.)

Army Form C. 2118

Place	Date	Hour	Summary of Events and Information	Remarks and references to Appendices
H.4.d.5.2	1-1-17	–	C.R.E. visited 7th Yorks & Lancs. (Pioneers) to see new duckboard tracks to forward area.	
do	2-1-17	–	do ——— do ———	
do	3-1-17	–	C.R.E. organizes laying of new duckboard tracks and visits WINTER Tr and Batt. H.Q.	
do	4-1-17		C.R.E. visits Field Companies and Tunnelling Company.	
do	5-1-17		C.R.E. visits Ciro's Trench and new duckboard tracks with O.C. 93rd Fld. Coy	
do	6-1-17		C.R.E. visits Field Coys. and three Brigade H.Q's.	
do	7-1-17		C.R.E. visits Intermediate Line and G.S. office.	
do.	8-1-17		C.R.E. receives orders for wiring of Reserve Line.	
do.	9-1-17		C.R.E. visits Field Coys. and dumps and arranges for wiring of Intermediate Line	
do	10-1-17		C.R.E. Inspects Reserve Line and completes arrangements for wiring of same.	
do	11-1-17		C.R.E. and adjutant walk through Reserve line at night while wiring is in progress.	
do.	12-1-17		Wiring of Reserve Line completed – 4500 yards.	
do.	13-1-17		Visited three Field Companies	
do.	14-1-17		C.R.E. visits and inspects work of D.O.R.E. in back area camps, also Div. Laundry at TREUX.	
do.	15-1-17		Consult with 29th Div C.R.E. about relief of Field Companies and handing over of work.	
do.	16-1-17		78th Field Coy is relieved by coy of 29th Div R.E.	
do.	17-1-17		93rd " " " " " " " "	
do	18-1-17		77th " " " " " " " " " H.Q. R.E. moves to CORBIE.	
CORBIE	19-1-17		Work in back area taken over from 29th Div.	
"	20-1-17		Arrangements for carrying on work in back area and supply of material for companies made.	
"	21-1-17		a/C.R.E. visits 77th Field Coy in MEAULT and sees work.	
"	22-1-17		" " 93rd " " " LA HOUSSOIRE	
"	23-1-17		" " 78th " " " CORBIE and inspects work.	

Instructions regarding War Diaries and Intelligence Summaries are contained in F. S. Regs., Part II. and the Staff Manual respectively. Title Pages will be prepared in manuscript.

WAR DIARY
or
~~INTELLIGENCE SUMMARY~~
(Erase heading not required.)

Army Form C. 2118

Place	Date	Hour	Summary of Events and Information	Remarks and references to Appendices
CORBIE	24-1-17		a/CRE arranges lecture to 17th Div. School DAOURS on Defense of Villages	[illegible]
"	25-1-17		" visits 78th and 93rd Coys. 93rd Coy in DAOURS.	[illegible]
"	26-1-17		a/CRE. visits CRE. 20th Div at Arrow Head Copse re reliefs. also C.E. 14th Corps and 77th Coy.	[illegible]
"	27-1-17		All work and dumps and Saw Mill in CORBIE handed over to C.E. 15th Corps. Works reports sent to C.E. 14th Corps	[illegible]
"	28-1-17		H.Q. CRE. moves up to Arrow Head Copse to relieve H.Q R.E of 20th Div.	[illegible]
Arrow Head copse.	29-1-17		C.R.E. visits Field Companies and 7th Yorks & Lancs Regt.	[illegible]
"	30-1-17		C.R.E. visits 77th Fld Coy and their work in forward area. Also H.Q. 51st Bde.	[illegible]
"	31-1-17		CRE visits Right sector support line with O.C 93rd Field Coy R.E., visits 52nd Bde and 77 Field Co.	[illegible]

K Travers Capt RE
Lieut. Colonel R.E.
C.R.E. 17. Div

1875 Wt. W593/826 1,000,000 4/15 J.B.C. & A. A.D.S.S./Forms/C. 2118.

Vol 17

Confidential

War Diary

of

C.R.E. – 17th Division

~~17th Field Co. R.E.~~ "

~~78th~~ do "

~~93rd~~ do "

for

February 1917

Instructions regarding War Diaries and Intelligence Summaries are contained in F. S. Regs., Part II. and the Staff Manual respectively. Title Pages will be prepared in manuscript.

WAR DIARY
or
~~INTELLIGENCE SUMMARY~~
(Erase heading not required.)

Army Form C. 2118

Place	Date	Hour	Summary of Events and Information	Remarks and references to Appendices
ARROW HEAD COPSE	1.2.17		C.R.E visits Bde H.Q and intermediate Line in left Sector with O.C. 77th Field Coy R.E.	
	2.2.17		C.R.E 29th Div. visits C.R.E with a view to taking over.	
	3.2.17		C.R.E. visits 52nd Bde., 3 Field Coys and Pioneers.	
	4.2.17		C.R.E attends gas lecture, visits pioneers and 78 Field Co. R.E.	
	5.2.17		C.R.E visits COMBLES R.E. Dump, 3 Field Coys and pioneers.	
	6.2.17		C.R.E visits 52nd Bde., 3 Field Coys and pioneers.	
	7.2.17		C.R.E visits 77th Field Coy R.E. and goes round support line with O.C. 93rd Field Coy R.E.	
	8.2.17		C.R.E visits pioneers and HARDECOURT Camp.	
	9.2.17		C.R.E visits 183rd Tunnelling Coy R.E., 3 Field Coys and pioneers.	
	10.2.17		C.R.E goes round trenches with G.S.O.1. D.H.Q. shelled by H.V. gun. CRE's mess and office destroyed.	
	11.2.17		C.R.E visits Field Coys in COMBLES.	
	12.2.17		C.R.E visits Field Coys in COMBLES and goes round NORTH COPSE Sector with G.S.O.1 by night.	
	13.2.17		C.R.E visits 78th Field Coy R.E. pioneers and inspects HARDECOURT CAMP.	
	14.2.17		C.R.E visits all 3 Field Coys. R.E. Adjutant inspects Div laundry at TREUX.	
	15.2.17		C.R.E. visits Field Coys. and goes round intermediate line with G.S.O.1.	
	16.2.17		C.R.E. inspects HARDECOURT camp, visits 78th Field Coy R.E. and pioneers.	
	17.2.17		C.R.E. inspects HARDECOURT camp with D.A.A. & Q.M.G. visits 3 Field Coys and goes round support Line.	
	18.2.17		C.R.E. visits 50th Bde. 77th and 93rd Field Coys. R.E. 78th Field Coy. moves.	
	19.2.17		C.R.E. visits 93rd Field Coy R.E. 77th Field Coy moves. Handing over to 29th Div.	
	20.2.17		C.R.E. visits 510th Field Coy R.E. and Pioneer Batt. 29th Div. 93rd Field Coy moves.	
	21.2.17		C.R.E 29th Div takes over. H.Q. R.E. moves to HEILLY.	
HEILLY	22.2.17		a/C.R.E sees O.C. 77th Field Co. R.E. and O.C. 78th Field Coy R.E. about work in back AREA.	
	23.2.17		a/CRE. visits 93rd Field RE at DAOURS.	
	24.2.17		O.C. 77th and 93rd Field Coys R.E. visits CRE. arrangements for Stores.	
	25.2.17		a/C.R.E visits 77th Field Coy R.E.	
	26.2.17		a/CRE. visits C.E. II CORPS and 77th Field Coy RE.	
	27.2.17		a/CRE. visits 93rd Field Coy R.E.	
	28.2.17		CRE. visits 93rd and 77th Field Coys RE.	

J E Travers Capt RE
for Lieut. Col. R.E.
C.R.E. 17th Div.

Instructions regarding War Diaries and Intelligence Summaries are contained in F. S. Regs., Part II. and the Staff Manual respectively. Title Pages will be prepared in manuscript.

WAR DIARY
or
INTELLIGENCE SUMMARY
(Erase heading not required.)

Army Form C. 2118

CRE 17 Div Vol 18

Place	Date	Hour	Summary of Events and Information	Remarks and references to Appendices
HEILLY	1.3.17		Division on the move C.R.E. visits CE II CORPS	[initials]
	2.3.17		H.Q. RE moves to CONTAY.	[initials]
CONTAY	3.3.17		CRE visits Field Coys.	[initials]
	4.3.17		H.Q. RE moves to VADENCOURT	[initials]
VADENCOURT	5.3.17		CRE visits CE V ARMY.	[initials]
	6.3.17 – 13.3.17		C.R.E. visits Field Coys. and arranges for Training. Visits CE. II CORPS + CE V ARMY. C.R.E. Inspects Field Coys :- 77th on 10th March, 78th " 14th March when moving off. 93th " 11th March	[initials]
	14.3.17 – 15.3.17		H.Q. R.E. on the move to WILLEMAN.	[initials]
WILLEMAN	16.3.17		CRE visits CE XIX CORPS	[initials]
	17.3.17 – 22.3.17		C.R.E. visits Field Coys. arranges Training. CRE visits CE XIX CORPS and CE III ARMY + arranges for supply of material for Area.	[initials]
	23.3.17		H.Q. RE moves to LE CAUROY.	[initials]
LE CAUROY	24.3.17		CRE visits 77th 78th + 93rd Field Coys.	[initials]
	25.3.17		CRE visits 78th + 93rd Field Coys.	[initials]
	26.3.17		CRE visits 77th Field Coy + CE III Army.	[initials]
	27.3.17		CRE holds Coy. Commanders conference. visits 77th Coy.	[initials]
	28.3.17		CRE visits CRE Cav. CORPS.	[initials]
	29.3.17		CRE visits CE III Army + 77th Coy in St Pol.	[initials]
	30.3.17		CRE visits Coys.	[initials]
	31.3.17		CRE goes round trenches in ARRAS Sector with CRE Cav. Corps.	[initials]

[signature] Capt RE
f. Lieut.-Col. RE
C.R.E. 17 Div.

1875 Wt. W593/826 1,000,000 4/15 J.B.C. & A. A.D.S.S./Forms/C. 2118.

Instructions regarding War Diaries and Intelligence Summaries are contained in F. S. Regs., Part II. and the Staff Manual respectively. Title Pages will be prepared in manuscript.

WAR DIARY

or

~~INTELLIGENCE SUMMARY~~

(Erase heading not required.)

Army Form C. 2118

APRIL 1917. HQ RE 17 D

Vol 19

Place	Date	Hour	Summary of Events and Information	Remarks and references to Appendices
LE CAUROY	1/4/17		CRE visits Field Coys.	
	2.4.17			
	3.4.17		CRE attends Div. Conference, later visits Field Coys.	
	4.4.17		CRE visits Cav. Corps and CRE's 3rd 14th 15th Divs.	
	5.4.17		CRE visits CE. VI Corps.	
	6.4.17		CRE visits CE. VI + VII Corps. CRE visits CRE Cav. Corps.	
HAUT AVESNES	8.4.17		H.Q. RE moves to Haut Avesnes.	
	9.4.17		Attack, division standing by.	
ARRAS.	10.4.17		H.Q. RE moves to 4 Place St CROIX ARRAS. CRE visits 3rd + 37th Divs.	
	11.4.17		H.Q. RE moves to 1 Rue Ste Barbe, CRE visits CRE 15th Div re taking over.	
	12.4.17		Div takes over from 15th Div. CRE visits 78 + 93rd Field Coys + 50th Bde in Feuchy.	
	13.4.17		CRE visits Field Coys and Bdes. Pontoons used for transport on canal.	
	14.4.17		CRE visits Field Coys and Bdes. 15th Div still using RE IVORY Dump. (G.22 d 4.7.) H.Q. RE moves to 22 Rue des Augustins	
	15.4.17 – 20.4.17		CRE visits Field Coys and Bdes daily. Preparations for attack, canal as a means of transport very successful. CRE. H.Q. shelled on 21.4.17.	
	21.4.17		H.Q. RE moves to Chateau D'Eau, CRE visits Field Coys + forward Bde	
	22.4.17		attack CRE visits 51st + 52nd Bdes with G.S.O. 2.	
	23.4.17			
	24.4.17		CRE visits Field Coys CRE 12th Div visits CRE re handing over.	
	25.4.17		Relief by 12th Div CRE 12th Div visits CRE.	
LE CAUROY.	26.4.17		H.Q. RE move to Le CAUROY.	
	27.4.17 – 30.4.17		Div in rest, CRE visits Field Coys and Bdes, CE XVIII Corps.	

H Travers Capt RE
for CRE 17 Div.

1875 Wt. W593/826 1,000,000 4/15 J.B.C. & A. A.D.S.S./Forms/C. 2118.

Army Form C. 2118

HQ RE 17 D

Vol 20

WAR DIARY
or
INTELLIGENCE SUMMARY
(Erase heading not required.)

Instructions regarding War Diaries and Intelligence Summaries are contained in F. S. Regs., Part II. and the Staff Manual respectively. Title Pages will be prepared in manuscript.

Place	Date	Hour	Summary of Events and Information	Remarks and references to Appendices
	1.5.17		Field Coys on move.	
	2.5.17		HQ RE moves to HERMAVILLE.	
HERMAVILLE	3.5.17			
	4.5.17		Coys in Rest at St NICHOLAS, CRE visits them Daily.	
	5.5.17			
	6.5.17			
	7.5.17			
	8.5.17		CRE visits 9th Div & goes round line, visits Field Coys.	
	9.5.17		CRE visits 9th Div & goes round line.	
	10.5.17		CRE visits 9th Div	
St NICHOLAS	11.5.17		CRE visits Field Coys & Bdes. HQ RE moves to St NICHOLAS.	
	12.5.17			
	13.5.17			
	14.5.17		CRE visits field Coys & Bdes.	
	15.5.17			
	16.5.17			
	17.5.17		as above and 180th T. Coy RE.	
	18.5.17			
	19.5.17			
	20.5.17			
	21.5.17			
	22.5.17		CRE visits field Coys & Bdes.	
	23.5.17		preparations for attack carried forward.	
	24.5.17			
	25.5.17			
	26.5.17			
	27.5.17			
	28.5.17		CRE with 9th Cos & Bdes.	
	29.5.17		CRE arranging relief	
	30.5.17			
	31.5.17		Relief.	

C. M. Carpenter
Lt. Col. RE
CRE 17th Div

1875 Wt. W593/826 1,000,000 4/15 J.B.C. & A. A.D.S.S./Forms/C. 2118.

Instructions regarding War Diaries and Intelligence Summaries are contained in F. S. Regs., Part II. and the Staff Manual respectively. Title Pages will be prepared in manuscript.

WAR DIARY
or
~~INTELLIGENCE SUMMARY~~

(Erase heading not required.)

HQ RE 17 D

Vol 21

Army Form C. 2118

Place	Date	Hour	Summary of Events and Information	Remarks and references to Appendices
COUTERELLE	1.6.17		H.Q. RE arrived COUTERELLE.	
"	2.6.17		78 + 93rd Field Coys to move to WANQUETIN, repairing Billets.	
"	3.6.17		Field Coys move. A/CRE goes round training Area.	
"	4.6.17		A/CRE visits WANQUETIN	
"	5.6.17		A/CRE arranging for supply of materials, targets etc.	
"	6.6.17		A/CRE arranges for material for billets, sports etc for Bdes.	
"	7.6.17		A/CRE visits 57th Bde.	
"	8.6.17		A/CRE go round work at WANQUETIN and visit 77th Field Coy in ST NICHOLAS.	
"	9.6.17		A/CRE arranges relief of 77 by 93rd Field Coy Relief Cancelled, after orders issued.	
"	10.6.17		Relief as above agreed to, to take place on 12th. orders issued.	
"	11.6.17		A/CRE visits WANQUETIN	
"	12.6.17		Relief of 77th by 93rd Field Coy Takes place.	
"	13.6.17		CRE visits WANQUETIN	
"	14.6.17		77 + 78th Field Coys to rejoin their Bdes, orders issued, move on 16th.	
"	15.6.17		CRE visits 57th + 52nd Bdes.	
"	16.6.17		CRE visits CRE 34th Div to make preliminary arrangements for Div. relief.	
"	17.7.17		CRE visits 77th Field Coy RE. Orders for relief of 34 div Coys by 17th Div issued.	
"	18.7.17		CRE visits 77 Field Coy RE. CRE's lecture at Army school postponed.	
"	19.7.17		CRE visits CRE 34 Div. 78th Coy moves.	
"	20.7.17		93rd Coy reverts to 17th Div. from CE XVII Corps.	
"	21.7.17		77th Coy moves. relief completed.	
ARRAS	22.7.17		H.Q. RE open in Camp at ST NICHOLAS Sheet 57.B.NW.(3) G. 17. 6. 5.8.	
"	23.7.17		CRE visits 77th + 93rd Coys and 52nd Bde.	
"	24.7.17		CRE goes round the trenches in left sector.	
"	25.7.17		CRE goes round right sector.	
"	26.7.17		CRE goes round trenches with O.C. 78th Field Coy.	
"	27.7.17		CRE inspects 77th Coys work on Dugouts.	
"	28.8.17		CRE goes round divisional sector.	
"	29.7.17		CRE visits 77 + 93rd Coys, Both Bdes + 77th Coy.	
"	30.7.17		CRE visits 77th Field Coy RE + CE. XVII Corps.	

H Travers Capt RE
for CRE 17 Div.

1875 Wt. W593/826 1,000,000 4/15 J.B.C. & A. A.D.S.S./Forms/C. 2118.

Instructions regarding War Diaries and Intelligence Summaries are contained in F. S. Regs., Part II. and the Staff Manual respectively. Title Pages will be prepared in manuscript.

WAR DIARY
or
INTELLIGENCE SUMMARY
(Erase heading not required.)

Army Form C. 2118

C.R.E. 17th Division

Vol 22

Place	Date	Hour	Summary of Events and Information	Remarks and references to Appendices
ARRAS	1.7.17.		C.R.E. goes round right sector, visits Field Coys, arranges work for 2 Coys of the Queens attached for work under division. Pioneers ordered to move.	[illegible]
	2.7.17.		Pioneers entrain. C.R.E. visits O.C. 1/4 Queens, who commence work. C.R.E. visits left sector [illegible]	[illegible]
	3.7.17.		C.R.E. visits right sector front line and Coy dugouts [illegible] 93rd Field Coy.	[illegible]
	4.7.17.		C.R.E. visits Bdes with G.S.O. II. Major Caton 78th Field Coy R.E. [illegible] to [illegible] H.Q. 17 Corps.	[illegible]
	5.7.17.		C.R.E. reconnoitres proposal for water supply in left sector with [illegible] water supply officer.	[illegible]
	6.7.17.		C.R.E. visits 78th Field Coy and goes round left sector.	[illegible]
	7.7.17.		C.R.E. visits C.E. III Army. Relief of 78th Field Coy by 77th Field Coy R.E. completed.	[illegible]
	8.7.17.		C.R.E. visits the trenches in right sector. Major J.F. Cubbon assumes command of 78th Field Coy R.E.	[illegible]
	9.7.17.		C.R.E. visits the trenches in both sectors.	[illegible]
	10.7.17.		C.R.E. visited by C.R.E. 63rd Division.	[illegible]
	11.7.17.		C.R.E. takes Army tramway officer round, & reconnoitre proposed tramway.	[illegible]
	12.7.17.		C.R.E. visits trenches in right sector, and visits Bdes.	[illegible]
	13.7.17.		C.R.E. visits 78 Field Coy to arrange details of work then 77th & 93rd Field Coys.	[illegible]
	14.7.17.		C.R.E. visits Field Coys and Bdes.	[illegible]
	15.7.17.		C.R.E. goes round with G.S.O. I.	[illegible]
	16.7.17.		C.R.E. visits Depot Batt. at SAVY and inspects R.E. work be done with G.S.O. II.	[illegible]
	17.7.17.		C.R.E. visits trenches and Field Coys.	[illegible]
	18.7.17.		C.R.E. visits work in hand on Strong points and dugouts with G.S.O. II	[illegible]
	19.7.17.		C.R.E. goes round Support line and right sector.	[illegible]
	20.7.17.		C.R.E. goes round left sector with O.C. 77th Field Coy.	[illegible]
	21.7.17.		C.R.E. visits all Field Coys and Bdes in the line.	[illegible]
	22.7.17.		a/C.R.E. visits Field Coys and inspects work in hand.	[illegible]
	23.7.17.		a/C.R.E. goes round right sector, CHEMICAL works and dugouts with O.C. 78th Field Coy R.E.	[illegible]
	24.7.17.		a/C.R.E. visits 77th and 78th Field Coys and arranges about dugouts, [illegible]	[illegible]
	25.7.17.		a/C.R.E. visits Field Coys and Bdes, arranges work on [illegible] dugouts and on C.T.s	[illegible]
	26.7.17.		a/C.R.E. visits right sector, more dugouts sited and walks round Strong points.	[illegible]
	27.7.17.		C.R.E. visited by O.C. 78th Field Coy R.E. re preparations for raid on night 28/29th.	[illegible]
	28.7.17.		C.R.E. visits Field Coys and Bdes in morning and C.E. 3rd Army in the afternoon.	[illegible]
	29.7.17.		C.R.E. goes round whole front and visits Field Coys. Raid [illegible] captured by 78 Field Coy	[illegible]
	30.7.17.		C.R.E. visits 78th Field Coy R.E. and dugouts in Support line.	[illegible]
	31.7.17.		C.R.E. visits all Field Coys and trenches in right sector.	[illegible]

[signature] Captain R.E.
for C.R.E. 17th Division

Instructions regarding War Diaries and Intelligence Summaries are contained in F. S. Regs., Part II. and the Staff Manual respectively. Title Pages will be prepared in manuscript.

WAR DIARY
or
INTELLIGENCE SUMMARY
(Erase heading not required.)

Army Form C. 2118

HQ RE 17 Div
Vol 23

Place	Date	Hour	Summary of Events and Information	Remarks and references to Appendices
ARRAS.	1.8.17.		C.R.E. visits 77th and 93rd Field Coys. R.E. in afternoon.	
	2.8.17.		C.R.E. visits all Field Coys and 2 Bdes in the line, goes round front trenches in left sector.	
	3.8.17		CRE. visits trenches in left sector & field coys.	
	4.8.17		CRE. goes round trenches & saps in right sector with the adjutant. visits Dept Battn.	
	5.8.17		CRE visits field coys, arranging work etc.	
	6.8.17		CRE visits trenches and field coys. Capt Moncrieff takes over duties of adjutant.	
	7.8th.17.		CRE visits Field Coy & Right & left Bgd HQrs with adjt.	
	8.8.17.		CRE visits trenches (left sector) and School at SAVY. where Lieut Beresford from 93rd Coy relieved " Stannier " 77th Coy who proceeded to 3rd Army H.Q.	
	9.8.17.		CRE visits right sector & field coys with adjt.	
	10.8.17		CRE " Field Coys.	
	11.8.17.		C.R.E. visits Coy. Horselines.	
	12.8.17.		C.R.E visits left sector front line inclusive, with G.S.O2 & adjt.	
	13 -		CRE visits Coys & Bgd Hqrs	
	14 -		CRE visits all right sector dugouts (with adjt)	
	15 -		Day spent in office & at H.Q.	
	16th		CRE visits left sector & all dugouts in that sector. also Coys with adjt.	
	17th		CRE " right "	
	18th		CRE. in rear.	
	19th		CRE. visits ~~left~~ Bgd. & Companies.	
	20th		CRE. visits Coys.	

1875 Wt. W593/826 1,000,000 4/15 J.B.C. & A. A.D.S.S./Forms/C. 2118.

Instructions regarding War Diaries and Intelligence Summaries are contained in F. S. Regs., Part II. and the Staff Manual respectively. Title Pages will be prepared in manuscript.

WAR DIARY
or
~~INTELLIGENCE SUMMARY~~
(Erase heading not required.)

Army Form C. 2118

Place	Date	Hour	Summary of Events and Information	Remarks and references to Appendices
ARRAS	21st		CRE visits 93rd Coy & 77th Coy. Lunches with CRE 63rd Div. on left. In evening, CRE visits Capt. Beresford RE at 17th Div. Depot Battn. SAVY.	AM
	22nd		CRE visits left sector up to support line.	AM
	23rd		CRE. visits right sector. new trench through CHEMICAL WORKS. Afternoon car to St Pol with 2nd Lt PEDDIE for interview with III Army workshops officer.	AM
	24th		Day spent in office clearing up reports. Evening, CRE visits coys	AM
	25th		CRE with adjt. & Corps Water supply officer visited Div front.	AM
	26th		Day in	AM
	27th		CRE visits trenches with O.C. 93rd Coy & inspects water supply	AM
	28th		CRE visits right Sector.	AM
	29th		CRE visits Coys in evening.	AM
	30th		CRE visits ~~Pioneers with 5th Army up north~~ trenches in left sector with Capt.	AM
	31st		CRE visits ~~Coys & Bgdes line with G.S.O~~ Pioneers with 5th Army up north	AM

Alan Moncrieff Capt. RE
for CRE 17th Div

1875 Wt. W593/826 1,000,000 4/15 J.B.C. & A. A.D.S.S./Forms/C. 2118.

Instructions regarding War Diaries and Intelligence Summaries are contained in F. S. Regs., Part II. and the Staff Manual respectively. Title Pages will be prepared in manuscript.

WAR DIARY
or
~~INTELLIGENCE~~ SUMMARY
(Erase heading not required.)

Army Form C. 2118

CRE 17th Divn

Vol 24

Place	Date Sept.	Hour	Summary of Events and Information	Remarks and references to Appendices
ARRAS	1st		CRE with G.S.O3. visited the Field Companies and Bgde Hqrs in the line	[illegible]
	2nd		CRE attends conference at 4th Div HQ with other CRE in the Corps & CE Corps concerning electric lighting of forward areas. In evening C.R.E. visits Coys with adjt	[illegible]
	3rd		O.C. 282 A.T. Coy sees CRE re water supply. CRE visits right sector with O.C. 78th (Field) Coy RE and adjt.	[illegible]
	4th		CRE visits Bgde Hqrs with representative of 352 M&E Coy RE & O.C. 93rd Coy RE with reference to lighting arrangements	[illegible]
	5th		CRE visits right sector & Quarry.	[illegible]
	6th		CRE went to 35R Coy VARENNES to collect M.G mountings. Thence to AMIENS to bring RE stores.	[illegible]
	7th		CRE. visits the two Bgde HQ. in the line & the 3 Field Coys	[illegible]
	8th		CRE visits right sector & CHEMICAL WORKS with OC 78th Coy RE & explores cellars & wells. Also visits left sector & railway. Night raid on left sector 1 officer & 15 sappers cooperate	[illegible]
	9th		C.R.E. visits Div. Depot Battn & relieves Lieut Beresford with II Lieut Peddie. Inspects work on pump at HERMAVILLE CHATEAU	

1875 Wt. W593/826 1,000,000 4/15 J.B.C. & A. A.D.S.S./Forms/C. 2118.

Instructions regarding War Diaries and Intelligence Summaries are contained in F. S. Regs., Part II. and the Staff Manual respectively. Title Pages will be prepared in manuscript.

WAR DIARY
or
~~INTELLIGENCE SUMMARY~~
(Erase heading not required.)

Army Form C. 2118

Place	Date	Hour	Summary of Events and Information	Remarks and references to Appendices
ARRAS.	10		GC Detachment 181 Tunnelling Coy RE & G.C. attached working parties visit C.R.E. concerning resting of infantry working parties. C.R.E. visits Coys in afternoon	Atw
do:-	11		C.R.E. proceeded on leave. Major Vasey RE. O.C. 77th (Field) Coy RE assumed acting C.R.E. & visited Coys:- in evening with adjt:-	Atw
do:-	12.		a/C.R.E. visited right sector & part of left with adjt. Also visited Coys	Atw
do:-	13		C.R.E. attended rehearsal of raid. SHERWOOD FORESTERS & 77th (Field) Coy Sappers CRE visited Coys.	Atw
do:-	14		CRE visited both sectors strong pts with adjt.	Atw
do:-	15		Morning spent at H.Q. Afternoon visited 79th Bgd D A sports & Horse show	Atw
do:-	16		CRE visited left sector. Two raids were made on the enemies trenches. In both of which sappers took part	Atw.
do:-	17th		Morning spent in office. CRE visits companies in afternoon	Atw
do:-	18		Morning at H.Q. Capt Sharp RE from NEWARK RE Training school arrived and visited right sector with CRE & adj.	Atw

1875 Wt. W593/826 1,000,000 4/15 J.B.C. & A. A.D.S.S./Forms/C. 2118.

Instructions regarding War Diaries and Intelligence Summaries are contained in F. S. Regs., Part II. and the Staff Manual respectively. Title Pages will be prepared in manuscript.

WAR DIARY
or
INTELLIGENCE SUMMARY
(Erase heading not required.)

Army Form C. 2118

Place	Date	Hour	Summary of Events and Information	Remarks and references to Appendices
ARRAS	19th		CRE and Adjt. visit new training area. Proposed Div HQ HERMEVILLE	[initials]
	20th		CRE 61st Div with adjt. visits CRE prior to relief	[initials]
	21st		CRE visits Coys & Bgds.	[initials]
	22nd		CRE 61st Div & his adjt. came to see CRE & partially take over. 2 CRE visit coys & Bgds also reserve line. 93rd Coy moved to HAUTEVILLE	[initials]
	23rd		Lt Col Carpenter returns & takes over CRE. Major Vasey returns to 77th Coy RE	[initials]
	24		CRE 61st Div. visits CRE.	[initials]
LE CAUROY	25		Div relieved by 61st Div at 10.0 am. CRE adjt. & Doctor rode to LE CAUROY Div H.Q. for training area	[initials]
	26th		CRE & Adjt. visited Coys & Bgd. H.Q. in their new billets	[initials]
	27th		CRE visited coys in training	[initials]
	28th		CRE inspected pumps at GRAND ROULECOURT & HERMAVILLE	[initials]
	29th		CRE attended conference at DHQ. & visited 78 Coy. Adjt. visited Coys	[initials]
	30th		CRE visited 77th & 93rd Coys in afternoon	[initials]

Alan Moncrieff Capt RE for CRE. 17th Div

1875 Wt. W593/826 1,000,000 4/15 J.B.C. & A. A.D.S.S./Forms/C. 2118.

"A" Form. Army Form C. 2121.

MESSAGES AND SIGNALS. No. of Message

Prefix ...... Code ...... m. Office of Origin and Service Instructions.	Words / Charge	This message is on a/c of: ...... Service. (Signature of "Franking Officer.")	Recd. at ...... m.
	Sent At ...... m. To ...... By		Date ...... From ...... By ......

TO C.R.E 17th Division

Sender's Number.	Day of Month	In reply to Number	
* G541	17th Sept		AAA

The Divisional Commander wishes you to convey to the detachments of the 77th and 93rd Field Companies R.E, who took part in last nights operations, his appreciation of the very excellent work done by them on the occasion

From 17th Div

Place

Time 4 pm

The above may be forwarded as now corrected. ...... *Censor.*

(Z) M. O'Connor Major GS

Signature of Addressor or person authorised to telegraph in his name.

* This line should be erased if not required.

(771-5) —McC. & Co. Ltd., London.— W 1789/1402. 150,000. 8/15. Forms C 2121/10.

"A" Form.

Army Form C. 2121.

MESSAGES AND SIGNALS.

No. of Message

Prefix Code m.	Words	Charge	*This message is on a/c of:*	Recd. at m
Office of Origin and Service Instructions.	Sent At m. To By		*Service.* (Signature of "Franking Officer.")	Date From By

TO
~~(1) 51 Bde~~
~~(2) 52 Bde~~
(3) CRE
~~(4) CRA~~

Sender's Number.	Day of Month	In reply to Number	
* G 540	17th		AAA

Following message received from Corps Commander AAA Many congratulations to you all on successful raids last night by ROSE and RENOWN AAA They deserve great credit for their enterprise and dash

From 17th Div

Place

Time 3.20 pm

The above may be forwarded as now corrected.

(Z) [illegible signature] Major

Censor. Signature of Addressor or person authorised to telegraph in his name.

* This line should be erased if not required.

McC. & Co. Ltd., London.— W 1789/1402. 150,000. 8/15. Forms C 2121/10.

XVII Corps No. G. 5/11.

17th. Division.

The following remarks, made by the Army Commander on your two raids of the night Sept. 16/17th., are forwarded for communication to the troops :-

"Two most successful and enterprising operations. The loss to the enemy is great in casualty and greater in moral. The conduct of all who took part is most commendable."

(Sd) J.R.C.CHARLES,
Brigadier-General,
General Staff.

H.Q., XVII Corps.
22nd. September, 1917.

- 2 -

17th. Division.
G. 747
23rd. Septr.,1917.

51st. Inf. Bde.
52nd. Inf. Bde.
C. R. A.
C. R. E.

Forwarded for communication to the troops concerned.

P.A.O'Connor

Major G.S.,
17th. Division.

77
78
93

Forwarded for your information

noted & returned
25-9/17 R.E

COPY.

17th. Division.

On the occasion of the Division leaving the XVII Corps, I wish to express to all ranks , my appreciation of the fine soldierly spirit which has been conspicuous in the Division during the last few months while serving on this front.

Its activity in patrolling, its keenness in Raids have both been admirable. But most conspicuous of all has been the splendid spirit shown in the work done in consolidating the line. In spite of weakness in numbers and the absence of the Pioneer Bn., the work done has been remarkable; showing not only excellent organisation on the part of the Staff, but also energy and zeal on the part of Regimental Officers and men. All ranks may be proud of their record in this respect, R.A. and R.E. a well as Infantry.

I wish goodbye, and good luck to all in the Division, with every confidence that they will fully maintain the reputation they have gained wherever their duty may call them.

(Sgd) CHARLES FERGUSON,
Lieutenant-General.,
Commanding, XVII Corps.

24-9-17.

17th. Division.
G.807.
25th. September 1917.

- 2 -

To all Units 17th. Division.

Forwarded for communication to all ranks.

Lieut.- Col.,
G.S., 17th. Division.

17th. Division

G. 782.

24th. September 1917.

C. R. E.

The G.O.C. Division wishes his appreciation for their uniformly good work during the present tour of the Division in the front line, conveyed to all ranks of the Divisional Engineers.

P. M. Birch

Lieut. Col.

G.S. 17th. Division.

Instructions regarding War Diaries and Intelligence Summaries are contained in F. S. Regs., Part II. and the Staff Manual respectively. Title Pages will be prepared in manuscript.

WAR DIARY
or
~~INTELLIGENCE SUMMARY~~
(Erase heading not required.)

C.R.E. 17th Division — Army Form C. 2118

Vol 25

Place	Date Oct.	Hour	Summary of Events and Information	Remarks and references to Appendices
LE CHAUROY	1st	–	CRE took G.S.O. II & III went North by car & visited XIV Corps	[signature]
	2nd		CRE visited 78th Coy in morning, 77th & 93rd Coys in afternoon. CRE innoculated.	[signature]
	3rd		CRE attends conference at Div: H.Q. O.C. 77 visits CRE	[signature]
PROVEN.	4th		Div: moved from XVII Corps to XIV Corps. CRE moved up to PROVEN by car. Adjt. & M.O. with H.Q.R.E. Personnel moved by rail arriving at PROVEN on morning of 5th	[signature]
	5th		CRE visited 93rd Coy & 78th Coy. met O.C. 77 at 78th Coy H.Q.; visited 5th Army H.Q. at LOVIE Chateau. Weather changes to wet & cold	[signature]
	6th		CRE visits CRE 29th Div at ELVERDINGE CHATEAU prior to proposed relief. On the way back to PROVEN C.R.E. calls at XIV Corps H.Q. at St SIXTE & see General Wilson C.E. There met CRE 34th Div. Lt Col Dobson RE & the question of forward road work was discussed. CRE dined with Army H.Q.	[signature]
	7th		Conference held at CRE's H.Q. concerning advanced roads. C.E. Corps & CRE 34th Div also 34th Div O.C.s concerned attended. Work definitely allotted at this conference. CRE visits 29th Div H.Q. Winter time assumed at 1.0 am.	[signature]
	8th		C.E. Corps & O.C.s 208 & 209 (Field) Coys RE visited CRE with reference to work on advanced roads to be carried out on morning of 9th. CRE went up to ELVERDINGHE CHATEAU & stayed there with CRE 29th Div. to be able to control road work in hand. The following units were working under CRE 209 & ½ 208 (Field) Coy RE & 2 Battns all of 34th Div. Pioneer Battn. 4th Div. REMAINDER of HQ RE remains with Div HQ at PROVEN	[signature] CRE. O.O. No. 14.

1875 Wt. W593/826 1,000,000 4/15 J.B.C. & A. A.D.S.S./Forms/C. 2118.

Instructions regarding War Diaries and Intelligence Summaries are contained in F. S. Regs., Part II. and the Staff Manual respectively. Title Pages will be prepared in manuscript.

WAR DIARY

~~or~~

~~INTELLIGENCE SUMMARY~~

(Erase heading not required.)

C. R. E. 17th Division

Army Form C. 2118

Place	Date Oct.	Hour	Summary of Events and Information	Remarks and references to Appendices
PROVEN.	9th		CRE at ~~[illegible]~~ ELVERDINGHE with CRE 29th Div. CRE went up the line in conjunction with work on advanced roads after attack which was launched by XIV Corps at 5. 0 a.m. & was reported as proceeding satisfactorily. Adjt. visited CRE in afternoon. The Coys (for the oncoming relief) were under orders from CRE for movements not under Brigades as had been the previous arrangement	[illegible]
	10th		O.C. Coys up forward taking over. 78 & 93 Coys moved up by train to ELVERDINGHE & relieved Coys of 29th Div. CRE at ELVERDINGHE. Adjt & remainder 1-H.Q. at PROVEN	[illegible]
ELVERDINGHE	11th		17th Div. relieved 29th Div. at ELVERDINGHE CHATEAU. CRE visited Coys.	[illegible]
	12th		CRE & adjt. went up line & visited work on Duckwalks & mule tracks forward.	[illegible]
	13th		Morning spent in office. CRE visited Coys in afternoon. Arrangements made for forming advanced RE Dump at BOESINGHE	[illegible]
	14th		CRE. visited the Coys. Advanced Dump started at BOESINGHE	[illegible]
	15th		CRE. in camp all day. Adjt. visits coys.	[illegible]
	16th		Adjutant went on leave + Lieut Holbrook took on acting adj. CRE visited the Coys in the morning	awH.
	17th		CRE + adj visited the 77th + 93rd Coys. Then to CRE 34th Div + CRE 58th Div. Div HQ moved back to PROVEN in morning.	awH
PROVEN	18th		CRE visited the Coys in the afternoon.	awH
	19th		Lieut Holbrook admitted to Hospital. Lieut Morris took over acting adjt. CRE visited Coys.	[illegible]
	20th		Div H.Q. moved to ZUTKERQUE. CRE to WOLPHUS	[illegible]

1875 Wt. W593/826 1,000,000 4/15 J.B.C. & A. A.D.S.S./Forms/C. 2118.

Instructions regarding War Diaries and Intelligence Summaries are contained in F. S. Regs., Part II. and the Staff Manual respectively. Title Pages will be prepared in manuscript.

WAR DIARY
or
~~INTELLIGENCE SUMMARY~~
(Erase heading not required.)

C. R.E. 17th Division Army Form C. 2118

Place	Date	Hour	Summary of Events and Information	Remarks and references to Appendices
WOLPHUS	21st		CRE in Billet all day	E.G.M.
	22nd		CRE & act adjt visited C.E. XIX Corps & 78th Fd Coy.	E.G.M.
	23		CRE visited 78th Coy RE, 50th Bde H.Q., and D.H.Q	E.G.M.
	24th		CRE visited Training Areas	E.G.M.
	25th		CRE visited D.H.Q, 78th Coy RE, & les ATTAQUES for materials	E.G.M.
	26th		CRE attended G.C.M. as a witness all day.	E.G.M.
	27th		CRE visited D.H.Q, Bde H.Q., & work in hand	E.G.M.
	28th		CRE visited P of W Cage under construction by 78 Co. RE, & D.H.Q	E.G.M.
	29th		CRE attended Tactical Exercise of 50th Bde in morning & visited works of 78th Co in afternoon	E.G.M.
	30th		CRE visited 77th & 93rd Coy RE in PROVEN Area. Duties of Adjt handed over to Capt Moncrieff RE	E.G.M.
	31st		CRE visited D.H.Q. & 78th Coy RE	A.M.

Alan Moncrieff Capt RE
for CRE 17th Div

1875 Wt. W593/826 1,000,000 4/15 J.B.C. & A. A.D.S.S./Forms/C. 2118.

Instructions regarding War Diaries and Intelligence Summaries are contained in F. S. Regs., Part II. and the Staff Manual respectively. Title Pages will be prepared in manuscript.

WAR DIARY C.R.E. 17th Division

or

~~INTELLIGENCE SUMMARY~~

(Erase heading not required.)

Army Form C. 2118

Place	Date Oct	Hour	Summary of Events and Information	Remarks and references to Appendices
LE CAUROY	1		NO 84475 Pioneer W. Ison joined from R.E. Base Depot.	
	2		1 Riding Horse transferred to 77th Field Coy. Pioneer Ison attached to 78th Field Coy	
	3			
PROVEN	4			
	5		61845 Pioneer Grisdale rejoined from Leave	
	6			
	7			
	8			
	9			
	10			
	11			
ELVERDINGHE	12		NO 33626. Sapper W.J. Isaac to 77th Field Coy. NO 23034 L Cpl G Saunders from 77th Field Coy	
	13			
	14		NO 63413. Sapper Randall T. from 93rd Field Coy	
	15			
	16			
	17			
PROVEN	18			
	19			
	20			
WOLPHUS	21			
	22			
	23			
	24			
	25			
	26		1 Riding Horse died suddenly at M.V.S.	
	27		NO 38879 Driver W. Norris granted leave to United Kingdom to 6.11.17	
	28		NO 51378 Driver S. Smith " " " " 7.11.17	
	29		NO 59269 RSM J.B. Pearce " " " " 8.11.17	
	30			
	31			

Alan Brunnell [?] Capt R.E.
for C.R.E. 17th Division

1875 Wt. W593/826 1,000,000 4/15 J.B.C. & A. A.D.S.S./Forms/C. 2118.

"A" Form,

MESSAGES AND SIGNALS.

Army Form C.2121
(in pads of 100.)
No. of Message 31

Prefix SM Code m.	Words	Charge	This message is on a/c of:	Recd. at m.
Office of Origin and Service Instructions. 79	Sent		Service.	Date
	At m.			From
	To			
	By		(Signature of "Franking Officer.")	By

TO ~~57 Div~~ ~~51 Div~~ CRE ...

Sender's Number	Day of Month.	In reply to Number.	AAA
* G892	2		

A conference will be held at Div HQ at [illegible] on the 3rd inst AAA The following officers will attend Brigadier and Brigade Major the CRA and OC Div Signals AAA Acknowledge

From 17th Div
Place
Time 7.50 am

The above may be forwarded as now corrected. (Z) [signature]

Censor. Signature of Addressor or person authorised to telegraph in his name.

* This line should be erased if not required.

(7107) Wt. W12093/M1217 50,000 pads. 1/17. D. D. & L. (E764.) Forms C/2121/11.

"A" Form.

Army Form C.2121
(in pads of 100.)

MESSAGES AND SIGNALS.

No. of Message ....

Prefix .... Code .... m.	Words	Charge	This message is on a/c of:	Recd. at .... m.
Office of Origin and Service Instructions.	Sent		.... Service.	Date ....
	At .... m.			From ....
	To			
	By		(Signature of "Franking Officer.")	By ....

TO			
	50th Bde	CRA	246 M.G. Coy
	51st Bde	CRE	Signals
	52nd Bde	ADMS	17 Div Q

Sender's Number	Day of Month	In reply to Number	AAA
* G 183	1[illegible]/10		

Following message received from Corps Commander AAA begins AAA Well done everybody AAA Wonderful performance in awful conditions AAA Hearty congratulations and thanks to you and all your great troops AAA Ends

War Diary

From	17 Div.
Place	
Time	3.35 pm

The above may be forwarded as now corrected. (Z)

.... Censor.

(Sd) J. J. O'Connor Major

Signature of Addressor or person authorised to telegraph in his name.

* This line should be erased if not required.

(7107) Wt. W12093/M1217 50,000 pads. 1/17. D. D. & L. (E764.) Forms C/2121/11.

"A" Form.

MESSAGES AND SIGNALS.

Army Form C.2121
(in pads of 100.)
No. of Message

Prefix	Code	m.	Words	Charge	This message is on a/c of:
Office of Origin and Service Instructions.			Sent		Service.
			At m.		
			To		
			By		(Signature of "Franking Officer.")

Recd. at m.
Date [illegible]
From
By

TO [illegible]

Sender's Number	Day of Month.	In reply to Number.	AAA
* G 849	25th		

There will be a conference at Div HQ at 3 pm the 27th inst AAA The following will attend the Inf Brigade Commanders the [illegible] [illegible] and [illegible] the CRE and the [illegible] [illegible] AAA Acknowledge

From 17 Div
Place
Time 10.50 pm

The above may be forwarded as now corrected. (Z) [illegible signature]

Censor. Signature of Addressor or person authorised to telegraph in his name.

* This line should be erased if not required.

(7107) Wt. W12093/M1217 50,000 pads. 1/17. D. D. & L. (E764.) Forms C/2121/11.

S E C R E T.

Operation Order No. 14. Copy.No. 7

by

Lieut.Colonel.C.M.CARPENTER.,D.S.O.,R.E.

Headquarters
17th Division.
9th October.1917.

17th Divisional Engineers will relieve [illegible]th Divisional Engineers as follows :-

1. 78th Field Co.,R.E., will relieve KENT Field Company R.E. on morning of 10th October.

93rd Field Company R.E., will relieve WEST RIDING Field Company R.E. on morning of 10th October.

77th Field Company R.E., will relieve LONDON Field Company R.E. on morning of 11th October.

2. ADVANCE PARTIES, will be sent up on 9th instant to take over Work, Company Billets, and Horse Lines.

3. LOCATIONS. 78th Field Co.,R.E. relieving KENT Field Co.,R.E.
Billets, B.14.b.9.8.
Horse Lines, A.11.a.4.4.

93rd Field Co.,R.E. relieving West Riding Field Co.R.E.
Billets. B.14.b.8.8.
Horse Lines. A.11.a.4.4.

77th Field Co.,R.E. relieving LONDON Field Co.,R.E.
Billets. B.14.a.9.8.
Horse Lines. A.11.a.3.4.

Field Companies less transport will entrain at PROVEN and detrain at ELVERDINGHE as follows :-

78th Field Co.,R.E.	10th Oct.	8.0 a.m.
93rd Field Co.,R.E.	10th Oct.	8.0.a.m.
* 77th Field Co.,R.E.	11th Oct.	8.0 a.m.

* Time liable to alteration.

4. Permanent attached Working Parties:-

4 Officers, 150 Other Ranks will be attached to each Field Company for Work. These will report as under.

To 78th Field Co.,R.E. at B.14.b.9.8. on 10th Oct at 12 noon.
To 93rd Field Co.,R.E. at B.14.b.8.8. on 10th Oct. at 12 noon. a.9.8.
To 77th Field Co.,R.E. at B.14.B.8.8. on 11th Oct. at 12 noon.

Field Companies will arrange to ration their attached working parties.

78th Field Co.R.E.) Supply rations for consumption
93rd Field Co.R.E.) on 10 instant.

77th Field Co.R.E. (Supply rations for consumption
(on 15th instant.

5. DUMP. Advance party will proceed to ONDANK Dump A.5.c. on 9th October.
R.S.M. will take over Dump from 29th Division at 10 a.m. on 10th October.
Field Companies will detail ONE N.C.O. and 15 men from permanent working party to report to R.S.M. at ONDANK Dump at 4 p.m. on date of arrival to act as permanent dump party.
Companies will continue to ration these parties.

6. Companies will be prepared to carry on work in afternoon of date of arrival.

7. ACKNOWLEDGE.

Alan [signature]
Captain, R.E.

for C.R.E., 17th Division.

Copies No.1. to 77th Field Co., R.E.
" 2. " 78th Field Co., R.E.
" 3. " 93rd Field Co., R.E.
" 4. " 17th Division "G". (For information).
" 5. " 17th Division "Q". (" ").
" 6. " C.R.E., 29th Division.
" 7. " War Diary.
" 8. " File.

S E C R E T.

Operation Order No.15. Copy.No. 6

by

Lieut.Colonel.C.M.CARPENTER.,D.S.O.,R.E.

Headquarters
17th Division.
15th October.1917.

In accordance with 17th Division Order No.236

1. XIV Corps front will be temporarily reorganized into a two Division Front.
17th Division will be withdrawn from the line and flanking Divisions extend their front on relief of 17th Division.

2. 77th & 93rd Field Companies R.E. will remain in their present billets for work as follows :-

From 16th instant 77th Field Company R.E. will be under orders of D.A.& Q.M.G., XIV Corps, in relief of one Field Company of 35th Division.
WORK: Construction of Camp Area near PILKEM.

From 17th instant 93rd Field Company R.E. will be under orders of G.O.C.R.A.,XIV Corps, in relief of one Field Company of Guards Division.
WORK: Tramline feeders to Guns.

3. 78th Field Company R.E. will concentrate at BOESINGHE with 50th Inf.Bde, and be moved by train to PROVEN.
Orders for move will be issued by 50th Infantry Brigade.
78th Field Company R.E. will be accomodated at PATAGONIA Camp. P.5. Area.

4. Attached working parties will rejoin their units on 17th instant independently.
They will take with them rations for consumption on 18th instant.

5. Dump parties will rejoin their working parties by 9.0.p.m. on 18th instant.

6. DUMPS. The dump at BOESINGHE WILL CLOSE.
R.S.M. and party will move to PROVEN CENTRAL CAMP independently on 17th instant.
List of Stores on charge at 17th Division R.E. is to be handed over to R.S.M. in charge of 14th Corps Dump. Copy to be sent to C.R.E's Office.
Billets will be vacated.

7. Location on 17th instant.

C.R.E. Central Camp. PROVEN.

	Billets.	Horse Lines.	Sheet.
77th Field Co.,R.E.	C.13.d.2.9.	B.15.b.7.8.	28.
78th Field Co.R.E.	E.17.d.5.2.	E.17.d.5.2.	27.
93rd Field Co.,R.E.	C.13.a.2.5.	A.5.c.7.2.	28.

5. ACKNOWLEDGE.

[signature] Capt RE
for
Lieut.Colonel.R.E.
C.R.E., 17th Division.

Copy No.1 to 77th Field Co.,R.E.
" " 2 " 78th Field Co.,R.E.
" " 3 " 93rd Field Co.,R.E.
" " 4 " 17th Division."G". (For information.)
" " 5. " 17th Division."Q" " "
" " 6. " War Diary.
" " 7. " File.
" " 8. " 50th Inf.Bde. (For information.)
" " 9 " 51st Inf.Bde. (" ")
" " 10 " 52nd Inf.Bde. (" ")

Army Form C. 2118

CRE 17th Division

Instructions regarding War Diaries and Intelligence Summaries are contained in F. S. Regs., Part II. and the Staff Manual respectively. Title Pages will be prepared in manuscript.

WAR DIARY
or
~~INTELLIGENCE SUMMARY~~
(Erase heading not required.)

VR 26

Place	Date	Hour	Summary of Events and Information	Remarks and references to Appendices
	November			
WOLPHUS	1st		CRE at Billets	[initials]
	2nd		C.R.E. went up forward with G.S.O.1. to see 57th Div. prior to relieving them. Visited 93rd (Field) Coy RE working under corps	[initials]
	3rd		CRE at Billets	[initials]
	4th		do:-	[initials]
	5th		CRE and adjt. visit CRE 57th Div at Canal Bank & make final arrangements for taking over. Return via 93rd (field) Coy RE & 77th (Field) Coy RE also visited XIX Corps H.Q. & saw the Chief Engineer.	[initials]
	6th		CRE attends Court Martial at NIELLES.	[initials]
PROVEN	7th		CRE moved by road to PROVEN.	[initials]
CANAL BANK	8th		CRE moved with advanced D.H.Q to Canal Bank & relieved CRE 57th Div. CRE visited rear D.H.Q at Welsh Farm also ONDANK Dump XIX Corps RE. CRE visited Coys	
"	9th		CRE visited forward brigade & field Coys	[initials]
	10th		CRE in billets	[initials]
	11th		CRE went up the line with G. S. O. 1	[initials]
	12th		CRE visited CE XIX Corps & Ondank Dump	[initials]

Instructions regarding War Diaries and Intelligence Summaries are contained in F. S. Regs., Part II. and the Staff Manual respectively. Title Pages will be prepared in manuscript.

WAR DIARY
or
~~INTELLIGENCE SUMMARY~~
(Erase heading not required.)

C.R.E. 17th Division

Army Form C. 2118

Place	Date	Hour	Summary of Events and Information	Remarks and references to Appendices
WELSH FARM.	13th		CRE moves with D.H.Q to WELSH FARM.	[initials]
ELVERDINGHE.	14th		CRE visited Coys	[initials]
	15th		CRE visited CE Corps & Coys	[initials]
	16th		CRE went on short leave to Paris. Major Vasey a/CRE. Brig: Gen: Liddell Deputy E in C came to visit us & stayed	[initials]
	17th		a/CRE & Gen: Liddell went up the line	[initials]
	18th		Gen: Liddell left. a/CRE visited Coys	[initials]
	19th		a/CRE & adjt: went up as far as SCHREIBOOM with O/C 77th Coy RE a/CRE visited Coys	[initials]
	20th		a/CRE in billets. Col: Carpenter returned from Paris. Bridge over STEENBEEK again repaired [illegible]	[initials]
	21		CRE visited Field Coys.	[initials]
	22		CRE & adjt: went up the line seeing the work. visited Bgd HQ at STRAYFARM and coys in Canal bank on return	[initials]
	23		CRE visited Coy Horse lines & Coys in Canal bank.	[initials]
	24th		CRE visited Corps HQ & Controller of mines at II corps HQ. also Army HQ. at CASSEL	[initials]
	25th		CRE visited Coys	[initials]
	26th		CRE went up the line & saw work on strong point line. visited Coys.	[initials]

1875 Wt. W593/826 1,000,000 4/15 J.B.C. & A. A.D.S.S./Forms/C. 2118.

CRE 17th Division

Army Form C. 2118.

Instructions regarding War Diaries and Intelligence Summaries are contained in F. S. Regs., Part II. and the Staff Manual respectively. Title pages will be prepared in manuscript.

WAR DIARY
or
~~INTELLIGENCE~~ SUMMARY.

(*Erase heading not required.*)

Place	Date	Hour	Summary of Events and Information	Remarks and references to Appendices
WELSH FARM	27th		CRE visited Field Coys	[illegible]
ELVERDINGHE	28th		CRE visited Field Coy.	[illegible]
	29th		CRE went round the line with G.S.I. and visited Field Coys.	[illegible]
	30th.		CRE visited Field Coys.	[illegible]
	~~1st Dec.~~		~~CRE visited Field Coys.~~	~~[illegible]~~
	~~2nd~~		~~CRE visited Field Coys and CRE 38th Div~~	~~[illegible]~~

Allan Moncrieff Capt RE
for CRE 17th Div

Map Ref.
Sheet
28.N.W.

S E C R E T.

Operation Order No.16. Copy No. 8

by

Lieut.Colonel.C.M.CARPENTER.,D.S.O.,R.E.
--*-*-*-*-*-*-*-*-*-*-*-*-*-*-*-*-*-*

Headquarters
17th Division.
6th November. 1917

1. In accordance with 17th Division Order No.241. 17th Divisional Engineers will relieve 57th Divisional Engineers,in right sector XIXth Corps, as follows :-

2. C.R.E., 17th Division relieves C.R.E., 57th Division on 8th November, 1917.
77th Field Coy R.E. relieves 505th Field Coy R.E. on 6th November 1917.
78th Field Coy relieves 421st Field Coy R.E. on 7th November.
93rd Field Coy R.E. will relieve 502nd Field Coy R.E.on 8th November 1917.

3. Location :-

Location	Billets.	Horselines.
77th Field Coy R.E.	C.19.a.0.2.	B.24.c.0.2.
78th Field Coy R.E.	B.23.b.5.4.	B.23.b.5.4.
93rd Field Coy R.E.	C.19.a.0.5	B.20.b.5.0.

C.R.E. at Advanced D.H.Q. C.19.c.0.9.

4. DUMPS. Back. ONDANK.(Corner og XIXth Corps Dump), taken over by C.R.E.
Forward. BARD CAUSWAY. Taken over by 77th Field Coy R.E. till further orders.
HAYMARKET. C.13.c.8.3., under construction, will replace BARD R.E.Dump as soon as completed.

5. 200 Infantry with suitable proportion of Officers and N.C.Os from each Brigade, will join affiliated Field Coys, as permanent working parties, after arrival of Brigades in XIXth Corps Area.

6. ACKNOWLEDGE.

Alan Moncrieff
Captain.,R.E.

for C.R.E., 17th Division.

Copy No	1	to	77th Field Coy R.E.
" "	2	"	78th Field Coy R.E.
" "	3	"	93rd Field Coy R.E.
" "	4	"	C.R.E., 57th Division.
" "	5	"	17th Division. "G". (For inofrmation)
" "	6	"	17th Division. "Q" (" ")
" "	7	"	File.
" "	8	"	War Diary.
" "	9	"	" " adj

Instructions regarding War Diaries and Intelligence Summaries are contained in F. S. Regs., Part II. and the Staff Manual respectively. Title pages will be prepared in manuscript.

WAR DIARY
or
~~INTELLIGENCE SUMMARY.~~
(Erase heading not required.)

Army Form C. 2118.

C=R=E
17th Div:–

VII 27

Place	Date Dec	Hour	Summary of Events and Information	Remarks and references to Appendices
WELSH FARM. ELVERDINGHE	1st		CRE visited Field Coys	[illegible]
	2nd		CRE visited Field Coys: and CRE 35th Div.	[illegible]
	3rd		CRE visited Field Coys. Visited by CRE 35th Div. Adjt. returned from PARIS leave	[illegible]
	4th		CRE visited Coys & Bgde. H.Q. in the line. also saw Field Coy work	[illegible]
	5th		CRE visited CE XIX Corps & Controler of Mines 2nd Army	[illegible]
	6th		CRE in billets and handed over all work to CRE 35th Div.	[illegible]
WOLPHUS	7th		CRE moved by car to WOLPHUS in RECQUES area. One day ahead of DHQ	[illegible]
	8th		CRE in billets	[illegible]
	9th		CRE rode over to HOCQUINGHEM & saw advanced party 77th Coy. Visited Div on return	[illegible]
	10th		CRE visited by O.C 78th Coy & O.C 77th Coy. Visited 93rd Coy at LOUCHES	[illegible]
	11th		CRE has reconnoitred Training at LICQUES with officers of 77th & 93rd Coys.	[illegible]
	12th		CRE rode round the 3 Companies whom had just moved their billets	[illegible]
EPERLECQUES	13th		CRE moved to EPERLECQUES. half way through the move orders were recd. to entrain at St OMER the following morning	[illegible]

Instructions regarding War Diaries and Intelligence Summaries are contained in F. S. Regs., Part II. and the Staff Manual respectively. Title pages will be prepared in manuscript.

WAR DIARY
or
~~INTELLIGENCE SUMMARY.~~

(Erase heading not required.)

Army Form C. 2118.

Place	Date	Hour	Summary of Events and Information	Remarks and references to Appendices
ACHIET-LE-PETIT.	14.		CRE entrained at St OMER at 8.0 am. Arrived BAPAUME at 4.30 pm. & marched to ACHIET-LE-PETIT. D.H.Q.	[illegible]
	15.		CRE visited 78th Coy & 93rd Coy RE	[illegible]
	16th		CRE visited 3 Field Coys RE & CE V Corps	[illegible]
	17th		CRE visited CE 5th Corps & proceeded with CE, OC 77, 78 & Pioneers to TRESCAULT to see rescue line to be constructed. All 3 Coys & pioneers work, under CE	[illegible]
	18th		CRE visited CE 5th Corps. 77th 78 & 93rd Coys. CRE 63rd Div & CRE 51st Div	[illegible]
	19th		CRE visited CRE 59th Div & CRE 47th Div at YTRES & discussed the proposed relief of the 6 field Coys & Pioneers by 17th Div RE & Pioneers. Visited Coys & CE Corps	[illegible]
	20th		CRE with CE 5th Corps & CRE 47th Div visited line	[illegible]
	21st		CRE visited CRE 59 & CRE 47 in YTRES. Visited 78th & 93rd Coys & [illegible]	[illegible]
YTRES	22nd		CRE moved to YTRES in relief of CRE 59th Div & CRE 47th Div	[illegible]
	23rd		CRE visited Corps line with CRE 63rd & handed over same. CRE visited Coys. Div moved into line.	[illegible]
	24th		CRE visited Coys & pioneers. also Div Dump at RUYAULCOURT & [illegible]	[illegible]
	25th		CRE visited Coys.	[illegible]
	26th		CRE visited Coys & 51st Bgde.	[illegible]
	27th		CRE with G.O.C 5th Corps & G.S.O.1. visited intermediate line, and visited Coys	[illegible]
	28th		CRE visited Coys & 51st Bgde. also own rescue line	[illegible]
	29th		CRE visited by C.O Pioneers. Afternoon visited CRE 2nd Div	[illegible]
	30th		CRE visited rescue line with GS.O1 & O.C 78th Coy RE	[illegible]
	31st		CRE & GSO1 visited HERMIES defences	[illegible]

Alan [illegible] Capt RE
for CRE 17th Div

A5834 Wt. W4973/M687 750,000 8/16 D. D. & L. Ltd. Forms/C.2118/13.

S E C R E T.

Copy No. 9....

OPERATION ORDER No. 17.

by

Lieut. Colonel. C.M. CARPENTER., D.S.O., R.E.

-=-

Headquarters, 17th Division.
4th December, 1917.

1. In accordance with 17th Division Order No. 264, and Administrative Instructions No.47, the 17th Divisional Engineers will be relieved by the 35th Divisional Engineers as follows :-

2. MOVEMENTS.

(a) The 77th Field Co. R.E. will be relieved by the 205th Field Co. R.E., and will move to PARDO Camp in the CANADA Area, and here rejoin the 51st Brigade Group, and will then proceed under 51st Brigade Orders to HOCQUINGHEN.

(b) The 78th Field Co., R.E. will be relieved by the 203rd Field Co. R.E. and will move with the 50th Brigade Group to LOSTRAT.

(c) The 93rd Field Co., R.E. will be relieved by the 204th Field Co. R.E., and will move to PORTLAND Camp in the PROOSDY Area on the 6th and rejoin the 52nd Brigade Group, and will then proceed under 52nd Brigade Orders to LOUCHE

3. RATIONS.

(a) 77th Field Co., R.E., rations ~~xx~~ for consumption on the 6th will be delivered on the 4th, at present Transport Lines.

(b) ~~78th Field Co., R.E., rations for consumption on the 7th will be delivered on the 6th, at present Transport Lines.~~ Cancelled

(c) 93rd Field Co., R.E. rations for ~~xx~~ consumption on the 6th will be delivered on the 4th at present Transporth Lines

4. INFANTRY WORKING PARTIES.

The Parties of the Duke of Wellington and Yorkshire Regiments at ONBANK Dump will rejoin the Transport Lines of their Units on the 4th.

The Parties supplied by the 50th Brigade at HAYMARKET Dump, will report to 50th Brigade Rear Headquarters at FUSILIER HOUSE, CANAL BANK, on the 5th.

5. DUMPS.

The R.S.M. will hand over the HAYMARKET Dump to a representative of the C.R.E., 35th Division at 10 a.m. on the morning of the 6th.

The Sappers attached to ONBANK & HAYMARKET Dumps, will rejoin their respective Field Coys on the 5th.

6. SAPPING PLATOONS.

The Sapping Platoons attached to the 77th, 78th, & 93rd Field Coys, should be ordered to rejoin their own Units under arrangements to be made between the Field Coys and Brigades concerned.

7. ACKNOWLEDGE.

for [signature] Capt R.E.
Lieut. Colonel. R.E.
C.R.E., 17th Division.

Copy	No.	1.	to	77th Field Co., R.E.
"	"	2	"	78th Field Co., R.E.
"	"	3	"	93rd Field Co., R.E.
"	"	4	"	C.R.E. 35th Division.
"	"	5	"	17th Division. "G". (for information)
"	"	6	"	17th Division. "Q". (for information)
"	"	7	"	R.S.M. HAYMARKET Dump. (for information)
"	"	8	"	File.
"	"	9	"	War Diary.
"	"	10	"	" "

All recipients of O.O.18.

Reference C.R.E's Operation Order No.18, para.3, line 4., between "relieve" and "467", insert "520 Field Coy in HAVRINCOURT and ".

Alan [signature]

Captain., R.E.

for C.R.E., 17th Division.

S E C R E T.

Copy No. 11

OPERATION ORDER NO.18.

by

Lieut. Colonel. C.M. CARPENTER., D.S.O., R.E.

Headquarters, 17th Division.
19th December, 1917.

1. In accordance with 17th Division G.80. dated 18-12-17, R.E. and Pioneers of 17th Division will relieve R.E. and Pioneers 47th Division, and R.E. of 59th Division, as follows :-

2. LOCATION OF UNITS to be relieved.

47th Division.

47th Division.	Forward Billets.	Resting Section.	Horse Lines.
517th Field Co., R.E.	(HAVRINCOURT.	(BROKEN HOUSE.	P.17.a.
518th Field Co., R.E.	(K.28.a.9.0.	(J.36.d.9.5.	P.17.a.
520th Field Co., R.E.	(	(	P.17.a.

59th Division.	Forward Billets.	Resting Section.	Horse Lines.
467th Field Co., R.E.	TRESCAULT. Q.10.a.45.45.		Q.10.c.2.5.
469th Field Co., R.E.	K.29.d.05.10z		Q.23.a.2.3.
470th Field Co., R.E.	K.30.a.5.9.		Q.10.c.2.5.

4th R.W.F. (Pioneers) at Broken House. J.36.d.9.5.
(47th Division).

3. BILLETS RELIEVED as follows :-

77th Field Co., R.E. relieve 517th Field Coy & 518th Field Coy in HAVRINCOURT, 518th Field Coy BROKEN HOUSE (1 Section) & 518th Horse Lines.
77th Field Coy. relieve 467th Field Coy in TRESCAULT & 520 th Field Coy BROKEN HOUSE (1 Section) & 520 Field Coy Horse Lines
93rd Field Coy relieves 469th & 470th Field Coys & 517th Field Coy at BROKEN HOUSE (1 Section) & 517th Field Horse Lines.
Pioneers relieve 47th Division Pioneers at BROKEN HOUSE & H.Qrs at HERTINCOURT.

4. WORK to be relieved as follows :-
77th Field Co., R.E. take over work in left sector from 517th & 518th Field Coys.
78th Field Coy. take over work from 520th, 467 & 469th Field Coys.
93rd Field Coys. take over work from 470th Field Coy.
Pioneers take over work from [illegible] 4th R.W.F., with exception of one Company working in 2nd Divisions Area.

5. MOVES.

Advance Parties will proceed on morning 20th inst as arranged verbally with C.R.E.
77th Field Coy relieves 517th & 518th Field Coys on 21st, billets & work.
78th Field Co relieves 520th Billets and Work on 21st. 467th Field Coy Billets and Work on 22nd & 469th Field Coy Work on 22nd.
93rd Field Co., R.E. relieves 469th Field Coy Billets on 22nd & 470th Field Co., R.E. Billets and work on 22nd.
Pioneers relieve Billets 4th R.W.F. on 21st & Work in left Sector [illegible] with 2 Companies. Relieve Work in Right Sector with One Company on 22nd.
[illegible] responding Coy to 4th R.W.F. now in 2nd Division Area will at [illegible] sent be resting Company.

6. Details of reliefs to be arranged between units concerned.

7. ATTACHED INFANTRY.
Companies will have attached Infantry (probably 100) after arrival in line.

8. DUMPS.
Divisional Dump at RUYALCOURT. R.S.M. to relieve 47th Div.R.E. at 10 a.m. on 21st inst.
METZ Dump. Corporal SMITH to relieve 59th Div.R.E. on 20th. This Dump will not bee carried on.
5th CORPS R.E.DUMP.YTRES. Sapper McLENNAN, C.R.E's representative will be already there.

Alan Armitage[?]

Captain.,R.E.

for C.R.E., 17th Division.

Copy No.1.	to	77th Field Co.,R.E.
" " 2.	"	78th Field Co.,R.E.
" " 3.	"	93rd Field Co.,R.E.
" " 4.	"	Pioneers (7th York & Lancs.)
" " 5.	"	C.R.E., 47thDivision. (for information).
" " 6.	"	C.R.E., 59th Division.(for information).
" " 7.	"	17th Div."G". (for information).
" " 8.	"	17th Div."Q". (for information).
" " 9.	"	R.S.M., 17th Div.
" " 10.	"	File.
" " 11.	"	War Diary.
" " 12.	"	" "

Instructions regarding War Diaries and Intelligence Summaries are contained in F. S. Regs., Part II. and the Staff Manual respectively. Title Pages will be prepared in manuscript.

WAR DIARY
or
INTELLIGENCE SUMMARY
(Erase heading not required.)

Army Form C. 2118

Headquarters RE
17th Division

Vol 28

Place	Date 1918	Hour	Summary of Events and Information	Remarks and references to Appendices
YTRES	Jan: 1st		CRE and adjt went up to HAVRINCOURT by Car & visited the 3 (Field) Coys CRE attended Q conference in afternoon	[illegible]
	2nd		CRE with G.S.O.1 went up to reserve line	[illegible]
	3rd		CRE stayed in. Adjt visited the Coys	[illegible]
	4th		CRE visited the Coys	[illegible]
	5th		CRE visited the Coys	[illegible]
	6th		CRE visited Pioneers. 77th Coy moved billets to SPOIL HEAP	[illegible]
	7th		CRE visited Coys & Pioneers	[illegible]
	8th		CRE in billets	[illegible]
	9th		CRE visited front line & 77th Coy	[illegible]
	10th		CRE in billets	[illegible]
	11th		CRE visited right sector & Coys	[illegible]
	12th		CRE visited new D.H.Q. Bertincourt & 77th Horselines	[illegible]
	13th		CRE went on Months Course. Major Lundie D.S.O. R.E. took over duties of CRE	[illegible]
	14th		a/CRE & adjt visited left sector front line. Coys & Pioneers	[illegible]
	15th		a/CRE visited line with G.S.O.1	[illegible]
	16th		a/CRE visited 93rd Coy RE & right sector front	[illegible]
	17th		a/CRE visited left sector & 77th Coy with adjt. D.O.R.E. went on course. Lt Bone 78th (Field) Coy RE took his place.	[illegible]
	18		a/CRE ~~visited right sector~~ in billets	
	19		a/CRE visited HERMIES defences	
	20		a/CRE visited right sector	

1875 Wt. W593/826 1,000,000 4/15 J.B.C. & A. A.D.S.S./Forms/C. 2118.

Instructions regarding War Diaries and Intelligence Summaries are contained in F. S. Regs., Part II, and the Staff Manual respectively. Title Pages will be prepared in manuscript.

WAR DIARY
or
~~INTELLIGENCE SUMMARY~~
(Erase heading not required.)

Army Form C. 2118

Headquarters R.E.
17th Division

Place	Date	Hour	Summary of Events and Information	Remarks and references to Appendices
YTRES	21		a/CRE visited right sector & part of left	[illegible]
	22		a/CRE visited left sector front line with O.C. 77th Coy	[illegible]
	23		a/CRE visited right sector	[illegible]
	24		a/CRE in billets. adjt. visited 77th & 78th Coys	[illegible]
	25		a/CRE in billets.	[illegible]
	26th		a/CRE visited right sector	[illegible]
	27th		a/CRE visited left sector	[illegible]
	28th		a/CRE & G.S.O.1 visited battle zone & right sector	[illegible]
	29th		a/CRE & adjt. visited right sector & support system. CRE attended corps commanders conference at Canal Cutting	[illegible]
	30th		CRE visited support system wiring & HERMIES defences	[illegible]
	31st		CRE and adjt. visited right sector front line	[illegible]

[signature] Capt. RE
for CRE
17th Div

S E C R E T.

Copy No....9...

OPERATION ORDER No. 19.

by

Lieut. Colonel. C.M. CARPENTER., D.S.O., R.E.

Headquarters, 17th Division.
1st January. 1918.

1. In accordance with 17th Division Order No.274. 17th Division will extend its front Northwards on 3rd/4th January, and take over the front of 2nd Division. On same date 19th Division will extend Northwards and take over front of 17th Division, as far as the BEETROOT FACTORY. (L.13.c.) exclusive.

2. The 17th Division Front being held by the 3 Brigades, each Field Company will work on the front of its affiliated Brigade. 78th Field Coy, Right. 93rd Field Coy, Centre. 77th Field Coy, left.

3. 77th Field Co., R.E. will take over Billets in SLAG HEAP K.20 Central, from 483rd Field Co., R.E., relief to be completed by midnight 3rd/4th January, 1918. Details to be arranged by Os.C, concerned.

4. SPECIAL WORK.

Companies will be employed as follows :-

77th Field Coy making new accomodation in SLAG HEAP, and Strong Point about K.14.b.3.4., details of which will be issued later.

78th Field Coy (less 2 Sections) are to work on Corps lines, as already arranged with C.R.E. 2Sections in Brigade Area, i.e. FLESQUIERES Defences.

93rd Field Coy, work on Strong Points in Centre Sector about K.17.c.7.8., K.10.b.4.8., K.16.d.5.6.,

Work will be commenced in these respective Areas on 4th inst.

Pioneers, work in Right Sector, 1 Company on Intermediate Line. Work in Centre Sector, 1 Company, GEORGE STREET, WIRING on North from HINDENBURG SUPPORT Line - Westwards.
Work in Left Sector. 2 Companies connecting CROSS AVENUE about K.9.a.7.3. to MULLEN TRENCH about K.9.a.5.4., and complete C.T. from WATSON TRENCH to HYDE STREET.

This work to be commenced on 4th inst.

5. ACKNOWLEDGE.

Lieut. Colonel., R.E.
C.R.E., 17th Division.

Copies Nos. 1. to 77th Field Co., R.E.
" 2 " 78th Field Co., R.E.
" 3 " 93rd Field Co., R.E.
" 4 " 7th York & Lancs.(Pioneers)
" 5 " 17th Division."G" (for information)
" 6 " 17th Division."Q" (for information)
" 7. " C.R.E., 2nd Division. (for information)
" 8 " War Diary.
" 9 " " "
" 10 " File
" 11 " File

S E C R E T.

Copy No. 8.

OPERATION ORDER No. 20.

by

Lieut. Colonel. C.M. CARPENTER., D.S.O., R.E.

Headquarters, 17th Division.
6th January, 1918.

1. In accordance with 17th Division Order No. [illegible]. 17th Division will hand over present Right Brigade Sector to 47th Division on the nights of 6th/7th, and 7th/8th January, 1918.

2. MOVES.
The following moves will take place on January 7th.

78th Field Co., R.E. will move to J.[illegible].
93rd Field Co., R.E. will move to TANK Trench and TANK Support, accomodation being allotted by G.O.C. 52nd Inf. Brigade, and to QUEEN'S Road K.[illegible].c.4.4. (Billets taken over from 77th Field Co., R.E.).
77th Field Co., R.E. will remain in present billets in Spoil Heap K.[illegible]. Central and [illegible].

3. WORK.
For 77th Field Co., R.E. as detailed in 17th Division G.[illegible].

For 78th Field Co., R.E. 2 Sections on Intermediate Line.

78th Field Co., R.E. less 2 Sections - [illegible].

For 93rd Field Co., R.E. as already in hand according to 17th Division G.439.

4. ACKNOWLEDGE.

Alan [illegible]

Captain., R.E.

For C.R.E., 17th Division.

Copy No. 1. to 77th Field Co., R.E.
" " 2 " 78th Field Co., R.E.
" " 3 " 93rd Field Co., R.E.
" " 4 " 17th Division. "G") (For information.)
" " 5 " 17th Division. "Q")
" " 6 " C.R.E., 47th Division. (For information.)
" " 7 " War Diary.
" " 8 " " "
" " 9 " File.

COMMANDING ROYAL ENGINEER
No. ....
Date ....
17th DIVISION

SECRET.

Copy No. 5...

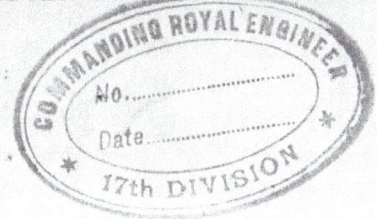

OPERATION ORDER NO. 21.

by

Major. R.C. LUNDIE.,D.S.O.,R.E.

Headquarters, 17th Division.
30th January, 1918.

1. 78th Field Company R.E. will relieve 77th Field Company R.E. in left sector on night 3rd/4th February 1918, relief to be completed by 6.0.a.m. on 4th inst.

2. 77th Field Company R.E. will become Divisional Reserve R.E. Company, and will take over all work now being carried out by 78th Field Coy.

3. No work must be interrupted owing to this relief. All details to be arranged between the Units concerned, and completion of relief to be reported to this office.

4. ACKNOWLEDGE.

Captain.,R.E.

for C.R.E., 17th Division.

Copy No.1. to 77th Field Co.,R.E.
" " 2. " 78th Field Co.,R.E.
" " 3. " 17th Division "G") For
" " 4. " Chief Engineer, Vth Corps.) information.
" " 5. " War Diary.
" " 6. " File.

Instructions regarding War Diaries and Intelligence Summaries are contained in F. S. Regs., Part II. and the Staff Manual respectively. Title Pages will be prepared in manuscript.

WAR DIARY
or
~~INTELLIGENCE SUMMARY~~
(Erase heading not required.)

Army Form C. 2118

HQ RE 17 D
Vol 29

CRE 17th Div

Place	1918 Date Feb	Hour	Summary of Events and Information	Remarks and references to Appendices
YTRES	1st		a/CRE visited 78th Coy RE & right & left Bdes in the line	
"	2nd		a/CRE visited right Bde Sector	
"	3rd		a/CRE visited do:- Lieut. G.F.H Reid RE came from 78th Coy RE to take over duties of acting Adjt.	
"	4th		a/CRE & adjt & a/adjt visited left sector	
"	5th		a/CRE visited right sector	
"	6th		a/CRE visited HERMIES DEFENCES	
"	7th		a/CRE visited left & right Sectors. Adjt proceeded on leave to U.K. Lt G.F.H. REID RE took over duties as act. Adjt.	
"	8th		a/CRE visited Right & left Bde H.Q's and Pioneer Battalion	
"	9th		a/CRE visited Right & left sectors; also left Bde, 77th & 78th Fd Coy HQ's	
"	10th		a/CRE & a/adjt visited right sector and 77th & 93rd Fd. Coys' H.Q's	
"	11th		a/CRE visited HERMIES DEFENCE with G.O.C. V Corps & a/CE. V Corps	
"	12th		a/CRE & a/adjt visited Right & left Sectors, Rt & left Bde H.Q's & 93rd Fd Coy	
"	13th		a/CRE visited 77th 78th & 93rd Fd Coy H.Q's.	
"	14th		a/CRE & a/adjt visited Right & left Sectors; also Rt Bde. H.Q. & 78th Fd Coy RE	
"	15th		CRE returned from leave to UK & took over from a/CRE	
"	16th		CRE & a/adjt visited right & left sectors: & 78th Fd Coy HQ.	
"	17th		CRE visited HERMIES DEFENCES with O.C 77th Fd Coy RE visited right & left Bde HQs	
"	18th		CRE visited Left. Bde. sector with O.C 78th Fd Coy RE	
"	19th		CRE visited Rt. Bde sector with OC 93rd Fd Coy RE	
"	20th		CRE visited 77th Fd Coy HQ	

Instructions regarding War Diaries and Intelligence Summaries are contained in F. S. Regs., Part II. and the Staff Manual respectively. Title Pages will be prepared in manuscript.

WAR DIARY
or
~~INTELLIGENCE SUMMARY~~
(Erase heading not required.)

Army Form C. 2118

Place	Date Feb 1918	Hour	Summary of Events and Information	Remarks and references to Appendices
YTRES.	21st		CRE visited left sector with G.S.O.1 + OC 78th Fd Coy RE.	[illegible]
	22nd		CRE visited 77th Fd Coy HQ + Pioneer Bn HQ.	[illegible]
	23rd		CRE visited right sector with O.C. 93rd Coy RE also Pioneers & Bde HQs	[illegible]
BERTINCOURT	24		Div. HQ moved to BERTINCOURT. Adjt returned from Leave.	[illegible]
	25th		CRE visited HAVRINCOURT Defences with O.C 77 & G.S.O1.	[illegible]
	26th		CRE visited left sector	[illegible]
	27		CRE visited Right sector	[illegible]
	28th		CRE in billets	

Alan Moncrieff Capt RE
for CRE
17th Div

1875 Wt. W593/826 1,000,000 4/15 J.B.C. & A. A.D.S.S./Forms/C. 2118.

Headquarters,

ROYAL ENGINEERS, 17th Division.

M A R C H

1 9 1 8

Instructions regarding War Diaries and Intelligence Summaries are contained in F. S. Regs., Part II. and the Staff Manual respectively. Title Pages will be prepared in manuscript.

WAR DIARY
or
INTELLIGENCE SUMMARY
(Erase heading not required.)

Army Form C. 2118

March 1918

Headquarters R E 17th Division

Vol 30

Place	Date	Hour	Summary of Events and Information	Remarks and references to Appendices
BERTINCOURT.	March 1st		CRE visited intermediate line, 3 (Field) Coys and Pioneers	[illegible]
	2nd		CRE went to AMIENS to buy stores	[illegible]
	3rd		CRE in billets	
	4th		CRE visited intermediate & switch systems. also 77th & 93rd Coys, Pioneers & left Bde	[illegible]
	5th		CRE went round trenches with CRE 19th Div	[illegible]
	6th		CRE went round reserve work with CRE 19th Div with view to taking over after relief	[illegible]
	7th		CRE visited 51st Infy Bde & 77th (Field) Coy RE	[illegible]
	8th		CRE visited HAVRINCOURT Defences with O.C. 77th Coy	[illegible]
	9th		CRE visited 77th Coy & Pioneers	[illegible]
	10th		CRE visited 93rd Coy. & 78th Coy & HAVRINCOURT Defences	[illegible]
	11th		CRE visited HERMIES defences. [illegible] 3 (Fd) Coy commanders at 77th H.Q.	[illegible]
	12		CRE do. do. do.	
	13		do. do. and HAVRINCOURT	[illegible]
	14th		CRE visited HERMIES defences. 77, 78 & 93 Fd Coys	[illegible]
	15th		do. do. with G.S.O.2 & then continued to HAVRINCOURT Defences with O.C. 93 Coy RE	[illegible]
	16		CRE visited left sector with G.S.O.3.	[illegible]
	17th		CRE in billets. [illegible] [illegible] to 51st Div sports.	[illegible]
	18		CRE visited HERMIES HAVRINCOURT line & the 3 field Coys	[illegible]
	19th		CRE went to AMIENS. Capt. Scrace (Border Regt) & Learner attached for 10 days	[illegible]
	20th		CRE took CRE 19 round the line prior to relief.	[illegible]
	21st		Heavy artillery bombardment started. D.H.Q. shelled in the morning. CRE at D.H.Q. all day. Fd Coys standing to. D.H.Q. moved to BEAULENCOURT	

1875 Wt. W593/826 1,000,000 4/15 J.B.C. & A. A.D.S.S./Forms/C. 2118.

Instructions regarding War Diaries and Intelligence Summaries are contained in F. S. Regs., Part II. and the Staff Manual respectively. Title Pages will be prepared in manuscript.

WAR DIARY
or
INTELLIGENCE SUMMARY
(Erase heading not required.)

COMMANDING ROYAL ENGINEER No. .... Date. .... 17th DIVISION

Army Form C. 2118

Headquarters R.E. 17th Division

Place	Date	Hour	Summary of Events and Information	Remarks and references to Appendices
Bertincourt	March 22nd		Heavy artillery bombardment continued. D.H.Q again shelled. C.R.E visited field Coys standing to in Canal West of Hermies.	EOH
"	23rd	midnight	D.H.Q moved to Beaulencourt 9 A.M. enemy within M.G fire of village of Bertincourt by then. C.R.E with Div. G. Staff.	EOH
Beaulencourt	24th	9 AM	In the early afternoon C.R.E reconnoitred defensive position for protection of transport route from Beaulencourt to Ligny-Thilloy and disposed the pioneer battalion and three field coys along the site chosen.	EOH
Courcelette		2 P.M	At 2 P.M. D.H.Q moved to a position on Albert Bapaume Rd between Le Sars and Courcelette. C.R.E with Division. The Adjutant Capt A. Moncrieff wounded at Beaulencourt and left R.E. HQ at Courcelette, adjutant's duties assumed by Lt E.O. Hutchinson R.E.	EOH
Meaulte	"	6 P.M.	D.H.Q moved from Courcelette to Meaulte at 6 P.M.	EOH
"	25th		C.R.E visited Coys in reserve positions S.E. of Fricourt. Interviewed stragglers from the R.E. from battle.	EOH
Henencourt	26th	5.30 AM	D.H.Q moved to Henencourt morning of 26th arriving 5.30 AM. Where later the Pnr. Battalion and Field Coys rejoined division and were in divisional reserve.	EOH
Senlis	"	6.30 PM	At 6.30 P.M. D.H.Q moved to Senlis.	
Contay	27th		D.H.Q retired to Contay arriving 2.30 A.M. C.R.E spent morning in office, in afternoon visited 'G' advanced H.Q at Senlis also visited Field Coys there and reconnoitred defensive line East of Senlis.	EOH
"	28th		C.R.E visited H.Q. of 50th & 51st Brigades. Went round line of posts dug by Field Coys the previous night also visited the Field Coys at Senlis.	EOH
"	29th		C.R.E. visited the Field Coys at Senlis and went round line of strong points with O.C. 17th M.G. Battalion	EOH
"	30th		C.R.E. visited the 50th Bgd. H.Q and the Field Coys.	EOH
"	31st		C.R.E. visited the Field Coys and went round Corps line with C.E. 5th Corps.	EOH

E.O. Hutchinson Lieut.
~~Captain~~ & Adjutant, R.E.
17th Division

1875 Wt. W593/826 1,000,000 4/15 J.B.C. & A. A.D.S.S./Forms/C. 2118.

AMENDMENT No 1
to
17TH DIVISIONAL ENGINEERS OPERATION ORDER No. 91

Ref: Para 4

Substitute 91st Field Coy for 92nd Field Coy R.E.

and

Substitute 92nd Field Coy for 91st Field Coy R.E.

Copies to all recipients of Divl:engrs: Orders No 91.

Captain R.E.

3/[illegible]/18 for C.R.E. 17th Division

War Diary

COMMANDING ROYAL ENGINEER
No. 4045
Date.
17th DIVISION

Secret

H. Q. R. E.

17th DIVISION

19/3/18

To all Recipients of C.R.E. O.O. 21 dated 7th March, 1918

1. Reference Division Order No 302.

The 19th Division Royal Engineers will relieve the 17th Division Royal Engineers in the CANAL Sector on the 22nd and 23rd Insts

On Relief the 17th Division will move into left Division reserve Area.

2. 94th Field Coy R.E. will relieve 77th Field Coy R.E. on 22nd & 23rd Inst.

82nd Field Coy R.E. " " 78th Field Coy R.E. on 22nd & 23rd Inst.

81st Field Coy R.E. " " 93rd Field Coy R.E. on 23rd & 24th Inst.

Pioneers

5th South Wales Borderers will relieve 7th Yorks & Lancs Regt on 22nd & 23rd Inst.

3. The following will be required for work under C.E. V Corps from 24th Inst Inclusive:-

77th Field Coy R.E.
78th Field Coy R.E.
Pioneer Battalion
3 Bdes of Infantry

C.R.E. 17th Division supervises work and will arrange details of taking over with C.R.E. 19th Division.

4. Infantry attached to Field Coys R.E. will rejoin their Units in sufficient time to proceed with them to the new Areas.
Necessary arrangements will be made by Field Coy Commanders And Brigades concerned.

Please acknowledge

War Diary

Alan Moncrieff Capt RE
for Lieutenant- Colonel.,R.E.

C.R.E. 17th Division

WAR
DIARY

C. R. E.

17th DIVISION

APRIL 1 9 1 8

Instructions regarding War Diaries and Intelligence Summaries are contained in F. S. Regs., Part II. and the Staff Manual respectively. Title Pages will be prepared in manuscript.

WAR DIARY
or
INTELLIGENCE SUMMARY
(Erase heading not required.)

COMMANDING ROYAL ENGINEER No. .... Date. .... 17th DIVISION

Army Form C. 2118

April 1918

Headquarters R.E. 17th Division

Vol 31

Place	Date	Hour	Summary of Events and Information	Remarks and references to Appendices
April Contay	April 1st		C.R.E visited all Field Coys at Senlis, also 51st Bgd. Assisted in organisation of Corps defences	[illegible]
	2nd		C.R.E. visited Field Coys. at Senlis	[illegible]
"	3rd		CRE in billets. Was visited by C.E. V Corps.	[illegible]
"	4th		Division moved to Flesselles for rest and training, two Field Coys & Pnr. Batt. remained at Warloy for work on Corps defences, C.R.E visited Field Coys & Pnr. Batt. at Henencourt before they moved to Warloy to arrange for the Corps work, also interviewed C.R.E 12th Div. at Warloy.	[illegible]
Flesselles	5th		C.R.E in billets	[illegible]
"	6th		C.R.E visited 93rd Field Coy	[illegible]
"	7th		C.R.E. visited Companies. Received orders to report as C.E. IV Corps	[illegible]
"	8th		Bt. Lt-Col C.M. Carpenter D.S.O., R.E. (promoted T/Brig-Genl.) left this H.Q. to be C.E. IV Corps. Major F.A. Ferguson R.E (promoted (T) Lt. Col.) assumed duties of C.R.E 17th Div.	[illegible]
"	9th		C.R.E visited Division and Pioneer Battalion. CRE attended Div conference	[illegible]
"	10th		C.R.E went round to each of the Field Coys. Capt. A Moncrieff returned from hospital & reassumed duties of Adjt.	[illegible]
PUCHEVILLERS	11th		D.H.Q moved to PUCHEVILLERS. Lt. E. Hutchinson rejoined 78th Coy R.E.	[illegible]
"	12th		CRE visited Corps line with C.E. In evening visited 77 & 78 Coys at work on this line. CRE moved to P. of W camp outside village.	[illegible]
"	13th		CRE visited intermediate line with G.S.O.1 & 93rd Coy in evening also CRE 63rd Div	[illegible]
"	14		CRE. visited ENGLEBELMER – MILLENCOURT line with O.C. Pioneers	[illegible]
"	15		CRE visited 78th Coy & 50th Inf. Bde also Pioneers & 93rd Coy R.E.	[illegible]
LEALVILLERS	16		D.H.Q. "A" Echelon moved to LEALVILLERS & Div went into the line taking over from 63rd Div. CRE visited Intermediate line with G.S.O.1 & O.C.s 77 & 78th Coys R.E.	[illegible]
"	17		CRE visited ENGLEBELMER – MILLENCOURT LINE with G.S.O.1.	[illegible]
	18		CRE visited Intermediate System. also All Fd Coys & Pioneers.	[illegible]
	19th		CRE up the line	[illegible]

Instructions regarding War Diaries and Intelligence Summaries are contained in F. S. Regs., Part II. and the Staff Manual respectively. Title Pages will be prepared in manuscript.

WAR DIARY
or
INTELLIGENCE SUMMARY
(Erase heading not required.)

COMMANDING ROYAL ENGINEER No. Date. 17th DIVISION

Army Form C. 2118

Place	Date	Hour	Summary of Events and Information	Remarks and references to Appendices
EALVILLERS	20		CRE in billets	Alan
	21		CRE visited left sector & Coys	Alan
	22		CRE visited right sector	Alan
	23		CRE and adjt visited Intermediate & left sector support line	Alan
	24		CRE in billets	Alan
	25		CRE visited Right sector with O.C 77 Coy RE and ENGLEBELMER Line with CE III Army and CE 5th Corps	Alan
	26			Alan
			CRE visited left sector	Alan
	27th		CRE visited intermediate system.	Alan
	28th		CRE visited Coys.	Alan
	29th		CRE visited ENGLEBELMER LINE & CE IV Corps	Alan
	30th		CRE in billets	

Alan [illegible] Capt RE
for CRE
17th Div

1875 Wt. W593/826 1,000,000 4/15 J.B.C. & A. A.D.S.S./Forms/C. 2118.

S E C R E T.

Copy No. 10.

OPERATION ORDER NO. 28.

by

Lieut. Colonel. C.M. CARPENTER., D.S.O., R.E.

Headquarters, 17th Division.
1st April., 1918.

1. The 17th Division (less Artillery) will be relieved by the 12th Division (less Artillery) on the present Divisional Front, on the night 2nd/3rd April.

2. The 3 Field Companies and Pioneers will be relieved as follows :-

87th Field Coy will relieve 77th Field Coy.
69th Field Coy will relieve 78th Field Coy.
70th Field Coy will relieve 93rd Field Coy.
12th Division Pioneers at HENENCOURT will relieve 17th Division Pioneers at SENLIS - arrangements to be made between C.Os. as to handing over work.

3. On relief Companies will be disposed of as follows :-

77th Field Coy. R.E. 78th Field Coy. R.E. 2 Companies of Pioneer.	To HENENCOURT for work on Corps Line.
93rd Field Coy. R.E. 1 Company Pioneers.	To CONTAY for work on Army Line.

Work will commence on Corps and Army Lines on 3rd instant.
Companies will arrange betweeb their respective relieving Companies as to change of Billets, which should take place after dinner on 2nd instant.

4. On 2nd instant, at 2 p.m., Companies of 12th Division will send representatives to Companies of 17th Division at SENLIS, to make arrangements for taking over 17th Division Forward work. Those of 87th Field Coy and 69th Field Coy will show 77th Field Coy and 78th Field Coy their work on Corps Line.
93rd Field Coy will send representative to be at junction of Army Line at VADENCOURT - WARLOY Road, about V.[illegible].d. at 12 noon, to take over the work on Army Line.

5. Horse Lines will remain as at present.

6. ACKNOWLEDGE.

C.M. Carpenter

Lieut. Colonel., R.E.

C.R.E., 17th Division.

Copy No.1. to 77th Field Co., R.E.
" " 2 " 78th Field Co., R.E.
" " 3 " 93rd Field Co., R.E.
" " 4 " 7th York & Lancs.
" " 5 " 17th Division. "G"
" " 6 " 17th Division. "Q"
" " 7 " C.R.E., 12th Division.
" " 8 " File
" 9 & 10 War Diary.

S E C R E T.

Copy No. 8

OPERATION ORDER No.1.

BY

Lieut.Colonel., F.FERGUSON., R.E.

****

Headquarters,
17th Division.
April.13th.1918.

1. 17th Divisional Engineers will relieve 63rd Divisional Engineers in the Line as follows :-

2. 78th Field Co.,R.E. relieves 248th Field Co.,R.E. Relief to be completed by 6.0.p.m. 14th inst.

77th Field Co.,R.E. relieves 249th Field Co.,R.E.. Relief to be completed by 6.0.p.m. 15th inst.

93rd Field Co.,R.E. relieves 247th Field Co.,R.E. Relief to be completed by 6.0.p.m. ~~16th~~ 15th inst.

3.

Locations :-	Billets.	Horse Lines.
248th Field Co.,R.E.	P.34.a.3.2.	CLAIRFAYE FARM.
249th) 247th) Field Coys.R.E.	FORCEVILLE, near Church.	

4. Os.C. of Field Companies to meet Os.C.Field Coys relieved at 11.0.a.m. at latter Companies Headquarters the day on which relief takes place.

They will acquaint themselves with work in hand of Company which they are taking over from.

5. It is intended that all the Companies shall eventually be accomodated in the open, i.e. dug into banks etc.

Os.C. will reconnoitre and report suitable positions for their billets.

If suitable positions can be found before the relief takes place, it may be possible to ar-range for Companies to go direct to their selected sites.

6. WORK. Companies will be employed in the ENGELBELMER - BOUZINCOURT Line, between Q.31.d.0.0. and Q.20.a.85.95. and on defences on spurs in Q.21., Q.26., and Q.27.

Companies affiliated to Brigades will maintain liaison and provide necessary assistance.

~~7.~~ Further details later.

~~8.~~ 7. Completion of reliefs to be reported to this of fice.

~~9.~~ 8. ACKNOWLEDGE.

Alan Moncrieff Capt RE
for Lieut.Colonel.,R.E.
C.R.E., 17th Division.

Copy No.1. to 77th Field Co.,R.E.
" " 2 " 78th Field Co.,R.E.
" " 3 " 93rd Field Co.,R.E.
" " 4 " 17th Division. "G"
" " 5 " 17th Division. "Q"
" " 6 " C.R.E., 63rd Division.
" " 7 " File.
" " 8 " War Diary.
" " 9 " " "

17th Divisional Engineers.
****

COMMANDING ROYAL ENGINEER
No.
Date.
17th DIVISION

Progres s Report.

for week ending 24th. April. 1918.

Unit.	Location.	Nature of Work.	Progress.
77th Field Co.,R.E.	Q.27.b.2.2.	S.P.3. Entrenching.	150 yards long. 6' wide. 5'6" deep. completed.
	Q.33.a.9.9.	S.P.5. do.	200 yards long. 8' wide. 6' deep. completed.
	Q.33.a.4.4.	S.P.5A. do	135 yards long. 5' wide. 3' deep.
	Q.33.a.2.0.	S.P.6. do	100 yards long. 50 yards 4'6" deep fire stepped. 50 yards 2'6" deep.
	Q.32.d.9.5.	S.P.7 do	70 yards long. 50 yards 4'6" deep fire stepped. 20 yard 3' deep.
	Q.27.c.1.7.	S.P.19. do	105 yards long. 80 yards firestepped and completed.
	Q.27.c.10.05.	S.P.20. do.	91 yards long. 5' deep. firestepped.
	Q.33.a.0.6.	S.P.21 do	90 yards long. 4'6" deep firestepped.
	Q.32.b.6.4.	S.P.22. do	220 yards long. 5'deep firestepped.
	Q.32.b.4.0.	S.P.23 do	95 yards long. 5' deep firestepped.
	Q.32.d.05.65.	S.P.24. do	110 yards long. 4'6" deep. firestepped.
	Q.26.d.7.6.	S.P.28 do	130 yards long. 2'6" deep.
	Q.32.b.50.95.	S.P.29. do	100 yards long. 5' deep firestepped.
	Q.32.a.9.5.	S.P.29A. do	65 yards long. 2'6" deep firestepped.
	Q.26.b.5.4.	S.P.25. do	100 yards long. 50 yards 4'6" deep firestepped. 50 yards 1'6" deep.
	Q.26.d.45.95.	S.P.26. do	110 yards long. 90 yards 4'6" deep firestepped. 20 yards 2'6" deep.
	Q.26.d.1.9.	S.P.26A. do	65 yards long. 5'6" deep firestepped.
	Q.26.d.0.6.	S.P.30. do	150 yards long. 2'6" deep.
	Q.26.d.3.4.	S.P.22 do	Old trench not yet cleared out.
	Q.32.c.9.6.) to) Q.27.a.2.0.)	Wiring.	Continuous belt. Inner belt medium entanglement. Outer belt not yet continuous, partly high, partly low. Same thickening done.
	P.24.d.4.4.	Bde. Hd.Qrs.	1 Officers Mess. Sleeping quarters for G.O.C. and 4 Officers. 1 Signal office. 1 Officers Cook House and quarters for 30 men, all completed. Office for Bde. Major., Staff Cant ain., and clerks 75% complete. Hut for R.F.A. Bde. 70% complete. Small deep dugout for Signals 25% complete.
	Q.34.a.3.0.	Battln. Hd.Qrs.	Completed and extended.
	Q.24.d.2.2.	do do	Retimbering old deep dugout. Erecting bunks. Signal Office and shelter for men. 50% complete.
	P.36.d.8.3.	Company Billets.	Accomodation for 3 Sections c ompleted.
	do.	Gas proofing.	4 Sappers with D.G.O.

(continued)

Unit.	Location.	Nature of Work.	Progress.
78th Field Co.,R.E.	Q.27.b.1.5.	S.P.5. Entrenching.	80 yards long.50 yards completed .
	Q.27.a.2.9.	S.P.14. do	150 yards long. completed.
	Q.27.a.7.9.	S.P.15 do	80 yards long. completed.
	Q.27.a.3.7.	S.P.16. do	160 yards long. completed.
	Q.26.b.8.6.	S.P.17 do	130 yards long. 120 yards completed.
	Q.27.a.3.3.	S.P.18 do	64 yards long. 54 yards completed.
	Q.20.d.8.0. to S.P.14.	C.T. do	110 yards from post.6' deep. 30 yards 4' deep.
	TERRACE to S.P.14.	C.T. do	90 yards 1' deep remainder 2'6" deep.
	S.P.14 to S.P.16.	C.T. do	40 yards 2'6" deep.
	S.P.16 to S.P.18.	C.T. do	67 yards 6' deep. 13 yards 4' deep.
	S.P.16 to S.P.17.	C.T. do	200 yards 1' deep.
	Q.27.a.3.0. to Left Div.Boundary.	Wire.	As shown on map.
	Q.20.a.1.9.	Demolition of road.	Craters blown.
	Q.28.d.3.8.	do	do do
	Q.28.d.7.3.	do	do do
	Q.28.d.15.35.	Stoppage of road.	3 Trees felled across road.
	Q.28.d.35.55.	do do	2 do do
	MESNIL.	Demolition of Wells.	5 prepared.
	Front System.	Taping	New Support Line and Line of Resistance taped.
	Bde. Hd.Qrs.	Accomodation.	Brigade of ice and quarters erected.
	P.29.c.5.2.	do	Billets for 3 Sections completed.
93rd Field Co.,R.E.	V.6.b.3.1.	S.P.42 Entrenching	95% Complete.
	V.6.b.75.55.	S.P.41. do	Completed.
	Q.31.c.2.1.	S.P.40 do	75% complete.
	Q.31.c.55.50.	S.P.39 do	Completed and drained.
	Q.31.c.95.35.	S.P.38 do	Completed.
	Q.31.d.25.65.	S.P.37 do	95% complete.
	Q.31.d.5.9.	S.P.36 do	80% complete.
	Q.32.b.45.25.	S.P.35. do	80% complete.
	Q.31.b.55.45.	S.P.34 do	Completed.
	Q.32.a.10.85.	S.P.33 do	90% complete

(continued)

Unit.	Location.	Nature of Work.	Progress.
93rd Field Co., R.E.	Q.26.c.30.15.	S.P.32. Entrenching.	Completed.
	Q.26.c.65.35.	S.P.31. do	Completed.
	Q.31.a.9.5.	S.P. Entrenchming	Completed
	Q.31.a.8.7.	do do	90% complete.
	S.P.34.to 35.	C.T. do	45% complete.
	Q.31.d.5.3.) to) Q.26.c.8.2.)	Wire.	Single belt double apron fence.
	Q.26.c.8.2.) to) Q.31.d.5.3.)	Wire	2nd belt completed.
	Q.31.b.7.1. toQ.32.aQ.4.	do	3rd belt completed.
	HEDAUVILLE) ENGLEBELMER) FORCEVILLE)	Demolition.	Wells prepared.
	FORCEVILLE	Baths b	Ready for use 8.0.a.m. ~~24-4-18~~.
7th York & Lancs.	INTERMEDIATE SYSTEM.	Entrenching & Wiring.	Working with Field Coys.
	CHARLES AVENUE.	Clearing & Deepening.	650 yards cleard and deepned.

Alan [signature]
Captain, R.E.
for C.R.E., 17th Division.

24/4/18

Instructions regarding War Diaries and Intelligence Summaries are contained in F. S. Regs., Part II. and the Staff Manual respectively. Title pages will be prepared in manuscript.

WAR DIARY
or
INTELLIGENCE SUMMARY.
(Erase heading not required.)

Army Form C. 2118.

HQRE 17 Div

Vol 32

Place	1918 Date MAY	Hour	Summary of Events and Information	Remarks and references to Appendices
LEALVILLERS	1st		CRE visited both sectors as far as support line. Adjt visited Coys in afternoon	[illegible]
	2nd		CRE visited ENGLEBELMER line with CE V Corps	[illegible]
	3rd		CRE and Adjt visited front system with O.C. 77th Coy RE	[illegible]
	4th		CRE visited 2 Bde HQ. ~~and~~ C.O. Pioneers visited CRE. CRE met 3 O.C. Fd Coys at 77th (Fld) Coy RE HQ at FORCEVILLE	[illegible]
	5th		CRE visited ENGLEBELMER LINE with O.C. 93	[illegible]
	6th		CRE visited left sector	[illegible]
	7th		CRE in billets. Capt F.G. FAHY RAMC rejoined as M.O. RE	[illegible]
	8th		CRE visited corps line with CE with a view to starting proposed work. 3 Fd Coys relieved by 3 Coys 63rd (Naval) Div. 77th moved to LA VICOGNE in back area. 78 & 93 moved to ACHEUX in preparation for work on Corps line	[illegible]
TOUTENCOURT	9th		CRE moved with D.HQ to TOUTENCOURT. Work was commenced by 78 & 93 & 2 Coys Pioneers also 3 Battns eight in Purple & Brown lines	[illegible]
	10th		CRE visited Coys 78 & 93 & reconnoitred tracks	[illegible]
	11th		CRE sick. Adjt accompanied CE & visited work in hand.	[illegible]
	12th		CRE and Adjt visited 77th Coy RE Training at LA VICOGNE	[illegible]
	13th		CRE in billets. 78th Coy moved out to [illegible] Training at PUCHEVILLERS. Major Cubbon wounded	[illegible]
	14th		CRE visited 78th Coy RE and Adjt visited 93rd Coy	[illegible]
	15th		CRE visited 93rd Coy & Adjt visited 77 & 78th Coys	[illegible]
	16.		V Corps Commander inspected 78th (Res) Coy with 50th Bde group & 77 Coy with 52nd Bde group. CRE saw both Coys on parade before inspection	[illegible]
	17th		CRE in billets in morning. Afternoon CRE visited Sherwood Foresters sports and then on to see Lt Col James (Pioneers)	[illegible]
	18th		77th Coy moved to BEAUQUESNE. CRE visited work on Purple system with O.C. 93rd Coy. Adjt visited proposed new Bde HQ with G.S.O. in 12th Div area	[illegible]
	19th		CRE went and saw Major Cubbon in hospital DOULLENS. Adjt visited 77th & 93 Coys	[illegible]

Instructions regarding War Diaries and Intelligence Summaries are contained in F. S. Regs., Part II. and the Staff Manual respectively. Title pages will be prepared in manuscript.

WAR DIARY
or
INTELLIGENCE SUMMARY.
(Erase heading not required.)

COMMANDING ROYAL ENGINEER No.......... Date.......... 17th DIVISION

Army Form C. 2118.

Place	Date	Hour	Summary of Events and Information	Remarks and references to Appendices
TOUTENCOURT	20th		CRE and Adjt attended G.O.C. Divs conference at ARQUEVES Bde HQ on practice tactical scheme. Weather continued very hot. CRE got a car in the evening & visited Coys	[illegible]
	21		CRE in billets. Attended gas lecture at D.H.Q in afternoon. Visited CRE 12th Div	[illegible]
	22		CRE visited Purple line with CE V Corps. Adjt visited Adjt 12th Div. Lt Hutchinson rejoined 77th Coy from R.A.	[illegible]
	23		CRE visited front with CRE 12th Div prior to taking over. CRE and adjt went to 51st Inf Bde Sports. CRE inspected 78th (Field) Coy at Transport. Lt SCHOFIELD 77th Coy came to D.H.Q. [illegible] attached to RA to give RE assistance.	
	25th		CRE in billets. O.C.s (field) Coys came to D.H.Q to discuss new policy of [illegible] with CRE	[illegible]
	26th		Field Coys moved into the line and relieved Field Coys of 12th Div. 77 & 93 forward. 78 reserve. CRE with O.C. 175 Tunnelling Coy visited new sites for Bde HQs near BEAUSART. CRE visited 77th Coy and 51st & 52nd Bde.	[illegible]
REINCHEVAL	27		D.H.Q moved to REINCHEVAL & relieved 12th Div in left sector of V Corps front. CRE went and saw experiment in blowing vertical shafts carried out. Adjt went to MAILLY-MAILLET fixed up billeting area for [illegible] attached to 175 Tunnelling Coy RE. Lt Brass RE was attached to CRE from 175 T. Coy RE to assist with tunnelling work	[illegible]
	28th		CRE went up the line with G.S.O.1 & O.C 78th Coy. R.S.M. wounded at [illegible] RE Dump	[illegible]
	29th		CRE in billets in morning visited Coy Horselines	
	30th		CRE went up line with O.C. 93 and G.S.O.1. New Div RE Dump formed at O.6 c. 3.0.	
	31st		CRE visited right sector. Major Dunlop O.C. 77 wounded & evacuated	[illegible]

[illegible signature] Capt RE
for CRE 17th Div

S E C R E T.

Copy No. 5....

OPERATION ORDER NO.2.

B Y

LIEUT. COLONEL., F.A. FERGUSON.,R.E.

C.R.E., 17th DIVISION.

Headquarters, Royal Engineers,
17th Division.
1st. May. 1918.

1. In accordance with 17th Division Order No.9, the 17th Division Front will be held by 3 Brigades in the Line with effect from the 5th May.

2. Attached plan shows new Brigade boundaries. Each Field Company will work in its affiliated Brigade Sector,i.e.

77th Field Coy with 51st Brigade.
78th Field Coy with 50th Brigade.
93rd Field Coy with 52nd Brigade.

3. Os.C. Field Companies will acquaint themselves, as soon as possible with all work now in progress, under Field Coys or Pioneers, in their new Sector.
Take over will be completed by 5.0. a.m. on the 5th instant.
Further details as to distribution of labour will be notified later.

4. Bdes Sectors extend from Front Line to ENGLEBELMER - MILLENCOURT Line inclusive.

5. There will no change or handing over of Field Companies Billets.

6. One Company of Pioneers will work in each Brigade Sector under orders of Division.
Infantry Brigades will be concentrating their energies on consolidation of the defences back to, but excluding, the INTERMEDIATE RINKX SYSTEM.

7. ACKNOWLEDGE.

Alan [signature]

Captain.,R.E.

for C.R.E., 17th Division.

Copy No.1. to 77th Field Co.,R.E.
" " 2 " 78th " " "
" " 3 " 93rd " " "
" " 4 " 17th Division "G".(for information)
" " 5 " War Diary.
" " 6 " File.

SECRET.

OPERATION ORDER No.3.

BY

LIEUT.COLONEL. R.A. FERGUSON., R.E.

C.R.E., 17th DIVISION.

Copy No. 9....

Headquarters, 17th Division.
May.6th. 1918.

1. In accordance with 17th Division Order No.12, 63rd (R.N.) Division Royal Engineers and Pioneers will relieve 17th Division Royal Engineers and Pioneers on 8th inst. Relief to be complete by 6.0. p.m. 8th inst.

2. The Field Companies will be relieved as follows, and hand over all details of work in Brigade Sector to relieving Companies, ~~xxx~~ including Maps, Demolition Schemes, etc. -

77th Field Coy. R.E. will be relieved by 248th Field Coy.R.E.
78th Field Coy. R.E. will be relieved by 249th Field Coy.R.E.
93rd Field Coy. R.E. will be relieved by 247th Field Coy.R.E.
7th York & Lancs (Pioneers) will be relieved by 63rd Division Pioneers.

3. After relief Field Coys and Pioneers will take over billets as follows :-

77th Coy. R.E. take over billets from 247th Coy.R.E. at N.21.a.7.8. (LA VICOGNE).

78th Coy.R.E. will move to billets at O.12.d.7.8. details of accomodation will be notified later.

93rd Coy.R.E. take over billets from 249th Coy. R.E. at O.12.d.7.8.

H.Q., and 1 Company of Pioneers take over billets from H.Q., and 1 Coy Pioneers 63rd Division in QUESNOY.

2 Companies Pioneers take over billets from 2 Companies Pioneers 63rd Division at ACHEUX.

4. Details of relief to be arranged between O.C. Field Companies and Pioneers Battalions concerned.

O.C. 247th Field Coy.R.E. will be at H.Q. 93rd Field Coy at noon on 7th inst. to arrange details.

5. ~~93rd~~ 78th Field Company and ~~78th~~ 93 Field Company R.E. and 2 Companies of Pioneers at ACHEUX will work on PURPLE RESERVE Line under C.R.E. commencing 9th inst. Details to follow.

6. Attached Infantry will be returned to their Units by 6.0.p.m. 7th inst.

7. Completion of reliefs to be reported to this office.

8. Field Companies will hand over all Trench Shelters to relieving Units.

9. ACKNOWLEDGE.

Allan Innes(?)

Captain., R.E.

for C.R.E., 17th Division.

Copy No.1. to 77th Field Co.,R.E.
" " 2 " 78th " " "
" " 3 " 93rd " " "
" " 4 " 7th York & Lancs.
" " 5 " 17th Division."G")
" " 6 " " " "Q") For information.
" " 7 " C.R.E.63rd Division.)
" " 8 " War Diary.
" " 9 " File.

8

To all recipients of C.R.E's. Operation Order No.4.

Amendment No.1.

Pioneer relief will be carried out as follows :-

7th York & Lancs. (Pioneers), to pass 12th Division Pioneers at ACHEUX, at 8.30.p.m. on 26th inst.

COMMANDING ROYAL ENGINEER
No. ....
Date ....
17th DIVISION

Captain., R.E.

24/5/18

for C.R.E., 17th Division.

SECRET.

Copy No. 8

OPERATION ORDER No.4.

B Y

LIEUT. COLONEL. F.A. FERGUSON., R.E.

C.R.E., 17th Division.

Headquarters, Royal Engineers.
17th Division.
May. 21st. 1918.

1. In accordance with 17th Division Order No.13., 17th Division Royal Engineers and Pioneers will relieve 12th Division Royal Engineers and Pioneers in the MAILLY Sector of Vth Corps Front as follows :-

2. Field Companies and Pioneers reliefs will be carried ~~xx~~ out as follows :-

Billets and Horselines. 77th Field Coy take over from 87th Field Coy at P.12.b.5.8.

78th Field Coy take over from 69th Field Coy at P.11.c.5.8.

93rd Field Coy take over from 70th Field Coy at P.17.a.4.7.

All Horselines at O.8.a.

Work. 77th Field Coy will take over from 70th Field Coy.
78th Field Coy will take over work from 69th Field Coy.
93rd Field Coy will take over work from 87th Field Coy.
7th Bn. York & Lancs (Pioneers) will take over Billets and work from 12th Division Pioneers.
Billets at P.17.c., and Horselines at O.12.b.8.0.

3. 77th Field Coy and 93rd Field Coy will each have one Section working in Front System with Brigade.

4. All reliefs to be completed by 6.p.m. 26th May.

5. O.C. 77th Field Coy will meet O.C. 70th Field Coy, and O.C. 78th Field Coy will meet O.C. 69th Field Coy at latter Company's Headquarters, respectively at 10.30.a.m. on 24th instant, to arrange details of taking over work.

6. All details to be arranged between O.C. Units concerned.

7. Completion of reliefs to be reported to this office.

8. 93rd Field Coy R.E. will hand over all work at present in hand on Corps Line to 87th Field Coy R.E. Details to be arranged direct between Os.C. Field Coys concerned.

9. ACKNOWLEDGE.

Captain., R.E.

for C.R.E., 17th Division.

Copy No.1. to 77th Field Co., R.E.
" " 2. " 78th Field Co., R.E.
" " 3. " 93rd Field Co., R.E.
" " 4. " 7th Bn. York & Lancs. (Pioneers).
" " 5. " 17th Division. "G".)
" " 6. " 17th Division. "Q".) For information.)
" " 7. " C.R.E., 12th Division) For information.)
" " 8. " War Diary.
" " 9. " File.

17th DIVISIONAL ENGINEERS & PIONEERS.

PROGRESS REPORT.

Week ending May.1st.1918.

Unit.	Location.	Nature of Work.	Progress.
77th Field Co.,R.E.	Q.33.a.9.9.	S.P.5. Digging.	Completed to Section.
	Q.33.a.4.4.	" 5.a. "	" " "
	Q.33.a.2.0.	" 6 "	Dug 5' deep 6'6" wide. firestepped.
	Q.32.d.9.5.	" 7 "	Dug 6' deep 7' wide. firestepped.
	Q.32.d.3.4.	" 8 "	Dug 3" deep 6' wide.
	Q.27.c.1.7.	" 19 "	Dug 5'6" deep 6' wide. firestepped.
	Q.27.c.10.05.	" 20 "	do do do
	Q.33.a.0.6.	" 21 "	do do do
	Q.32.b.6.4.	" 22 "	do do do
	Q.32.b.4.0.	" 23 "	do do do
	Q.32.d.05.65.	" 24 "	Completed to section.
	Q.26.b.5.4.	" 25 "	do do
	Q.26.d.45.95.	" 26 "	do do
	Q.26.d.1.9.	" 26.a. "	do do
	Q.26.d2.4.	" 27 "	10% complete.
	Q.26.d.7.6.	" 28 "	Completed to section.
	Q.32.b.50.95.	" 29 "	5' deep.otherwise complete.
	Q.32.a.9.5.	" 29.a. "	6' wide 3' deep.
	Q.27.d.2.4. to Q.33.a.7.5.	Wiring.	850 yds double apron erected.
	Q.26.c.8.0. to Q.27.c.3.0.	Wiring	1,500 yds double apron erected, with low wire in front.
	Q.27.a.4.0. to Q.27.c.4.1.	do	750 yds double apron added to belt already there.
	S.P.22. Forward.	C.T.	550 yds dug 6' wide 2' deep. 240 yds 6' wide 6' deep.
	P.24.d.4.4.	Bde. H.Q.	Completed.
	Q.34.a.3.0.	Battn. H.Q.	Completed.
	Q.24.d.2.2.	do	Completed.

P. T. O.

Unit.	Location.	Nature of Work.	Progress.
78th Field Co., R.E.	Q.27.a.2.9.	S.P. 14. Digging.	Completed to section &fire stepped.
	Q.27.a.7.9.	" 15 "	do do
	Q.27.a.3.7.	" 16 "	do do
	Q.28.b.8.6.	" 17 "	do do
	Q.27.a.3.3.	" 18 "	do do
	Q.21.a.2.8.	" 9 "	do do
	Q.21.a.1.6.	" 10 "	do do
	Q.21.a.5.2.	" 11 "	do do
	Q.21.c.3.6.	" 12 "	do do
	Q.21.c.5.5.	" 13 "	do do
	S.P.16 to S.P.18.	C.T. Digging	Completed to section.
	" 16 " " 17.	" "	do do
	Bank to S.P.17.	" "	125 yards completed. 65 yards 75% completed.
	S.P.14 " " 16.	" "	Completed to section.
	BANK " " 14.	" "	76 yards completed. 74 yards 75% completed.
	" " " 15.	" "	112 yards completed. 64 90% completed. 113 yards 50% complet(ed
	S.P.11. " Q.20.b.9.0.	" "	82 yards completed. 230 yards 3' deep.
	FLANK POST.) Q.21.b.6.7.)	Digging.	Southern portion excavated to section.
	Q.21.c.9.3.) to) Q.20.d.9.6.)	Wiring.	One belt completed 4 yards wide, less 100 yards which is only 70% complete.
	Q.27.a.4.0.) to) Q.26.b.8.5.)	Wiring.	One belt 4 yards wide completed. 4 strand fence erected.
	Q.21.b.7.2.) to) Q.21.d.9.1.)	Wiring.	Double apron fence commenced.
	Q.21.b.	S.P.1.	5% old trench cleared.
	Q.27.b.3.9.	S.P.2.	10% do do
93rd Field Co., R.E.	Q.32.b.45.25.	S.P.35. Digging.	Completed.
	S.P.34.to.S.P.35.	C.T. Digging.	Completed.
	Q.31.b.3.2.) to) Q.31.a.5.7.)	" "	85% complete.
	S.P.35.to S.P.36.	" "	30% complete.

P.T.O.

Unit.	Location.	Nature of Work.	Progress.
93rd Field Co.,R.E. (contd)	S.P.37.to Q.31.c.7.7.	C.T. Digging.	15% complete.
	S.P.33.to Bank.	" "	75% complete.
	S.P.32. to Bank.	" "	15% complete.
	S.P.39.	Duckboarding.	Completed.
	Q.31.c.	C.T. Digging.	85% complete.
	Q.31.a.	" "	85% complete.
	Q.20.a.	" "	10% complete.
	Q.31.a.5.8.	S.P.45 "	75% complete.
	Q.25.c.6.5.	" 46 "	" "
	Q.25.c.7.6.	" 47 "	" "
	Q.25.c.9.9.	" 48 "	" "
	Q.25.b.3.4.	" 49 "	" "
	Q.25.b.5.6.	" 50 "	" "
	Q.32.a.10.85.	S.P.33 "	Completed.
	- -	Wiring.	As shewn on map.
7th York & Lancs.	CHARLES AVENUE.	Clearing & Deepening.	Q.22.c.6.4. to Q.22.d.7.3. completed.
	" "	do.	Q.22.c.5.4. to Q.22.c.0.3. in hand.
	-	---	One Company on ~~Left~~ Right Sector. One Company on ENGLEBELMER Line.

Captain.,R.E.

1/5/18 for C.R.E., 17th Division.

COMMANDING ROYAL ENGINEER
No. ....
Date. ....
17th DIVISION

17th DIVISIONAL ROYAL ENGINEERS AND PIONEERS.

PROGRESS REPORT : : : : : : WEEK ENDING 7th MAY, 1918.

Unit,	Location.	Nature of Work.	Progress.
77th Field Co. R. E.	Q33b & 34a	Digging	500 yds dug to average 5ft.-6ft. wide.
	S.P. 26 & 30	Cuting Resesses	Excavated S.A.A. recesses in bays.
	S.P. 27	Digging	145 yds old trench dug to depth & firestepped.
	S.P. 30	"	Completed.
	S.P. 20 to 28	"	C.T. - cut 6ft. wide x 3ft. for Bomb Stop.
	S.P. 26 to 28	"	C.T. - dug to 6ft. firestepped.
	S.P. 22 to 6	"	C.T. - completed to Section.
		WIRING AS PER PROGRESS MAP.	
78th Field Co. R. E.	P29c,6-2.	Company H.Q.	5 Bivouacs completed.
	Q28c.7.3.	Excavation	Excavation for demolition charge in well completed.
	Q34a & 34b	Digging C.T.	350 yds 4ft x 3ft x 2ft. Appromimate head of C.T. is about Q34a. 8.8.
		WIRING AS PER PROGRESS MAP.	
93rd Field Co- R.E.	S.P. 12	Digging	Post extended 6ft. wide at top, 3ft. deep.
	S.P. 39	Digging C.T.	C.T. from Post to road completed.
	Q31b 3.2 to) Q31a 5.7.)	" "	Completed.
	Q31a 4.4.	" "	Dug to average depth of 5ft. 6in.
	Q22d	" Supt:Line	200 yds trench North of Charles Avenue dug out. Average depth 5ft.
	S.P.31 to) Bank)	" C.T.	45 yds - 6ft. x 3ft.
	Q22b 3.4.	" New Support Line	180 yds dug - 4ft wide x 2ft 3in deep.
	Q31c 6.5.	Duckboarding	Sunken road, - Road cleared, 124 yds duckboarding laid on pickets.
		WIRING ASX PER PROGRESS MAP.	
7th Y. & L. Pioneer Regt.	S.P. 13 to 2 (Charles Av)	Digging	Clearing old trench - completed.
	Q33b to 34a	Digging C.T.	950yds dug to average depth of 3ft.
	S.P. 37 to) Bank)	" "	6ft x 3ft x 4ft.
	Road. 35 & 36 S.P. 39 to	" "	6ft x 3ft x 4ft.

Capt: R.E.
for C.R.E. 17th Division.

11

WAR DIARY
or
INTELLIGENCE ~~SUMMARY.~~
(Erase heading not required.)

Instructions regarding War Diaries and Intelligence Summaries are contained in F. S. Regs., Part II. and the Staff Manual respectively. Title pages will be prepared in manuscript.

Army Form C. 2118. 17

COMMANDING ROYAL ENGINEER No. Date. 17th DIVISION

VR 33

Place	June Date	Hour	Summary of Events and Information	Remarks and references to Appendices
REINCHEVAL	1		CRE went up the line with G.S.O.1	[illegible]
	2.		CRE in billets And went to G.O.C. 38th Div "At Home" and officers jumping competition	[illegible]
	3.		CRE visited Field Company billets & Pioneers	[illegible]
	4.		CRE went up the line Adjt demonstrated use of [illegible] charges to 50th Bde.	[illegible]
			Major a/Lt Col. F.A. Ferguson C.R.E. awarded D.S.O. in Despatch 3-6-18	[illegible]
	5.		CRE sick in billets. Adjt visited Coys.	[illegible]
	6th		CRE in billets Adjt went up line in left sector Capt A [illegible] adjt RE awarded M.C.	[illegible]
	7th		CRE in billets adjt went up line with O.C. 77 & O.C. 175 Tunnelling Coy	[illegible]
	8th		CRE visited CRE 12th Div:-	[illegible]
	9th		CRE visited line with O.C. 77	[illegible]
	10th		CRE " " O.C. 78. Major Harman from 97th (Field) Coy RE joined as O.C. 77	[illegible]
	11th		CRE took Major Harman up to 77	
	12th		CRE in billets saw O.C. 175 Tunnelling Coy	[illegible]
	13th		CRE up the line	
	14th		CRE up the line	
	15th		CRE in billets adjt up the line with G.S.O. 3	
	16th		CRE up the line	
	17th		CRE up the line	
	18		CRE up the line	
	19th		do	
	20th		CRE and Adjt up the line Adjt [illegible] CRE 63rd [illegible] relief	
	21st		CRE 63 visited CRE.	[illegible]

(A7092). Wt. W12839/M1293. 750,000. 1/17. D. D. & L., Ltd. Forms/C.2118/14.

Instructions regarding War Diaries and Intelligence Summaries are contained in F. S. Regs., Part II. and the Staff Manual respectively. Title pages will be prepared in manuscript.

WAR DIARY
or
INTELLIGENCE SUMMARY.
(*Erase heading not required.*)

Army Form C. 2118.

Place	Date	Hour	Summary of Events and Information	Remarks and references to Appendices
REINCHEVAL	22	–	CRE and CRE 63 went round the trenches	[illegible]
	23.	–	CRE to Abville Coy relieved in the line	[illegible]
HERISSART.	24	–	Div relieved by 63rd Naval Div. and moved to Herissart	[illegible]
	25.		CRE saw CE V Corps re forward work	[illegible]
	26		1 sect 77 send forward for work on SENLIS defences. CRE went over the work	[illegible]
	27.		CRE in billets & round the Field Coys	[illegible]
	28		CRE up forward with CE Corps. 77th Coy sent 2nd Section forward	[illegible]
	29th		77th Coy held sports.	[illegible]
	30th		CRE in billets	[illegible]

Alan [illegible]
Capt and Adjt RE
for CRE 17th Div

S E C R E T.

Copy No. 8

OPERATION ORDER NO, 5.

****

B Y

***

LIEUT-COLONEL F.A.FERGUSON D.S.O.,R.E.

****

C.R.E.17th DIVISION.

****

Headquarters, R.E.
17th Division.
20th June, 1918.

---

1. In accordance with 17th Division Order No.26, 17th Division Royal Engineers will be relieved by 63rd Division Royal Engineers in the Line as follows :-

Reliefs to be completed

2. 77th Field Co.R.E.relieved by 249th Field Co.R.E. by 3-0 p.m. 22nd instant.

78th Field Co.R.E.relieved by 247th Field Co.R.E. by 5-0 p.m. 23rd instant.

93rd Field Co.R.E.relieved by 249th Field Co.R.E. by 3-0 p.m. 23rd instant.

3. On completion of reliefs Field Companies will take over billets as follows, and join their Brigade Group :-

77th Field Co.R.E.take over billets from 247th Field Co.R.E. at HERISSART (T.5.a.6.5.)
78th Field Co.R.E.take over from 248th Field Co.R.E. at RUBEMPRE (T.14.a.2.7.)
93rd Field Co.R.E.take over from 249th Field Co.R.E. at TOUTENCOURT WOOD (T.6.d.2.3.)

4. Attached Infantry Working Parties will rejoin their Units at Horselines as follows :-

From 77th Field Co.R.E. by 3-0 p.m. 22nd instant.
" 78th " " " " Mid-day 23rd instant.
" 93rd " " " " 6-0 p.m. 22nd instant.

5. All maps, defence schemes, trench stores, and tools, etc., should be handed over to relieving Units and receipts obtained and forwarded to this office.

6. Field Companies will take over Pontoon Equipment from relieving Companies at their new horselines.

7. Parties moving from Forward Billets by daylight must not be more than 20 strong, and waggons will move singly.

8. Completion of reliefs to be reported to this office.

9. On completion of reliefs Companies will be ready to move at 9 hours notice.

10. Acknowledge.

[signature]

Captain, R.E.
for C.R.E.17th Division.

Copy to 77th Field Coy.R.E.
78th Field Coy.R.E.
93rd Field Coy.R.E.
"G" 17th Division.)
"Q" 17th Division.)For information.
C.R.E.63rd Division.)
No 8 —War Diary, File (2)

To all recipients of C.R.E's Operation Order No.5 dated 20th June, 1918.

Amendment No.1.

8

Para. 8, line 5. For 249th Field Co. read 248th Field Co.

77th Field Co.R.E. will stage for one night 22/23rd in billets of 249th Field Co.R.E. at TOUTENCOURT.

On 23rd, 77th Field Co.R.E. will hand over these billets to 93rd Field Co.R.E. and proceed to HERISSART where they will take over billets from 247th Field Co.R.E.

21/6/18.

Captain, R.E.
for C.R.E. 17th Division.

O.C.77th Field Coy.R.E.
O.C.78th Field Coy.R.E.
O.C.93rd Field Coy.R.E.

Reference attached order -

Para: 4. Infantry are to rejoin their Units with two days rations.

Para: 7. Pontoon Equipment should be carefully checked before taking it over.

Captain, R.E.
for C.R.E.27th Division.

20/6/18.

WAR DIARY
or
~~INTELLIGENCE SUMMARY.~~
(Erase heading not required.)

Instructions regarding War Diaries and Intelligence Summaries are contained in F. S. Regs., Part II. and the Staff Manual respectively. Title pages will be prepared in manuscript.

Army Form C. 2118.

COMMANDING ROYAL ENGINEERS
No. ....
Date ....
17th DIVISION

July.

Vol 34

Place	Date July	Hour	Summary of Events and Information	Remarks and references to Appendices
HERISSART	1st	–	CRE visited 93rd Coy and training	[illegible]
	2nd	–	CRE and Adjt. attended G.O.C. Div's Conference on Tactical Scheme	[illegible]
	3rd	–	CRE in billets in morning. training in afternoon. Major Lundie joined to act CRE while CRE	[illegible]
	4th	–	CRE, Major Lundie & O.C. 77 visited forward ... work in BROWN Line under Corps. on leave	[illegible]
	5.	–	CRE went on leave to U.K. Major R.C. Lundie D.S.O. R.E. took over acting CRE	[illegible]
	6th	–	CRE visited CRE 12th Div. also Rosel. RE Dump to see MOIR Pill box	[illegible]
	7th	–	CRE up the line with G.S.O.1. Div. Horse show. Practice stand too 11.0 pm	[illegible]
	8th	–	Stood down 7.0 am. CRE attended conference. Adjt visited CRE 12.	[illegible]
	9th	.	C.R.E up the line with G.S.O.1. C.R.E. visited C.R.E. 12th Div. also 77th 78th & 93rd Field Coys.	[illegible]
	10th		C.R.E. toured Right line with G.S.O.1 & O.C. 77 Field Coy. Field Coys relieved Coys of the 12th Div in the line, 93rd on right, 78th on left, 77th in support.	[illegible]
Toutencourt	11th		C.R.E moved to Toutencourt & relieved C.R.E. 12th Div. C.R.E. visited Pioneer Bn in line.	[illegible]
	12th		C.R.E toured line with G.S.O.1.	[illegible]
	13th		C.R.E toured line with O.C. 178 Tunnelling Coy, also O.C. 78 Field Coy, also O.C. 77 Field Coy. visited 50 & 52 Bde. [illegible]	[illegible]
	14th		C.R.E toured line with G.S.O.1.	[illegible]
	15		C.R.E toured line	[illegible]
	16		C.R.E attended conference with C.E. & V.S.E.	[illegible]
	17		C.R.E visited C.R.E 38 Division, held conference Field Coy Commanders, visited Brigade Coy. Capt Moncrieff	[illegible]
	~~18~~		2nd Lieut Partridge joined from the 178 Tunnelling Coy ~~C.R.E toured line with G.S.O.~~ / joined the 77th Field Coy as 2nd in command. Lieut J. Bone assumed the duties of Adjutant	[illegible]
	~~19~~ 18		C.R.E toured new left Brigade area with G.S.O.1. 78 & 93 Field Coys changed billets.	[illegible]
	~~20~~ 19		C.R.E toured line with G.S.O.2. O.C. 77 Coy R.E & Tunnelling Officer. met C.R.E. 38 Division. changed billets	[illegible]
	20		C.R.E toured line with Corps camouflage officer and O.C. 151 Field Coy. Visited O.C. 50 Brigade. 77 & 78 Field Coys. Colonel Ferguson the C.R.E. returned from leave.	[illegible]
	21.		Major Lundie acting C.R.E. handing over to C.R.E. C.R.E. visited 175 & 178 Tunnelling Coys. Major Cubbon left Division for England. Major [illegible] assumed command of 77 Field Coy R.E.	[illegible]

(A7092). Wt. W12839/M1293 750,000. 1/17. D. D. & L., Ltd. Forms/C.2118/14.

Army Form C. 2118.

Instructions regarding War Diaries and Intelligence Summaries are contained in F. S. Regs., Part II. and the Staff Manual respectively. Title pages will be prepared in manuscript.

WAR DIARY
or
INTELLIGENCE SUMMARY.
(Erase heading not required.)

Place	Date JULY	Hour	Summary of Events and Information	Remarks and references to Appendices
	22		C.R.E. round line with Major Hendrie. Inspected Northern sector with O.C. 77 Field Coy R.E. Visited 78 Field Coy R.E.	
	23.		C.R.E round southern sector with Major Hendrie. Attended conference with C.E and O.C. 151 Field Coy R.E	
	24		C.R.E visited Pioneer Battalion, 175 and 178 Tunnelling Coys R.E and V.S.E.	
	25.		C.R.E round left sector with O.C. 77 Field Coy. R.E. Attended conference with V.S.E and O.C.s Field Companies.	
	26.		C.R.E round centre sector with O.C. 78 Field Coy. R.E. Visited V.S.E. & Pioneer Battalion. Attended Conference with C.E with reference to size of monolithic concrete M.G. emplacements.	
	27.		C.R.E. visited site of monolithic M.G. emplacement, also visited 93 Field Coy. R.E.	
	28		C.R.E round right sector, visited 151 Field Coy R.E, Pioneer Battalion, and 1st Bn, 305 V.S.E	
	29		C.R.E in office all day.	
	30		C.R.E round left sector, visited 77 Field Coy R.E. Conferred with C.E on subject of concrete M.G. emplacements	
	31		C.R.E round line with O.C. 1st Bn, 305 V.S.E.	

Captain & Adjutant, R.E.
17th Division.

S E C R E T.

OPERATION ORDER NO. 7

by

MAJOR R.C.LUNDIE D.S.O., R.E.

A/C.R.E. 17th DIVISION.

COMMANDING ROYAL ENGINEER
No. ....
Date. ....
17th DIVISION

Headquarters R.E.
17th Division.
17th July, 1918.

1. In accordance with 17th Division Order No. 34 of 17th July, 1918.
The 38th Division will be withdrawn from the Line and Vth Corps front held by 2 Divisions.
Dividing line between Divisions GRID Line East & West through P.30. central.

2. The adjustment of the front will take place on the nights 18/19th and 19/20th instant.
52nd Infantry Brigade will relieve troops of 38th Division.

3. One Field Company R.E. will work in each Brigade area (including PURPLE SYSTEM), each with 1 Section working under G.O.C., Infantry Brigade in the Advanced Forward Zone, as follows :-

93rd Field Coy. R.E. in 50th Infantry Brigade Sector.
78th " " " 51st " " "
77th (less 1 Section)" 52nd " " "
under V Corps)

O.C. 77th Field Coy. R.E. will arrange to take over all work in Sector to be taken over by 52nd Brigade from Field Coys. of 38th Division.

4. Each Field Coy. will be responsible for
(a) Providing N.C.O's and men for supervision of all R.F.A. Dugouts (under 2 Lieut. SCHOFIELD R.E.) in its Brigade Sector, and
(b) For all Demolitions in its Brigade Sector.

5. Following changes of locations will take place -

(a) 93rd Field Coy. R.E. (less 2 Sections already in Forward Billets) will move into billets in V.10.d. at present occupied by 10th Lancs. Fusiliers.
As Pioneers are also moving into this area allocation of billets between R.E. and Pioneers to be arranged between O.C. 93rd Field Coy. R.E. and O.C. 7th Btn. York & Lancs. direct.

(b) 78th Field Company R.E. (less 1 Section already in Forward Billets) take over billets in bank in P.30.b. at present occupied by Pioneers (19th Welsh Regt.) of 38th Division.
As Pioneers are also moving into this area allocation of billets between R.E. and Pioneers to be arranged between O.C. 78th Field Coy. R.E. and O.C. 7th Btn. York & Lancs. direct.

(c) 77th Field Company R.E. (less 1 Section under Vth Corps which remains at present location) will take over billets at P.24.c.1.3. at present occupied by 114th Brigade as Hd.Qtrs.

6. R.E. Dump and Company Horse Lines remain as at present.

7. [illegible]
Moves will be completed by 6 a.m. 19th instant, with the exception of move of 77th Field Coy. (less 1 Section) to P.24.c.1.3. which will be completed by 6-0 pm. 20th instant.

8. Copies of all receipts for Tentage & Trench Stores taken over will be forwarded to this office.

9. Completion of moves will be reported by wire to this office as follow

93rd Field Coy.R.E.		"Forty"
78th " " "		"Thousand"
77th " " "		"Seven"

10. ✗ Defence Instructions Instructions as to handing over present Billets to incoming Units of 38th Division will be issued later.

11. ACKNOWLEDGE.

John Bray
Lieut & Adjutant
for Major, R.E.
A/C.R.E., 17th Division.

Copies to :-

O.C. 77th Field Coy.R.E.
O.C. 78th Field Coy.R.E.
O.C.93rd Field Coy.R.E.
C.O. 7th Bn.Yorks.& Lancs.Rgt.
"G" 17th Div.)
"Q" 17th Div.) For information.
C.R.E.38th Divn.)
C.R.E.63rd Divn.)
War Diary
File.

17th Divl.
Engineers

C. R. E.

17th DIVISION,

A U G U S T 1 9 1 8.

24

Instructions regarding War Diaries and Intelligence Summaries are contained in F. S. Regs., Part II. and the Staff Manual respectively. Title pages will be prepared in manuscript.

WAR DIARY
or
INTELLIGENCE SUMMARY.
(Erase heading not required.)

Army Form C. 2118.

HQ RE 17 D

VR 35

Place	1918 Date AUG	Hour	Summary of Events and Information	Remarks and references to Appendices
TOUTENCOURT	1		C.R.E. round line with O.C. 1st Bn 305 [illegible] S.E. Conferred with C.E. V. Corps	[illegible]
	2.		C.R.E. round line with C.R.E. 38 Division. Conferred with C.R.E. 38 Division in reference to handing over	[illegible]
	3.		C.R.E. in round line with O.C. M.G. Bn. & C.R.E. 21 Div settling boundaries. C.R.E. conferring with C.E.	[illegible]
	4		C.R.E. engaged in reference to handing over to 38 Division	[illegible]
	5		C.R.E. " " " " Conferring with C.R.E. 38 Division	[illegible]
	6		C.R.E. handed over to C.R.E. 38 Division. 77th Field Coy moved to Toutencourt. 93 Field Coy to Herissart. ~~Field~~ 78 Field Coy remained in line	[illegible]
	7		C.R.E. visited 77th & 93rd Field Coys.	[illegible]
ALLONVILLE	8.		Conference of O's.C. the 3 Field Coys with C.R.E. C.R.E. moved Allonville and the three Field Coys moved with the Division	[illegible]
	9.		C.R.E. visited Field Coys. Three Field Coys moved in the evening to another location	[illegible]
	10.		C.R.E. spent day in Allonville.	[illegible]
	11		C.R.E. visited Field Coys.	[illegible]
HAMELET	12		C.R.E. attended Divisional Conference. C.R.E. moved to neighbourhood of Hamelet. Field Coys relieved Field Coys of 3rd Australian Division	[illegible]
	13.		C.R.E. round line with Field Coy Commanders	[illegible]
	14		C.R.E. round line. Major E. Harman O.C. 77 Field Coy R.E. relieved from [illegible]	[illegible]
	15		C.R.E. round left sector. Lieut E.O. Hutchinson rejoined 78 Field Coy R.E. from sick leave. 2nd Lieut [illegible] joined the Division & was posted to Field Coy. C.R.E. conferred with C.R.E. 5 Australian Division	[illegible]
	16.		C.R.E. engaged handing over to C.R.E. 5th Australian Division. Capt A. [illegible] M.C. ~~[illegible]~~ struck off the strength of 77 Field Coy on becoming Staff Officer to C.E. V Corps	[illegible]

(A7092). Wt. W12839/M1293. 750,000. 1/17. D. D. & L., Ltd. Forms/C.2118/14.

Instructions regarding War Diaries and Intelligence Summaries are contained in F. S. Regs., Part II. and the Staff Manual respectively. Title pages will be prepared in manuscript.

WAR DIARY
or
INTELLIGENCE SUMMARY.
(Erase heading not required.)

Army Form C. 2118.

Place	Date 1918 AUG	Hour	Summary of Events and Information	Remarks and references to Appendices
ALLONVILLE	17		C.R.E moved to Allonville. The 3 Field Coys changed their locations	[illegible]
TOUTENCOURT	18		C.R.E moved to Toutencourt Do. Do.	[illegible]
	19		C.R.E visited Field Coys.	[illegible]
	20		Do. Do. The 3 Field Coys changed their location	
	21		C.R.E visited C.R.E's 21st & 38th Division. Conferred with O.C's 77 & 93 Field Coys	[illegible]
			Attended C.E. V. Corps. 77 & 93 Field Coys changed their location	[illegible]
	22		C.R.E in Office	[illegible]
BEAUSSART	23		C.R.E making reconnaissance of crossings over Ancre. Attended V. Corps Commander's Conference. Moved Beaussart 78 Field Coy went into line and worked at crossings over the Ancre. Pioneers in line clearing forward roads.	[illegible]
HAMEL	24		77 Field Coy went into line worked on crossings over the Ancre. 78 Field Coy worked at crossing over Ancre. Pioneers on road repairing. C.R.E inspected road crossings etc. C.R.E moved to Hamel	[illegible]
	25		C.R.E inspecting forward roads & bridge crossings. 77 & 78 Field Coys continued work on crossings. Pioneers on road repair. 93 Field Coy went into line prepared road parallel to & east of [illegible] crossings	[illegible]
	26.		C.R.E inspecting forward roads. 77 & 78 Field Coys worked on crossings and roads. Pioneers on road. 93rd Field Coy searched for & repaired wells in forward area	[illegible]
COURCELETTE	27		C.R.E moved to neighbourhood of Courcelette. Field Coys & Pioneers worked as on previous day	
	28.		C.R.E inspected forward zone. 78 Field Coy worked on tank crossings and Thiepval Pozières Road. 77 Coy on forward roads and 93rd Coy on wells.	[illegible]
	29		C.R.E conducted forward zone with O.C's 77th & 93rd Field Coy. Field Coys and Pioneers worked as on previous day. C.R.E conferred	[illegible]

Instructions regarding War Diaries and Intelligence Summaries are contained in F. S. Regs., Part II. and the Staff Manual respectively. Title pages will be prepared in manuscript.

WAR DIARY
or
INTELLIGENCE SUMMARY.
(Erase heading not required.)

Army Form C. 2118.

Place	Date 1918	Hour	Summary of Events and Information	Remarks and references to Appendices
	AUG			
MARTINPUICH	30		C.R.E moved to neighbourhood of Martinpuich. C.R.E inspected forward roads.	[initials]
	31		C.R.E inspected forward water supply	[initials]

[signature]
Capt RE
for C.R.E [illegible] Div
1-9-18.

(A7092). Wt. W12839/M1293. 75,000. 1/17. D. D. & L., Ltd. Forms/C.2118/14.

OPERATION ORDER NO.9.   **S E C R E T**

BY   Copy No. 8...

LIEUT.COLONEL. .N.A. FERGUSON., D.S.O.,R.E.

C.R.E., 17 th DIVISION.

1. The 17th Division will relieve the 3rd Australian Division in the line immediately South of the SOMME to-night.

2. 50th Brigade will be on the right. 51st Brigade on the left. and 52nd Brigade in reserve. Reliefs to be completed by 12 midnight.

3. R.E ,Field Companies and Pioneers will move from their present billets in Brigade Groups, and will relieve the Australian Field Companies and Pioneers Bn. taking over work including forward section, and billets as follows :-

77th Fld. Coy.	will relieve	10th	Aust.Fld.Co.	Billets.	J.32.a.
78th Fld. Coy.	" "	9th	" " "	"	Q.21.a.
93rd Fld. Coy.	" "	11th	" " "	"	Q.21.b.

Pioneers will relieve Australian Pioneers at Billets Q.16.d.9.

4. Advance Parties should be sent forward by Field Coys and Pioneers forthwith XXXXXXXX * All details of relief will be arranged direct between Os.C.

5. As soon as possible Os.C. Field Coys and Pioneers will send details to this office, of state and nature of work taken over.

6. ACKNOWLEDGE.

[signature]

Captain.,R.E.

12/8/18   for C.R.E., 17th Division.

Copy No. 1. to O.C. 77th Field Co.,R.E.
" " 2 " O.C. 78th Field Co.,R.E.
" " 3 " O.C. 93rd Field Co.,R.E.
" " 4 " 17th Division. "G". } For information.
" " 5 " 17th Division. "Q". }
" " 6 " C.R.E. 3rd Australian Division. }
" " 7 " XXXXXXXX. 7th York & Lancs. (Pioneers).
" " 8 " War Diary.
" " 9 " File.

* in order if possible to see all work in hand before dark.

S E C R E T.

Copy No. 9

OPERATION ORDER No.10

by

LIEUT.COLONEL F.A.FERGUSON, D.S.O., R.E.

C.R.E., 17th DIVISION.

1. 17th Division, less Artillery will be relieved in the Line by the 5th Australian Division on the 15/16th and 16/17th instants.

2. Field Coys. and Pioneer Battalion reliefs will be carried out in accordance with attached table.

3. Advance parties of the relieving Field Coys. and Pioneer Battalion will visit their opposite numbers at 10 am tomorrow morning the 16th inst.

4. Details of reliefs will be arranged between the respective C.O's.

5. Field Coys. will take their Bridging Equipment with them.

6. On completion of march Field Coys. will rejoin the Brigade Groups to which they are properly affiliated.

7. C.R.E's Office will open at ALLONVILLE by 8 am on August 17th inst.

8. ACKNOWLEDGE.

D.H.Q.,
15/8/18.

Capt.R.E.
for C.R.E.,17th Division.

Copy No. 1 to O.C.,77th Field Coy.,R.E.
" " 2 " O.C.,78th Field Coy.,R.E.
" " 3 " O.C.,93rd Field Coy.,R.E.
" " 4 " O.C.,7th York & Lancs. (Pioneers)
" " 5 " 17th Division "G")
" " 6 " 17th Division "Q") For
" " 7 " C.R.E.,5th Australian Division.) information.
" " 8 " War Diary
" " 9 " File.

Unit.	From.	To.	Relieving Unit.	Time and Date.	Remarks.
77th Field Coy., R.E.	P.8.d.9.3.	FOUILLOY	8th Australian Field Coy.	Hours of march to be arranged by C.O's so that their Units will arrive at their new destination about dusk on the 16th inst.	Billets in new area are being arranged by the Staff Captains of the respective Brigades.
78th Field Coy., R.E.	Q.21.a.9.1.	AUBIGNY	15th Australian Field Coy.	do do	do do
93rd Field Co R.E.	Q.21.b.2.8.	VECQUEMONT	14th Australian Field Coy.	do do	do do
7th Bn. Y.& L. Pioneers	Q.23.a.4.3.	FOUILLOY	5th Australian Pioneer Bn.	do do	do do

<u>NOTE</u> :- All movement in forward areas will be by small parties at considerable intervals. For moves by daylight most concealed routes to be used.

Instructions regarding War Diaries and Intelligence Summaries are contained in F. S. Regs., Part II. and the Staff Manual respectively. Title pages will be prepared in manuscript.

WAR DIARY
or
INTELLIGENCE SUMMARY.
(Erase heading not required.)

HQ RE 17 D

Army Form C. 2118.

VIII 36

Place	Date 1918	Hour	Summary of Events and Information	Remarks and references to Appendices
	SEPTEMBER			
MARTINPUICH	1		C. R. E visited 78 Field Coy and inspected crossings over Ancre and roads which they were maintaining. 93 Field Coy opened out wells in Flers and neighbourhood. 77 Field Coy worked on forward roads	[illegible]
	2.		C. R. E visited 93 Field Coy & their water supply work. 77 Field Coy worked on forward reconnaissance of roads. 78th on crossings over Ancre. 77 Field Coy discovered & land mines on roads in neighbourhood of Le Transloy.	[illegible]
LE TRANSLOY	3.		C. R. E moved Le Transloy. 77 + 93 Field Coys and Pioneers moved same neighbourhood. 93 Field Coy opened out wells in Le Transloy & Rocquigny blown by the enemy. 77th on forward roads. 78th maintained crossings over Ancre	[illegible]
	4		C. R. E conferred with C. E. V Corps in reference to roads, water supply and bridges. 78 Field Coy moved to neighbourhood of Le Transloy. 77 Field Coy commenced construction of wooden girder bridge over Canal du Nord. 93 Field Coy erected troughs and tanks at Tunnel mouth near [illegible] station. 78 Field Coy worked on roads in neighbourhood.	[illegible]
	5.		C. R. E inspected roads and water supply. 77 Field Coy's work on bridge impeded by shell fire. 78th on roads in neighbourhood. 93rd erected more troughs in Equancourt.	[illegible]
	6.		C. R. E inspected forward roads and bridge under construction by 77 Field Coy over Canal du Nord. 78th worked on roads in neighbourhood. 93rd maintained water supply. C. R. E conferred with C. E. V Corps	[illegible]
LECHELLE	7.		C. R. E. inspected work of 3 Field Coys and Pioneers who worked as before. C. R. E. moved to Lechelle.	[illegible]
	8.		C. R. E. spent day in his Office. 3 Field Coys worked as before.	[illegible]
	9.		77 Field Coy completed bridge which was opened for lorry traffic in afternoon. 78 + 93 Field Coys worked as before. C. R. E conferred with C. E. V Corps	[illegible]
	10		C. R. E conferred with C. R. E's 21st and 38th Divisions	[illegible]
	11.		C. R. E handed over work to C. R. E. 38 Division. 17 Division went in rest.	[illegible]
	12.		C. R. E spent day in his Office and attended Divisional Conference. 3 ~~[illegible]~~ C. R. E's [illegible] were wounded by shell fire	[illegible]
	13.		C. R. E visited the 3 Field Coys.	[illegible]
	14		C. R. E in his Office.	[illegible]
	15.		C. R. E held conference of Field Company Commanders	[illegible]

(A7092). Wt. W12839/M1293. 750,000. 1/17. D. D. & L., Ltd. Forms/C.2118/14.

Instructions regarding War Diaries and Intelligence Summaries are contained in F. S. Regs., Part II. and the Staff Manual respectively. Title pages will be prepared in manuscript.

WAR DIARY
or
INTELLIGENCE SUMMARY.
(Erase heading not required.)

Army Form C. 2118.

Place	Date	Hour	Summary of Events and Information	Remarks and references to Appendices
	SEPT			
LECHELLE	16		C.R.E. attended Divisional Conference. 78 Field Coy worked forward marking tracks for Infantry	JB
	17		77 Field Coy moved forward for work under Brigade and made tracks through Anti-tank mined areas and erected warning Notice Boards	JB
	18		78 Field Coy moved forward for work under Brigade and worked on consolidation in forward zone. C.R.E visited line. Pioneer Coy worked on consolidation.	JB
	19		Three Field Coys worked on consolidation. C.R.E visited line. Pioneers also worked on consolidation. 93 Field Coy moved forward	JB
	20		C.R.E visited three Field Coys and 50th & 52nd Brigades and visited line. Coys and Pioneers worked as before.	JB
	21.		C.R.E visited line in morning. Lieut Hutchinson 78 Field Coy R.E. died of wounds. Coys & Pioneers worked as before.	JB
	22.		C.R.E in Office in morning & attended conference of C.E. V. Corps in afternoon. Coys & Pioneers worked as before, the 78th Field Coy also erecting barricade across road.	JB
	23.		C.R.E visited line. Coys and Pioneers worked as before.	JB
	24.		C.R.E engaged handing over to C.R.E. 21 Division. Coys and Pioneers worked as before.	JB
	25.		3 Field Coys and Pioneers moved back on Division being relieved by 21 Division. C.R.E inspected their new billets	JB
	26		C.R.E conferred with C.E. V. Corps	JB
	27		C.R.E held conference with O.C. 77th & 93 Field Coys R.E. C.R.E visited C.R.E. 21 Division.	
	28.		C.R.E visited C.R.E 21 Division	
	29		C.R.E inspected Field Companies.	
	30		C.R.E. conferred with Field Company Commanders	

John Bone
Capt R.E.
for C.R.E. 17 Div

1-10-18.

A5834 Wt. W4973/M687 750,000 8/16 D. D. & L. Ltd. Forms/C.2118/13.

S E C R E T.

Copy No.....

WARNING ORDER No.11.

by

LIEUT.COLONEL F.A.FERGUSON, D.S.O.,R.E.

C.R.E., 17th DIVISION.

The 17th Division will probably be relieved by the 58th Division in the near future.

In view of this relief, please prepare to hand over to your opposite numbers as below, who will probably call upon you this afternoon or tomorrow morning.

77th Field Coy.,R.E.	will be relieved by	151st Field Coy.,R.E.
78th Field Coy.,R.E.	" " " "	124th Field Coy.,R.E.
93rd Field Coy.,R.E.	" " " "	123rd Field Coy.,R.E. and 1 Section of 151st Field Coy.,R.E. and possibly 1 Section of 124th Field Coy.,R.E.
17th Divisional Pioneers	" " "	58th Divisional Pioneers.

J. Ferguson
~~Capt.~~ Lt.Col R.E.
~~for~~ C.R.E.,17th Division.

10/9/18.

Distribution :-

Copy No.1 to 77th Field Coy.,R.E.
" " 2 " 78th " " "
" " 3 " 93rd " " "
" " 4 " 17th Divisional Pioneers.
" " 5 " War Diary
" " 6 " File

S E C R E T.

Copy No. 7...

OPERATION ORDER No.17

by

Lieut.Col. F.A.FERGUSON, D.S.O.,R.E.

C.R.E., 17th DIVISION.

1. The 17th Division (less Artillery) will be relieved by 38th Division (less Artillery) in the left Sector V Corps front on 11th September and night 11/12th September.

On completion of relief 17th Division will be in V Corps Reserve.

2. The Command of the Divisional Front will pass from G.O.C., 17th Division to G.O.C.,38th Division on completion of Infantry Reliefs on night 11/12th September.

The command of the Artillery covering the Divisional front will pass from C.R.A.,17th Division to C.R.A.,38th Division at the same hour.

3. Moves will be completed before dark tomorrow as follows :-

(a) 77th Field Coy.,R.E. will remain in their present location on completion of relief by 151st Field Coy.,R.E.

(b) 78th Field Coy.,R.E. will move to ROCQUIGNY Area on completion of relief by 124th Field Coy.,R.E. Billets will be allotted by Assistant Staff Captain, Lieut.BUSH, at "B" Echelon, 50th Brigade, with whom 78th Field Coy.,R.E. should get in touch.

(c) 93rd Field Coy.,R.E. will move to LE TRANSLOY Area on completion of relief by 123rd Field Coy.,R.E. Billets will be allotted by Staff Captain, 52nd Brigade, with whom 93rd Field Coy.,R.E. should get in touch.

(d) 17th Divisional Pioneers will move to O.36.c. on completion of relief by 38th Divisional Pioneers.

4. Work will be carried on till noon tomorrow.

5. Bridge at V.8.b.5.5. will be handed over by 77th Field Coy.,R.E. to 21st Division under arrangements to be made direct between O.C.,77th Field Coy.,R.E. and representative C.R.E.,21st Division. This representative will call at the 77th Field Coy's. Headquarters tomorrow morning.

6. After completion of reliefs, units will be in their normal Brigade Groups.

7. 17th Divisional Headquarters will remain at P.30.d.8.8.

8. ACKNOWLEDGE.

Capt. R.E.
for C.R.E., 17th Division.

10/9/18.

Distribution :-

Copy No. 1 to O.C., 77th Field Coy., R.E.
" " 2 " O.C., 78th Field Coy., R.E.
" " 3 " O.C., 93rd Field Coy., R.E.
" " 4 " O.C., 17th Divisional Pioneers.
" " 5 " 17th Division G.S.
" " 6 " 17th Division "Q".
" " 7 " War Diary.
" " 8 " File.

S E C R E T.

Copy No. 7....

OPERATION ORDER No.13.

by

Lieut.Col. F.A.FERGUSON, D.S.O., R.E.

C.R.E., 17th DIVISION.

Following moves will be carried out on the night of the 17/18th September. Units will not move till 8.15 pm.

(1) 77th Field Coy., R.E. from present billets to trenches in V.8.c. and d.

(2) One Company 7th Bn. Y. & L. (Pioneers) from present billets to trenches in V.8.c. and d.

The above will be prepared to commence work on consolidation of objectives gained as soon as dark on the night of the 18/19th and should have the necessary tools with them.

(3) 93rd Field Coy., R.E. will move from present billets to billets vacated by 77th Field Coy., R.E. about V.7.b.7.8.

Above moves will be by cross country tracks.

Northern Divisional Boundary runs East and West through V.8.c. and d.central and bivouacs should as far as possible be within Divisional boundary.

Section Transport only will accompany 77th Field Coy., R.E and a suitable site for such transport will be reconoitred beforehand.

Remainder of transport will not move from their present billets.

93rd Field Coy., R.E. horselines will bivouac in the neighbourhood of the 77th Field Coy., R.E. horselines, taking over such billets as have been vacated.

Reference Divisional Administrative Instructions No.29 para.7, Os.C. Units will use their own discretion as to dumping packs, overcoats and blankets.

ACKNOWLEDGE

Copy No.1 to 77th Field Co. R.E.
" 2 78th " " "
" 3 93rd " " "
" 4 7th Bn. Y. & L. (Pioneers)
" 5 17th Division 'G'
" 6 " " 'Q'
" 7 War Diary

16/9/18.

" 8 File

[signature]
Capt. R.E.
for C.R.E., 17th Division.

S E C R E T.

Copy No....6..

OPERATION ORDER No.14.

by

Lieut.Col. W.A.FERGUSON, D.S.O., R.E.

C.R.E., 17th DIVISION.

1. Consolidation will be pushed on energetically.

2. The FORWARD ZONE for the Defence of which Brigades in the line will be responsible will be Eastwards of the following line :-

W.12.a.central - Trench junction W.5.a.1.7. - Q.28.c.9.4.

3. The front line of MAIN ZONE will run along LOWLAND TRENCH to W.5.d.1.2. - C.T. to HEATHER SUPPORT - HEATHER SUPPORT to W.5.a.1.7. - thence along trench in Q.34.d. and c. - This line will be the line of resistance of the MAIN ZONE.

The Division will be responsible for the construction of defences in and the defence of the Main Zone.

4. C.R.E. will arrange for the construction of defended localities in the MAIN ZONE as follows :-

Q.34.d.2.2.)
W.5.a.1.7.)
W.5.a.2.0.)
W.5.c.4.4.) Each to accommodate 2 Platoons.
W.5.d.1.2.)
W.11.b.3.9.) Order of priority front to rear.
W.11.b.4.6.)
W.12.a.0.0.)
W.11.a.9.4.)
W.4.d.8.2.)
W.4.b.5.1.)

5. In the case of heavy bombardment indicating attack or in the case of actual attack the front line of the MAIN ZONE will be occupied immediately as under -

Reserve Bn. of Reserve Brigade - LOWLAND TRENCH from W.11.b.9.1. - W.5.d.1.2. - C.T. to HEATHER SUPPORT - HEATHER SUPPORT to W.5.c.4.5.
77th., 78th., and 93rd Field Coys., R.E. - W.5.c.4.5. - trench junction W.5.a.1.7.
Pioneer Bn. - W.5.a.1.7. - trench to Q.34.c.central.

The three Field Companies will be disposed as follows :-
77th Field Coy.,R.E. on right.
78th Field Coy.,R.E. in centre.
93rd Field Coy.,R.E. on left.

6. Detailed instructions as to work will be issued later.(The 93rd Field Coy.,R.E. will commence work on the construction of defended localities set out in para.4 as soon as ground has been reconnoitred. Any work already done by 93rd Field Coy., R.E. forward of Main line of Resistance will be handed over to the Field Coy., in whose Brigade area such work is in.

7. ACKNOWLEDGE.

Capt. R.E.
for C.R.E., 17th Division.

22/9/18.

Distribution :-

Copy No. 1 to 77th Field Coy., R.E.
" " 2 " 78th Field Coy., R.E.
" " 3 " 93rd Field Coy., R.E.
" " 4 " 17th Division G.S.
" " 5 " 17th Division "Q".
" " 6 " War Diary.
" " 7 " File.

S E C R E T.

Copy No. 8

OPERATION ORDER No. 15.

by

Lieut.Col. F.A.FERGUSON, D.S.O.,R.E.

C.R.E.,17th DIVISION.

1. The Field Companies and Pioneer Bn. of the 17th Division will be relieved on the 25th inst., by Field Coys., and Pioneer Bn. of the 21st Division.

2. Field Company reliefs as follows :-

77th Field Coy.,R.E. will be relieved by 97th Field Coy.,R.E.
78th " " " " " " " 98th " " "
93rd " " " " " " " 126th " " "

3. 21st Division Companies & Pioneer Bn. will take over forward billets and work from 17th Division Companies.

4. 17th Division Companies will take over any work in rear areas now in hand by 21st Division Companies.

5. 17th Division Companies will move to neighbourhood of their present Transport Lines.

6. 17th Division Transport Lines are remaining in their present locations.

7. Os.C. of the 21st Division Companies will visit Os.C. 17th Division Companies this afternoon at 4.30 pm.

8. Details of relief will be arranged direct between Os.C. Field Companies and Os.C. Pioneer Bns.

9. Reliefs will be completed by 6 pm. on the 25th inst.

10. ACKNOWLEDGE.

Lieut.Col.R.E.
C.R.E.,17th Division.

24/2/18.

Distribution :-

Copy No.1 to 77th Field Coy.,R.E.
" " 2 " 78th Field Coy.,R.E.
" " 3 " 93rd Field Coy.,R.E.
" " 4 " C.R.E.,21st Division.
" " 5 " 17th Division G.S.
" " 6 " 17th Division "Q".
" " 7 " O.C.,7th Bn. Y. & L. Regt.
" " 8 " War Diary.
" " 8 " File.

S E C R E T.

Copy No. 4.

OPERATION ORDER No. 16.

by

Lieut.Col. F.A.FERGUSON, D.S.O., R.E.

C.R.E., 17th DIVISION.

1. 17th Division will be at two hours notice to move from 11 am September 29th.

2. Movements to either of the undermentioned areas may be ordered at short notice :-

(a) DESSART WOOD - FINS - EQUANCOURT
(b) HEUDECOURT - PEIZIERE - SOREL-LE-GRAND

3. In the event of either of the above being ordered, movements will be in accordance with either TABLE 'A' or TABLE 'B'.

4. (a) Later moves of the Division will be dependent on the tactical situation.

(b) If the Division is ordered to follow the left Division (21st.) of the Corps, route of supply will be -

FINS - GOUZEAUCOURT - thence VILLERS GUISLAIN or GONNELIEU to BANTOUZELLE.

(c) If ordered to follow the Right Divisions (33rd. and 38th.) of the Corps, route of supply will be :-

FINS - PEIZIERE - VILLERS GUISLAIN - HONNECOURT - LATERRIERE.

5. In the event of the Division moving Eastwards of CANAL DE L'ESCAUT units must be prepared to employ pack transport until bridges suitable for wheeled transport are available.

6. ACKNOWLEDGE.

[signature]
Capt.R.E.
29/9/18. for C.R.E.,17th Division.

Distribution :-

Copy No. 1 to 77th Field Coy.,R.E.
" " 2 " 78th Field Coy.,R.E.
" " 3 " 93rd Field Coy.,R.E.
" " 4 " War Diary.
" " 5 " File.

T A B L E 'A'

(AREA:- DESSART WOOD - FINS - EQUANCOURT.)

SERIAL NO.	UNIT.	STARTING POINT.	TIME.	ROUTE	DESTINATION	REMARKS.
No. 1	No.1 GROUP (G.O.C.51st Bde.Comdg) (51st Inf. Bde. ('C' M.G.Coy. (77th Field Coy.,R.E. (93rd Field Coy.,R.E. (Mobile 6" Newtons. (51st Field Amb.	CANAL DU NORD Crossings South of main ETRICOURT - EQUANCOURT Bridge.	ZERO	TRACKS South of ETRICOURT - EQUANCOURT - FINS Road	Bde. H.Qs.P.35.d.5.9. Units & Echelon 'A' 1st Line Transport W.7.c. & d. W.8.c. & d. W.13.a. & b. Echelon 'B' and Baggage wagons V.6.a. and c.	
No.2	No.2 GROUP. (G.O.C.50th Bde.Comdg.) (50th Inf. Bde. ('D' M.G.Coy. (78th Field Coy.,R.E.	O.38.b.9.0.	ZERO	Tracks to Tunnel mouth at P.32 - P.35. thence N. of FINS - GOUZEAUCOURT Road.	Bde. H.Qs. P.35.d.5.9. Units & Echelon 'A' 1st Line Transport W.3.a., W.2.b. Q.32. Ech. 'B' and Baggage wagons V.1.a. and c.	

NOTE :- ZERO will be the time at which No. 1 Group will commence movement.

T A B L E 'B'

(AREA :- PRIZIERES - HEUDECOURT - SOREL-LE-GRAND)

SERIAL NO.	UNIT.	STARTING POINT.	TIME.	ROUTE	DESTINATION	REMARKS.
No.1	No.1 GROUP. (G.O.C.51st Bde.Comdg.) 51st Inf. Bde. 'C' M.G. Coy. 77th Field Coy.,R.E. 93rd Field Coy.,R.E. Mob.6" Newtons ~~51st Field Amb.~~	CANAL DU NORD CROSSINGS South of main ETRICOURT -EQUANCOURT bridge.	ZERO	Tracks South of ETRICOURT - EQUANCOURT - FINS - BAILTON (W.16.d.9.0) Road.	Units and Ech. 'A' 1st Line Transport - W.22 Bde. H.Qs. -Dugouts in Road W.9.c. Ech. 'B' Transport & Baggage Wagons - W.20.b.	

T ABB L E 'B' continued.

No.9	No.2 GROUP G.O.C.50th Inf.Bde. (Commanding) 50th Inf. Bde. 'D' M.G.Coy. 78th Field Coy.,R.E.	Cross Roads O.35.b.9.0.	ZERO	Tracks to Tunnel mouth at P.32 - P.35 - V.6. - DESSART Valley.	Units & Ech. 'A' 1st. Line Transport - FINS RIDGE. Bde. H.QS. dugouts in road W.9.d. Ech. 'B' Transport and Baggage wagons W.1.a. & c.

S E C R E T.

Copy No....6.

OPERATION ORDER No. 17.

by

Lieut. Col. F.A. FERGUSON, D.S.O., R.E.

C.R.E., 17th DIVISION.

1. 93rd Field Coy., R.E. will move at 7 am tomorrow to forward billets which should be in the neighbourhood of FINS RIDGE or RAILTON.

2. 93rd Field Coy., R.E. will commence work as already arranged on lorry bridge over canal as soon as tactical situation permits.

3. As the 21st Division is constructing foot and light transport bridges, the construction of lorry bridge is not a matter of extreme tactical urgency, and work will not be undertaken in face of serious enemy opposition.

4. 93rd Field Coy., R.E. will report completion of move and map location to this office and to C.R.E., 21st Division.

5. 77th Field Coy., R.E. will be prepared to move forward on receipt of instructions from this office.

6. ACKNOWLEDGE.

Lieut.Col., R.E.
C.R.E., 17th Division.

30/9/18.

Distribution :-

Copy No. 1 to 77th Field Coy., R.E.
" " 2 " 78th Field Coy., R.E.
" " 3 " 93rd Field Coy., R.E.
" " 4 " 17th Division G.S.
" " 5 " 17th Division "Q".
" " 6 " War Diary.
" " 7 " File.

Instructions regarding War Diaries and Intelligence Summaries are contained in F. S. Regs., Part II. and the Staff Manual respectively. Title Pages will be prepared in manuscript.

WAR DIARY
or
INTELLIGENCE SUMMARY
(Erase heading not required.)

Army Form C. 2118

HQ RE 17 D

Place	Date 1918	Hour	Summary of Events and Information	Remarks and references to Appendices
LECHELLE	OCTOBER 1		93 Field Coy R.E moved forward under orders to bridge canal at Honnecourt for lorry traffic as soon as situation permitted. 7th Bn York & Lancaster (Pioneer) Regt moved forward and came under direction of C.R.E. V. Corps Troops for work on railways. C.R.E visited 77 and 78 Field Companies	JB3
	2.		C.R.E went round forward area with C.E. V. Corps	JB3
	3.		C.R.E visited 93 Field Coy R.E.	JB3
	4.		C.R.E conferred with C.R.E. 21 Division	JB3
HEUDECOURT	5.		C.R.E moved with D.H.Q. to neighbourhood of Heudecourt. 93 Field Coy R.E commenced constructing R.S.J. bridge for 12 ton axle loads over Canal d'Escaut at Honnecourt. C.R.E inspected work. C.R.E conferred with C.R.E. 21 Division. 77 and 78 Field Coy R.E moved forward	JB3
	6.		C.R.E inspected work on bridge at Honnecourt. 93 Field Coy R.E. completed bridge at 6 a.m. when same was opened for traffic. C.R.E went forward with G.S.O.1. 78 Field Coy worked on roads in neighbourhood of Gonnelieu.	JB3
	7.		C.R.E visited 3 Field Coys & Pioneer Battalion. One section 77 Field Coy R.E became attached to 51 Brigade. C.R.E conferred with C.R.E. 21 Division.	JB3
	8		C.R.E. conferred with O.C. 93 Field Coy R.E.	JB3
GUILLEMIN 57b N17a 2.4	9		C.R.E moved with ~~H.Q.~~ D.H.Q. to Guillemin. Three Field Coys moved forward. 78 Field Coy made roads passable for Divisional Transport. 93 Field Coy established water points. 17 Division relieved 21 Division in line	JB3
MONTIGNY	10		C.R.E moved with D.H.Q. to Montigny. 77 Field Coy worked forward on making roads passable. 78 Field Coy worked on road repairs. 93 Field Coy R.E searched for and removed mines in Montigny & made water supply reconnaissance. Three Field Coys moved forward	JB3

Instructions regarding War Diaries and Intelligence Summaries are contained in F. S. Regs., Part II. and the Staff Manual respectively. Title pages will be prepared in manuscript.

WAR DIARY
or
INTELLIGENCE SUMMARY.
(Erase heading not required.)

Army Form C. 2118.

Place	Date	Hour	Summary of Events and Information	Remarks and references to Appendices
MONTIGNY	OCTOBER			
	11		C.R.E. went forward with G.S.O.1. 93 Field Coy. R.E. relieved 77 Field Coy R.E. as forward Company. 93rd erected 8 Infantry Bridges over River Selle at Neuvilly which enabled advance Brigade to cross to the attack. One of these bridges was supported by sappers standing in the stream and supporting same. 77 Field Coy R.E. made reconnaissance of river with view to the construction of tank bridge. 78 Field Coy worked on road. The Pioneer Battalion came under orders of C.R.E.	[initials]
	12.		C.R.E. conferred with C.R.E. 33 Division & visited the three Field Coys. O.C. 77 Field Coy R.E. was wounded when making reconnaissance of Selle River. 78 Field Coy R.E. worked on road repairs. 93 Field Coy R.E. maintained the infantry crossings on the river. Pioneers worked on roads	[initials]
	13.		77 Field Coy R.E. worked on assembling Tank Bridges. 78 Field Coy R.E. and 2 Coys of Pioneers commenced construction of trench system to form a Main Line of Resistance. C.R.E. went forward. 93 Field Coy R.E. maintained Infantry Bridges. One Coy Pioneers worked on roads	[initials]
	14		C.R.E. conferred with O.C. Tank Battalion. C.R.E. conferred with C.R.E. 21 & 38 Divisions and with C.E. V Corps. Field Coys and Pioneers worked as before.	[initials]

(A7092). Wt. W12839/M1293. 750,000. 1/17. D. D. & L., Ltd. Forms/C.2118/14.

Instructions regarding War Diaries and Intelligence Summaries are contained in F. S. Regs., Part II. and the Staff Manual respectively. Title pages will be prepared in manuscript.

WAR DIARY
or
INTELLIGENCE SUMMARY.
(*Erase heading not required.*)

Army Form C. 2118.

Place	Date	Hour	Summary of Events and Information	Remarks and references to Appendices
MONTIGNY	OCTOBER			
	15		Field Coys and Pioneers worked as before. C.R.E. conferred with C.E. V Corps, O.C. Tank Battalion, C.R.E. 21 & C.R.E. 38 Division. C.E. Third Army visited C.R.E. Major R.C. LUNDIE. D.S.O. R.E. reported missing, believed killed. 93 Field Coy R.E. made forward road reconnaissance. 77 Field Coy R.E. constructing stone abutments of Tank Bridge	[illegible]
	16		C.R.E. visited C.E. V Corps & visited 3 Field Coys. The 3 Field Coys and Pioneers worked as before save that ~~one Coy~~ two Coys worked on roads and one on trench consolidation.	[illegible]
	17		E in C. GHQ, C.E. 3rd Army & C.E. V. Corps called upon C.R.E. E in C. congratulated Lieut Lucas & 4 O.R. of 93 Field Coy R.E. on their gallantry in connection with placing Infantry bridges over the ~~river~~ Selle. C.R.E. conferred with C.R.E.s 21 & 38 Divisions.	[illegible]
	18		C.R.E. conferred with C.R.E. 21 Division. Field Coys & Pioneers worked as before.	[illegible]
	19		C.R.E. attended conference C.E. V Corps. C.R.E. conferred with Field Coy commanders and C.O. Pioneers. 97 Field Coy R.E. 21 Division was lent C.R.E. for bridge building. 77 Field Coy R.E. constructed bridge for Tanks over Selle River. 93 Field Coy R.E. constructed 2, Infantry Bridges.	[illegible]
	20		C.R.E. visited Field Coys and Advanced Brigade. 77th Field Coy commenced construction of another tank bridge. 97 Field Coy R.E. commenced construction of 12 ton arch trench bridge. 93 Field Coy R.E. constructed 2 First line Transport Bridges. 78 Field Coy & 1 Coy Pioneers worked on consolidation.	[illegible]

Army Form C. 2118.

Instructions regarding War Diaries and Intelligence Summaries are contained in F. S. Regs., Part II. and the Staff Manual respectively. Title pages will be prepared in manuscript.

WAR DIARY
or
INTELLIGENCE SUMMARY.
(Erase heading not required.)

Place	Date	Hour	Summary of Events and Information	Remarks and references to Appendices
MONTIGNY	21		C.R.E visited 97 Field Co R.E & 93rd Field Co R.E. Inspected work on bridges in NEUVILLY & footbridges & 1 tier transport bridge on North of river. C.E V Corps conferred with C.R.E.	[initials]
	22		97th Field Co R.E rejoined 21st Division. Tank Bridge at K8a.16 completed at 16.00 hrs by 77th Field Co RE. C.R.E ~~[illegible]~~ inspected bridges. Division relieved by 21st Division night of 22/23	[initials]
INCHY	23		C.R.E H.Q moved to INCHY with Division H.Q. 78th & 93rd Field Cos moved into INCHY. 93rd Field Co RE selected Tank bridge K1c6.8. & foot bridges & formed a dump.	[initials]
	24th		C.R.E inspected roads in Divisional area. 77th Field Co moved into AUDENCOURT	[initials]
	25th		78th Field Co moved up to OVILLERS & worked on roads. 7th Yorks & L Pioneers moved to NEUVILLY & worked on roads.	[initials]
OVILLERS	26		C.R.E moved with Division H.Q to OVILLERS. 77th Field Co moved to VENDEGIES. 78th Field Co to POIX-DU-NORD. 17th Division relieved 21st night of 26/27	[initials]
	27		C.R.E went up the line & selected defensive position with O.C. 77th Field CoRE. 93rd Field Co moved to VENDEGIES. 7th Yorks & L Pioneers moved to VENDEGIES. 1 Co to POIX-DU-NORD. 78th Field Co worked under 52nd Inf Bde on consolidation. 77th continue on communication in forward zone. 93rd on water supply	[initials]

Instructions regarding War Diaries and Intelligence Summaries are contained in F. S. Regs., Part II. and the Staff Manual respectively. Title pages will be prepared in manuscript.

WAR DIARY
or
INTELLIGENCE SUMMARY.
(Erase heading not required.)

Army Form C. 2118.

Place	Date	Hour	Summary of Events and Information	Remarks and references to Appendices
OVILLERS	28		Coys worked as for 27th	[initials]
	29th		C.R.E. moved back to INCHY with Division H.Q. Division relieved by 21st Division night of 29th/30th. All Field Coys & Pioneers moved to NEUVILLY.	[initials]
	30		Coys training & cleaning up. Pioneers worked on roads	[initials]
	31		As for 30th	[initials]

A. Lyons Lieut. R.E.
for C.R.E. 7th Division
2/10/18.

S E C R E T.

Copy No....6...

OPERATION ORDER No. 18.

by

Lieut. Col. F.A.FERGUSON, D.S.O., R.E.

C.R.E., 17th Division.

1. 77th and 78th Field Coys.R.E. will move forward today in accordance with Table 'A' of my Operation Order No.16.

2. ZERO hour will be 12.30 pm.

3. After arrival in positions given in Table 'A' further forward movements will be ordered as advance of 21st Division progresses.

4. ACKNOWLEDGE.

Capt.R.E.
for C.R.E., 17th Division.

8/10/18.

Distribution :-

CopyNo. 1 to 77th Field Coy., R.E.
" " 2 " 78th Field Coy., R.E.
" " 3 " 93rd Field Coy., R.E.
" " 4 " 17th Division G.S.
" " 5 " 17th Division "Q".
" " 6 " War Diary.
" " 7 " File.

SECRET.

Copy No.4....

OPERATION ORDER No.19.

by

Lieut.Col. F.A.FERGUSON, D.S.O., R.E.

C.R.E., 17th DIVISION.

1. Three Field Companies less 1 section 77th Fld: Coy. will move forthwith and concentrate in X.3.a. or b.

2. After concentration in this area they will remain at one hour's notice and be prepared for a further advance.

3. In the event of this advance taking place the three Bridging Wagons of each Company would probably move with Divisional Train.

4. Completion of move to be reported.

5. ACKNOWLEDGE.

F Ferguson

Lieut.Col.R.E.

8/10/18. C.R.E.,17th Division.

Distrubution :-

Copy No. 1 to 77th Field Coy.,R.E.
" " 2 " 78th " " "
" " 3 " 93rd " " "
" " 4 " War Diary.
" " 5 " File.
" " 6 " 17th Div: Q.

S E C R E T.

Copy No. 6

OPERATION ORDER No.90.

by

Lieut. Col. W.A.FERGUSON, D.S.O., R.E.

C.R.E., 17th DIVISION.

1. Situation at 18.00 hrs. on 8/10/18 is reported to be as follows :-

(a) Troops of 38th Division - South West edge of VILL WOOD - N.38.central - DEHERIES.

(b) Troops of 37th Division IVth Corps - N.10 and Northwards.

(c) 21st Division attacking under a barrage from the WALINCOURT - AUDIGNY Line with the object of gaining the line - high ground N.18. East of WALINCOURT to O.19.c.0.0. - O.25.central.

2. (a) The enemy is to be followed up on the 9th with the greatest vigour.

(b) The 17th Division will pass through the 21st Division at 05.20 hrs. on the 9/10/18. Objectives CAULLERY, exploiting towards MONTIGNY and TRONQUOY. Southern Divisional boundary O.17.a.0.0. to P.5.b.0.0.

3. The Field Companies less one Section 77th Field Coy., R.E. will move under the command of Major R.C.LEWDIS D.S.O., R.E. to trenches at N.33. Move to be completed by 03.00 hrs. on 9/10/18, route via HAUTMUX: not to commence crossing lock at HAUTMUX before 04.30 hrs.

4. C.R.E's Headquarters will open at W.30.c.5.3. at 07.00 hrs.

5. ACKNOWLEDGE.

Capt.R.E.
for C.R.E., 17th Division.

9/10/18.

Distribution :- Copy No. 1 to 77th Field Coy.,R.E.
" " 2 " 78th Field Coy.,R.E.
" " 3 " 93rd Field Coy.,R.E.
" " 4 " 17th Division G.S.
" " 5 " 17th Division "Q".
" " 6 " War Diary.
" " 7 " File.

S E C R E T.

Copy No. 6

OPERATION ORDER No.21.

by

Lieut.Col. F.A.FERGUSON, D.S.O., R.E.

C.R.E., 17th DIVISION.

1. In the event of enemy attack the Line of Resistance of the outpost line will be maintained by the Advance Brigade at all costs.

2. Tactical points will be selected and constructed by G.O.C., Advance Brigade between the outpost line of resistance and the line RAMBOURLIEUX FARM - J.12. These posts will be permanently garrisoned by Advance Guard Brigade and the garrisons will in case of attack maintain their positions at all costs.

3. In the event of attack or of heavy bombardment presaging attack -

(a) The INCHY Brigade will move at once and occupy the RAMBOURLIEUX LINE.

(b) MONTIGNY Brigade will be moved to H.27. and H.28. on receipt of message "MOVE" - Brigade H.Q. being established at those of the INCHY Brigade.

(c) R.E. Field Companies and Pioneer Battalion will 'Stand to' at their present locations and be prepared to move as required.

(d) Working parties working East of the RAMBOURLIEUX FARM - J.12. line will report to the nearest O.C. Unit and be despatched by him to rejoin their units as soon as the tactical situation permits.
Parties working West of the above line will rejoin their units at once.

4. ACKNOWLEDGE.

Capt.R.E.
for C.R.E.,17th Division.

14/10/18.

Distribution :-

Copy No. 1 to 77th Field Coy.,R.E.
" " 2 " 78th Field Coy.,R.E.
" " 3 " 93rd Field Coy.,R.E.
" " 4 " 17th Division G.S.
" " 5 " 17th Division "Q".
" " 6 " War Diary.
" " 7 " File.

SECRET.

OPERATION ORDER No.22. Copy No. 6..

by

Lieut.Col. F.A.FERGUSON, D.S.O.,R.E.

C.R.E., 17th DIVISION.

1. Third Army will continue advance on October 23rd. The advance on this front will be carried out by 21st Division.

2. The task of the 17th Division will be to advance through the 21st Division on October 23rd or later according to the situation.

3. Objective of 21st Division is about 7,000 yds in front of present front line.

4. 77th and 78th Field Coys.,R.E. will be at half hours notice to move after 11.00 hrs.on the 23rd. In the event of a forward move the 78th Field Coy.,R.E. will be leading Company.

5. 78th Field Coy.,R.E.,less one Section, will move to INCHY on the morning of the 23rd inst. Move to be completed by 11.00 hours.

6. Stringent precautions against gas will be taken in crossing the SELLE Valley.

7. O.C.,78th Field Coy.,R.E. will place one Section at disposal of 51st (Advance Guard) Brigade.

8. 51st Brigade will be on AMERVAL Ridge, K.4. at 09.00 hrs, moving from Eastern outskirts of INCHY at 08.00 hrs.

9. 93rd Field Coy.,R.E. will be prepared on receipt of further orders from this office to salve all bridges, including foot bridges and tank bridge, and bridging Equipment on the River SELLE with the exception of the two main bridges in NEUVILLY.

Company Equipment will be returned to Units to whom it belongs and all other material from the River or from any other Company Dumps in Divisional area will be collected into a dump at a suitable site on the road about K.9.a.0.5. Location of dump and list of material will be forwarded to this office.

10. All roads East of INCHY will be kept clear after 08.00 hr for troops of 21st Division moving Eastwards. Any troops of the 17th Division on the road after 08.00 hrs. must give way to troops moving Eastwards.

11. C.R.E's Office will close at MONTIGNY at 11.00 hrs. on the 23rd and re-open in INCHY at the same hour.

12. ACKNOWLEDGE.

A Rhees

Lieut.R.E.

22/10/18. for C.R.E.,17th Division.

Distribution as for C.R.E's O.O. No.21.

SECRET.

Copy No. 6.

OPERATION ORDER No. 23

by

Lieut.Col. F.A.FERGUSON, D.S.O.,R.E.

C.R.E.,17th DIVISION.

1. Fifth Corps operations today were successful.

2. 33rd and 21st Divisions will continue the advance early on the 24th inst. 17th Division will not advance on the 24th.

3. Companies will take this opportunity for resting, refitting and bathing.

4. 78th Field Coy.,R.E. may be required for work on roads after 12.00 hours on the 24th inst.

5. ACKNOWLEDGE.

A.L. [signature]
Lieut.R.E.
for C.R.E.,17th Division.

23/10/18.

Distribution :-

Copy No. 1 to 77th Field Coy.,R.E.
" " 2 " 78th Field Coy.,R.E.
" " 3 " 93rd Field Coy.,R.E.
" " 4 " 17th Division G.S.
" " 5 " 17th Division "Q".
" " 6 " War Diary.
" " 7 " File.

S E C R E T.

Copy No. 6..

OPERATION ORDER No. 24.

by

Lieut.Col. F.A.FERGUSON, D.S.O.,R.E.

C.R.E., 17th Division.

1. 17th Division will not advance on 25th October but will be prepared to replace 21st Division in left sector Vth Corps during 26th and night 26/27th October.

2. All moves will be carried out across Country by troops, transport by tracks or roads according to the weather.
Transport moving by road will follow traffic routes laid down.

3. ACKNOWLEDGE.

Lieut.R.E.
for C.R.E.,17th Division.

24/10/18.

Distribution :-
Copy No. 1 to 77th Field Coy.,R.E.
" " 2 " 78th Field Coy.,R.E.
" " 3 " 93rd Field Coy.,R.E.
" " 4 " 17th Division G.S.
" " 5 " 17th Division "Q".
" " 6 " War Diary.
" " 7 " File.

S E C R E T.

Copy No. 6...

WARNING ORDER No.25

by

Lieut.Col., F.A.FERGUSON, D.S.O.,R.E.

C.R.E., 17th DIVISION.

1. 17th Division (less Artillery) will relieve 21st Division (less Artillery) in left Sector of Vth Corps front during 26th October and night 26/27th October.

2. (a) Units relieving in daylight will move in small parties forward of OVILLERS, and will take all precautions against observation by enemy aircraft.
(b) Infnatry will move across Country, transport by tracks or roads according to weather. Transport moving by road will adhere to traffic route laid down.

3. Engineer and Pioneer reliefs will be carried out on 26th and night 26/27th inst. under arrangements to be made by C.R.E's 17th and 21st Divisions.

4. Orders as to relief of Companies of 21st Division will be issued later.

5. 78th Field Coy.,R.E. will not go out to work on morning of 26th inst., but will be prepared for work at short notice.

6. Administrative Instructions will be issued separately.

7. Command of the Divisional Sector and of the Artillery in it will pass from G.O.C.,21st Division to G.O.C.,17th Division on completion of Infantry reliefs on night of 26/27th inst.

8. Advanced D.H.Q. will open at OVILLERS on completion of Infantry reliefs. Rear D.H.Q. will remain at INCHY.

9. ACKNOWLEDGE.

A. P. Lucas
Lieut.R.E.
for C.R.E.,17th Division.

25/10/18.

Distribution :-

Copy No. 1 to 77th Field Coy.,R.E.
" " 2 " 78th Field Coy.,R.E.
" " 3 " 93rdField Coy.,R.E.
" " 4 " 17th Division G.S.
" " 5 " 17th Division "Q".
" " 6 " War Diary.
" " 7 File.

SECRET.

Copy No..7..

OPERATION ORDER No. 26.

by

Lieut.Col.,F.A.FERGUSON, D.S.O.,R.E.

C.R.E.,17th DIVISION.

1. Moves of Field Coys.,R.E. and Pioneer Bn. of 17th Division will be carried out in accordance with attached table.

2. 78th Field Coy.,R.E. and one Company Pioneers will be at disposal of 52nd Brigade to assist in consolidation.

3. 77th Field Coys,R.E. and 93rd Field Coy.,R.E. will work under C.R.E. Details of work will be issued later.

Lieut.R.E.
for C.R.EW,17th Division.

26/10/18.

Distribution :-

Copy No. 1 to 77th Field Coy.,R.E.
" " 2 " 78th Field Coy.,R.E.
" " 3 " 93rd Field Coy.,R.E.
" " 4 " 17th Division G.S.
" " 5 " 17th Division "Q".
" " 6 " 7th Bn. Y & L.
" " 7 " War Diary.
" " 8 " File.

TABLE TO ACCOMPANY C.R.E's OPERATION ORDER No. 26.

UNIT	FROM	TO	TIME	REMARKS.
77th Field Coy., R.E.	AUDENCOURT	VENDEGIES	16.00 hours 26th inst.	
78th Field Coy., R.E.	OVILLERS	POIX DU NORD	16.00 hours 26th inst.	
93rd Field Coy., R.E.	INCHY	VENDEGIES	08.00 hours 27th inst.	
One Company Pioneers	OVILLERS	POIX DU NORD	Afternoon 26th inst.	
Two Companies Pioneers	NEUVILLERS	VENDEGIES	Afternoon 26th inst.	Take over accommodation from 21st Divisional Pioneers.

<u>NOTE.</u> Accommodation in VENDEGIES and PIOX DU NORD will be allotted by Area Commandant, OVILLERS.

S E C R E T.

Copy No. 7...

WARNING ORDER No.27.

by

Lieut.Col. F.A.FERGUSON, D.S.O.,R.E.

C.R.E.,17th DIVISION.

1. 17th Division will be relieved by 21st Division in Left Divisional Sector on 29th and night of 29/30th inst.

2. Field Companies R.E. and 7th Bn. Y. & L. will be relieved on the afternoon of the 29th inst.

3. Os.C. Field Coys.,R.E. and O.C. Pioneer Bn., 21st Division will call on xxxxxxxxxxxxxxx respective OsC. 17th Division at 10.00 hours on 29th inst. to take over work.

4. Two Companies Pioneers working on forward Roads will carry on with work on 29th inst.

5. Further details will be issued later.

6. ACKNOWLEDGE.

Lieut.R.E.
for C.R.E.,17th Division.

28/10/18.

Distribution :-

Copy No. 1 to 77th Field Coy.,R.E.
" " 2 " 78th Field Coy.,R.E.
" " 3 " 93rd Field Coy.,R.E.
" " 4 " 7th Bn. Y. & L.
" " 5 " 17th Division G.S.
" " 6 " 17th Division "Q".
" " 7 " War Diary.
" " 8 " File.

<u>S E C R E T.</u>

Copy No. 8..

<u>OPERATION ORDER No.28.</u>

by

<u>Lieut.Col.,F.A.FERGUSON, D.S.O.,R.E.</u>

<u>C.R.E.,17th DIVISION.</u>

1. Reliefs of Field Coy.,R.E. and 7th Bn. Y. & L. by corresponding units of the 21st Division will be carried out in accordance with attached table on the afternoon of the 29th inst.

2. All work now in progress will be handed over by Os.C. and details of relief arranged direct.

3. (a) Units moving in daylight will move in small ~~in each~~ parties East of OVILLERS and will take all precautions against observation by enemy aircraft.
   (b) Dismounted parties will move across country. Transport by main road via MONTAY.

4. Bridging equipment of the 78th Field Coy.,R.E. across the river at K.27.c.9.1. will be left in situ. Arrangements have been made for the corresponding bridging material to be handed over by 21st Division on arrival in new billets.

5. C.R.E's office will close in OVILLERS at 18.00 hours and open in INCHY same hour.

6. ACKNOWLEDGE.

A. Chivers

Lieut.R.E.

28/10/18. for C.R.E.,17th Division.

Distribution:-

Copy No. 1 to 77th Field Coy.,R.E.
" " 2 " 78th Field Coy.,R.E.
" " 3 " 93rd Field Coy.,R.E.
" " 4 " 7th Bn. Y. & L.
" " 5 " 17th Division G.S.
" " 6 " 17th Division "Q".
" " 7 " C.R.E.,21st Division.
" " 8 " War Diary.
" " 9 " File.

SECRET.

Copy No. 7....

DEFENCE INSTRUCTIONS No.3.

by

Lieut.Col. F.A.FERGUSON, D.S.O.,R.E.

C.R.E.,17th DIVISION.

1. In the event of attack or heavy bombardment presaging attack, the 77th Field Coy.,R.E. and 93rd Field Coy., R.E. and Pioneers (less one Company with Advance Guard) will stand to at their present locations and be prepared to move as required.

2. 78th Field Coy.,R.E. and one Company of Pioneers with Advance Guard will stand to and report to G.O.C.,Advance Brigade for instructions.

3. Working parties working East of a line X.23.d.7.0. - X.16.c.4.0. will report to the nearest O.C.,Unit and be despatched by him to rejoin their units as soon as the tactical situation permits.

Parties working West of the above line will rejoin their units at once.

4. ACKNOWLEDGE.

Lieut.R.E.
for C.R.E.,17th Division.

28/10/18.

Distribution:-

Copy No. 1 to 77th Field Coy.,R.E.
" " 2 " 78th Field Coy.,R.E.
" " 3 " 93rd Field Coy.,R.E.
" " 4 " 7th Bn. Y. & L.
" " 5 " 17th Division G.S.
" " 6 " 17th Division "Q".
" " 7 " War Diary.
" " 8 " File.

TABLE TO ACCOMPANY C.R.E. O.O. No.28.

UNIT	TO BE RELIEVED BY	FROM	TO	BILLETS AND HORSELINES FROM	TRANSPORT. STARTING POINT	TIME
77th Field Coy., R.E.	Field Co. R.E., 21st Div.	VENDEGIES	NEUVILLY	Field Coy., R.E., 21st Div.	Cross Roads F.21.c.8.8.	14.30
78th Field Coy., R.E.	Field Co. R.E., 21st Div.	POIX	NEUVILLY	Field Coy., R.E., 21st Div.	Cross Roads F.21.c.8.8.	14.45
93rd Field Coy., R.E.	Field Co. R.E., 21st Div.	VENDEGIES	NEUVILLY	Field Coy., R.E., 21st Div.	Cross Roads F.21.c.8.8.	15.00
7th Bn. Y. & L.	Pioneer Bn., 21st Div.	VENDEGIES	NEUVILLY	Pioneer Bn., 21st Div.	Cross Roads F.21.c.8.8.	15.15.

S E C R E T.

Copy No. 7....

OPERATION ORDER No. 99.

by

Lieut.Col. F.A.FERGUSON, D.S.O.,R.E.

C.R.E.,17th DIVISION.

1. 17th Division (less Artillery) will relieve 21st Division (less Artillery) in Left Sector of V Corps Front during 2nd inst and night 2/3rd inst.

2. Movements of Field Coys.,R.E. and 7th Bn. Y. & L. will be carried out as follows.

3. Infantry will move by tracks. There will be no movement East of the River SELLE before 17.00 hours.

4. Transport.

Unit.	From	To	Route.	
78th Field Co.,R.E.	NEUVILLY	~~[illegible]~~ VENDEGIES area.	Via OVILLERS. To pass cross roads K.9.a.9.7.	18.15 hrs.
93rd Field Co.,R.E.	do	do	do	18.25 hrs.
7th Bn. Y. & L. (less one Coy.)	do	do	do	18.35 hrs.

Transport will adhere to traffic routes laid down.

5. No billets are available for Field Coys.,R.E. or 7th Bn. Y. & L. Cs.C. Units will reconnoitre a suitable bivouac ground during daylight.

Neighbourhood of battery positions and villages to be avoided.

Positions selected by Field Coys.,R.E. for bivouacs will be reported to this office not later than 14.00 hours, tomorrow.

Horse lines to be West of River HARPIES.

6. 77th Field Coy.,R.E. and one Company 7th Bn. Y. & L. will vacate billets now occupied and will bivouac: 77th Field Coy., R.E. in neighbourhood of VENDEGIES and Pioneer Company with remainder of Battalion.

7. 77th Field Coy.,R.E. and one Company 7th Bn. Y. & L. now at VENDEGIES will carry on with work tomorrow night as arranged by C.R.E.,21st Division.

8. Canvas will be drawn from the Area Commandant's Office at VENDEGIES. Time and quantity will be notified later.

9. C.R.E's H.Q. will close at INCHY at 17.00 hours and open at VENDEGIES same hour.

10. ACKNOWLEDGE.

A.L. Lee
Lieut.R.E.
for C.R.E.,17th Division.

1/11/18.

Distribution as for O.O.98.

S E C R E T.

Copy No. 8...

C.R.E., 17th DIVISION.

OPERATION ORDER No. 30.

1. The V Corps will resume the advance in conjunction with neighbouring Corps on a date (Z day) and an hour to be notified later.

2. The boundaries and objectives of the attack of the 17th Division are shewn on tracing "A".

3. The 52nd Brigade will capture the first objective starting from present front line at Zero.

4. 51st Brigade will capture the second objective starting from the jumping off line with 52nd Brigade, then loosing distance and following 52nd Brigade to first objective at approximate distance of 500 yards, eventually passing through the 52nd Brigade

5. The 50th Brigade will capture the third objective, passing through the 51st and 52nd Brigades.

6. Barrage maps are forwarded herewith.

7. 78th Field Coy., R.E. and one Pioneer Company will follow 51st Brigade across the starting line at one hours distance and follow up the advance to the third objective or as far as the situation allows.

The role of these Companies will be to clear roads and tracks within Divisional Boundaries from neighbourhood of present front line forward precedence being given to the route X.8.a.9.9. - S.19.b.0.0. - S.26.a.8.8. - S.26.a.2.1. thence North along main road to S.20.d.3.0. - S.22.c.9.3. - S.24.a.3.6.

Every effort should be made to get at least one route passable for first line transport as far forward as the tactical situation permits during the day.

8. O.C., 78th Field Coy., R.E. will report to C.R.E. at frequent intervals on condition of roads and progress in clearing etc.

9. Os.C., 78th Field Coy., R.E. and Pioneer Company will keep in touch with G.Os.C. leading Brigades throughout in order to keep themselves acquainted with the situation, and will render such technical assistance as may be necessary.

10. 77th and 93rd Field Coys., R.E. and two Companies Pioneers will cross the existing front line as soon as first objective has been captured.

O.C., 77th Field Coy., R.E. will arrange liaison with the 52nd Brigade tow ascertain when this occurs.

11. Companies will take with them such Company Transport as they can make available for cartage of material.

12. The Companies referred to in para.10 will work on main road from front line in S.20.d. to MAISON FORET DE L'OPERA and ROUTE DE CHENE COUPLET in left Divisional Sector. The former will be completed for lorry traffic, and the latter for horse traffic.during the day.

[illegible]
13. Major A.G.MITCHELL R.E. will be responsible for the co-ordination and direction of the work of these four Companies and will report to this office as early as possible on condition of roads and his estimate of material, time and labour required to complete.

14. 93rd Field Coy., R.E. will erect six horse troughs at a suitable site in neighbourhood of S.16.c. as soon as the situation permits. Completion to be reported to this office.

15. Arrangements are being made to assemble wagon loads of Bridging Stores in F.16.central. Details and contents of material dumps will be forwarded as soon as possible.

16. Special Anti-gas precautions will be enforced both during and after completion of attack.

17. Attention is called to Administrative Instructions 5, 6, and 9 in 17th Division A.I. No.97 dated 8/11/18.

18. C.R.E's H.Q. will be at F.5.b.5.6. from 08.00 hours on Zero day.

19. ACKNOWLEDGE.

Lieut.R.E.
for C.R.E., 17th Division.

8/11/18.

Distribution :-

Copy No. 1 to 77th Field Coy., R.E.
" " 2 " 78th Field Coy., R.E.
" " 3 " 93rd Field Coy., R.E.
" " 4 " 7th Bn. Y. & L.
" " 5 " 17th Division G.S.
" " 6 " 17th Division "Q".
" " 7 " C.R.E., 21st Division.
" " 8 " War Diary.
" " 9 " File.

NOTE. Tracing "A" and Barrage maps to Field Coys., R.E. only.

SECRET.

Copy No. 8

AMENDMENTS TO OPERATION ORDER No. 29.

by

Lieut.Col. F.A.FERGUSON, D.S.O.,R.E.

C.R.E.,17th DIVISION.

1. Cancel para. 2 and substitute the following.

2. 78th and 93rd Field Coys.,R.E. and 7th Bn. Y. & L., (less one Company) will move to POIX DU NORD Area as follows.

2. In para. 9 for VENDEGIES read OVILLERS.

Lieut.Col.R.E.
C.R.E.,17th Division.

2/11/18.

Distribution as for O.O.29.

Instructions regarding War Diaries and Intelligence Summaries are contained in F. S. Regs., Part II. and the Staff Manual respectively. Title pages will be prepared in manuscript.

CRE 17th Div

WAR DIARY
or
INTELLIGENCE SUMMARY.
(Erase heading not required.)

CRE

Vol 38

Army Form C. 2118.

Place	Date	Hour	Summary of Events and Information	Remarks and references to Appendices
INCHY	1/11/18		77th Field Co & 167th [illegible] [illegible] moved forward to work under C.R.E. 21st Division. C.R.E. attended conference at D.H.Q.	App
OVILLERS	2/11/18		C.R.E. moved with D.H.Q. to OVILLERS. 77th Company & 167th [illegible] [illegible] working under C.R.E. 21st Division. 78th & 93rd Field Coys & 2 Coys Pioneers moved to POIX-DU-NORD. C.R.E. visited C.R.E. 21st Division.	App
	3/11/18		C.R.E. held a conference of Field Co Commanders & C.O. 7th Y&L.	App
	4/11/18		17th Division attacked FORET-DE-MORMAL. 77th & 93rd Field Coys + 2 Coys Pioneers worked on forward roads. 78th Field Co & 1 Coy 7th Y&L followed up advance. C.R.E. inspected all forward roads. C.R.E. at advanced D.H.Q. POIX-DU-NORD. Field Coys in billets at POIX	App.
POIX-DU-NORD	5/11/18		C.R.E. moved forward to POIX-DU-NORD. Inspected forward roads. 77th & 93rd Field Coys + 2 Coys 7th Y&L worked on forward roads. C.R.E. moved with advanced D.H.Q. to LOCQUIGNOL. Field Coys & Pioneers moved forward to LOCQUIGNOL.	App
LOCQUIGNOL	6/11/18		C.R.E. inspected forward roads. 78th & 93rd Field Coys & 2 Coys Pioneers worked on roads	App.
	7/11/18		C.R.E. moved with Division H.Q. to AULNOYE. 93rd Field Co worked on craters at T.23.c.5.1 with 1 Coy of Pioneers	App
AULNOYE	8/11/18		C.R.E. inspected forward roads. Conference [illegible] to BACHANT	App
	9/11/18		C.R.E. inspected all roads in forward area. 77th & 78th Field Coys & 2 Coys Pioneers worked on roads, bridges, [illegible] & craters	App

A5834 Wt. W4973 M687 750,000 8/16 D. D. & L. Ltd. Forms/C.2118/13.

Instructions regarding War Diaries and Intelligence Summaries are contained in F. S. Regs., Part II. and the Staff Manual respectively. Title pages will be prepared in manuscript.

WAR DIARY
or
INTELLIGENCE SUMMARY.
(Erase heading not required.)

Army Form C. 2118.

Place	Date	Hour	Summary of Events and Information	Remarks and references to Appendices
	NOVEMBER			
AULNOYE	10		77 & 78 Field Coys R.E. completed bridges over ~~Sambre~~ River at Limont Fontaine. 93 Field Coy R.E. and Pioneers on roads. C.R.E. inspected work.	[illegible]
	11		77 & 78 Field Coys R.E. moved back to Berlaimont, Pioneers to Tête-Noir. 17 Div relieved by 21 Division. Coys worked on roads. Armistice signed	[illegible]
	12.		Coys and Pioneers worked on roads	[illegible]
	13.		Do Do C.R.E. inspected work	[illegible]
INCHY	14		C.R.E. moved with D.H.Q. to INCHY. 3 Field Coys to ENGEL FONTAINE. Pioneers ceased to be under orders of C.R.E.	[illegible]
	15.		77 Field Coy R.E. moved Troisvilles, 78 Field Coy to Bertry, 93 Field Coy R.E. to INCHY. C.R.E. inspected Field Coys on the march	[illegible]
	16.		Field Coys worked on re-equipping, training & education	[illegible]
	17		Do Do Do	[illegible]
	18		Do Do Do	[illegible]
	19		Do Do Do	[illegible]
	20		Do Do Do	[illegible]
	21		C.R.E. inspected 93 Field Coy R.E.	[illegible]
	22		Do Do Do	[illegible]

Instructions regarding War Diaries and Intelligence Summaries are contained in F. S. Regs., Part II. and the Staff Manual respectively. Title Pages will be prepared in manuscript.

WAR DIARY
or
INTELLIGENCE SUMMARY
(Erase heading not required.)

Army Form C. 2118

Place	Date 1918	Hour	Summary of Events and Information	Remarks and references to Appendices
INCHY	NOVEMBER			
	23		C.R.E. inspected 78 Field Coy. R.E.	[illegible]
	24		Church Parades etc.	[illegible]
	25		C.R.E. inspected 77 Field Coy R.E. Lt-Col F. A. Ferguson D.S.O. R.E. went on leave. Major A. C. Nesbitt R.E. O.C. 77 Field Coy R.E. became acting C.R.E.	[illegible]
	26		The three Field Coys were inspected in their Brigade Groups by the Divisional Commander	[illegible]
	27		C.R.E. visited 77 Field Coy R.E. Field Coys worked on training & education	[illegible]
	28		C.R.E. visited 78 and 93 Field Coys R.E. Do	[illegible]
	29		Do	[illegible]
	30		Do	[illegible]

1875 Wt. W593/826 1,000,000 4/15 J.B.C. & A. A.D.S.S./Forms/C. 2118.

S E C R E T.

Copy No. 8....

C.R.E.'s OPERATION ORDER No. 31.

1. (a) 77th Field Coy.,R.E. and one Company of Pioneers will start at 07.00 hours tomorrow and move to BERLAIMONT.

(b) Road from T.19.d.central into BERLAIMONT will probably be required for transport tomorrow. O.C.,77th Field Coy.,R.E. will take such steps as may be necessary to prevent transport from sticking, and O.C., Pioneer Company will assist.

(c) These Companies will be prepared for work in forward area at short notice

(d) Route for transport.

CARREFOUR TAPPERIE - T.15.a.4.6. - T.29.a.3.7. - LAGRAND CARRIERE unless crater now being worked on by 78th Field Coy.,R.E. at T.23.c.45.15. is completed, when main route will be used.

2. (a) 78th Field Coy.,R.E. and one Company of Pioneers will billet in TETE-NOIR. Units now occupying TETE-NOIR will be moving about 09.00 hours and billets should be available.

(b) 78th Field Coy.,R.E. will go direct from the crater unless work is finished sufficiently early to allow of them returning to LOCQUIGNOL for the night.

3. (a) 93rd Field Coy.,R.E. and one Company of Pioneers will remain in LOCQUIGNOL until further orders. They will probably be moved forward in the course of the day.

(b) 93rd Field Coy.,R.E. will be prepared to send out two Sections (with tool carts) to complete trestle bridge over crater at T.23.c.45.15. if ordered. In this case they will start work at the site at 08.00 hours tomorrow. If this work is ordered arrangements should be made to enable these Sections to rejoin their Company in forward billets in the event of the Company moving up during the day, without returning to LOCQUIGNOL.

4. ACKNOWLEDGE.

Lieut.R.E.
for C.R.E.,17th Division.

6/11/18.

Distribution :- Copy No. 1 to 77th Field Coy.,R.E.
" " 2 " 78th Field Coy.,R.E.
" " 3 " 93rd Field Coy.,R.E.
" " 4 " 7th Bn. Y. & L.
" " 5 " 17th Division G.S.
" " 6 " 17th Division "Q".
" " 7 " C.R.E.,21st Division.
" " 8 " War Diary.
" " 9 " File.

SECRET.

Copy No. 9

C.R.E's OPERATION ORDER No. 82.

1. 77th Field Coy., R.E. will move tomorrow to BEAUFORT.

2. 78th Field Coy., R.E. will move tomorrow to LIMONT - FONTAINE or ECLAIBES.

3. 93rd Field Coy., R.E. will remain at BACHANT.

4. One Company of Pioneers will move today to BEAUFORT.

5. H.Q. and one Company of Pioneers will move tomorrow to LIMONT - FONTAINE - ECLAIBES.

6. One Company of Pioneers will remain at BACHANT.

7. Acting Town Majors have been appointed in all above villages, and billets should be obtained from them.

8. Completion of moves and new locations to be reported to this office.

9. ACKNOWLEDGE.

Lieut. R.E.
for C.R.E., 17th Division.

9/11/18.

Distribution :-

Copy No. 1 to 77th Field Coy., R.E.
" " 2 " 78th Field Coy., R.E.
" " 3 " 93rd Field Coy., R.E.
" " 4 " 7th Bn. Y. & L.
" " 5 " 17th Division G.S.
" " 6 " 17th Division "Q".
" " 7 " C.R.E., 21st Division.
" " 8 " War Diary.
" " 9 " File.

S E C R E T.

Copy No. 8....

C.R.E.'s OPERATION ORDER No. 33.

1. 17th Division (less Artillery) will be relieved by 21st Division in left Sector of V Corps front today.

2. Movements will be carried out as follows

3. 77th and 78th Field Coys., R.E. will move from BEAUFORT and LIMONT-FONTAINE respectively to BERLAIMONT, marching under orders of G.O.C., 52nd Brigade Group, to whom they will apply for orders as to starting time etc.

4. Billets will be taken over from Field Coys., R.E. of the 21st Division and billeting parties should report to this office at 10.30 hours for orders as to the Companies they are taking over from.

5. 93rd Field Coy., R.E. will remain in their present billets.

6. 7th Bn. Y. & L. will move in accordance with 17th Division Order No.32.

7. Work on bridges at present in hand by the 77th and 78th Field Coys., R.E. will be completed and if necessary small party left behind.

8. Pioneers will not work.

9. ACKNOWLEDGE.

Lieut. R.E.
for C.R.E., 17th Division.

11/11/18.

Distribution :-

Copy No. 1 to 77th Field Coy., R.E.
" " 2 " 78th Field Coy., R.E.
" " 3 " 93rd Field Coy., R.E.
" " 4 " 7th Bn. Y. & L.
" " 5 " 17th Division G.S.
" " 6 " 17th Division "Q".
" " 7 " C.R.E., 21st Division.
" " 8 " War Diary.
" " 9 " File.

S E C R E T.

Copy No. 7...

C.R.E's OPERATION ORDER No. 34.

1. The three Field Companies and the 7th Bn. Y. & L. will move to ENGLEFONTAINE tomorrow the 14th inst.

Units will leave their present billets at the following times :-

77th Field Coy.,R.E.	09.00 hours.
78th Field Coy.,R.E.	09.30 "
93rd Field Coy.,R.E.	09.30 "
7th Bn. Y. & L.	09.00 "

Route via LOCQUIGNOL, south towards LES Q.des PATURES - HECQ.

2. Move will be continued on 15th inst. to BERTRY. Further instructions will be sent as to this move.

3. A representative of the 147 Army Troops Coy.,R.E. will be at my office early tomorrow morning to take over construction of AYMERIES Bridge. A representative from the 78th Field Coy., R.E. will be at my office at 09.00 hours in order to hand over this work.

4. Os.C. Field Coy.,R.E. will personally supervise the march discipline of their units.

5. C.R.E's office will close in AULNOYE at 10.00 hours tomorrow and open in INCHY the same hour.

6. ACKNOWLEDGE.

[signature]

Capt.R.E.

13/11/18. for C.R.E.,17th Division.

Distribution :-

Copy No. 1 to O.C.,77th Field Coy.,R.E.
" " 2 " O.C.,78th Field Coy.,R.E.
" " 3 " O.C.,93rd Field Coy.,R.E.
" " 4 " O.C.,7th Bn. Y. & L.
" " 5 " 17th Division G.S.
" " 6 " 17th Division "Q".
" " 7 " War Diary.
" " 8 " File.

S E C R E T.

Copy No....7...

C.R.E's OPERATION ORDER No. 35.

1. On the 15th inst., the three Field Companies R.E. will join the Brigades to which they are ordinarily affiliated ~~xx~~ viz :

77th Field Coy., R.E.	51st Brigade.
78th Field Coy., R.E.	50th Brigade.
93rd Field Coy., R.E.	52nd Brigade.

and will leave their present billets on the above date as follows :-

	Time of starting	Destination.	
77th Field Coy., R.E.	09.00	TROISVILLES	Route via MONTAY
78th Field Coy., R.E.	09.20	BERTRY	
93rd Field Coy., R.E.	09.40	INCHY	

Billeting parties will be sent in advance to report to the Staff Captains of the respective Brigades.

2. 7th Bn. Y. & L. will leave their present billets at 10.00 hours tomorrow the 15th inst. and proceed to BERTRY, via Montay

Billeting party should be sent in advance to BERTRY to report to D.A.A.G., 17th Division at Area Commandant's Office, BERTRY at 11.00 hours.

3. 7th Bn. Y. & L. will hand over all canvas in their charge to Area Commandant, ENGLEFONTAINE and report quantity to 17th Division "A".

4. Paragraph 2 of my Operation Order No. 34 is cancelled.

5. ACKNOWLEDGE.

John Orme
Capt. R.E.
for C.R.E., 17th Division.

14/11/18.

Distribution :-

Copy No. 1 to 77th Field Coy., R.E.
" " 2 " 78th Field Coy., R.E.
" " 3 " 93rd Field Coy., R.E.
" " 4 " 7th Bn. Y. & L.
" " 5 " 17th Division G.S.
" " 6 " 17th Division "Q".
" " 7 " War Diary.
" " 8 " File.

Instructions regarding War Diaries and Intelligence Summaries are contained in F. S. Regs., Part II. and the Staff Manual respectively. Title Pages will be prepared in manuscript.

WAR DIARY
or
INTELLIGENCE SUMMARY
(Erase heading not required.)

Army Form C. 2118

CRE. 17 D

Vol 39

Place	Date 1918 DEC	Hour	Summary of Events and Information	Remarks and references to Appendices
INCHY	1		C.R.E. visited 77 & 78 Field Coys R.E.	
	2		C.R.E. went to HALLENCOURT to reconnoitre new area for Division. C.R.E's Hd Qrs remained at INCHY.	
	3.		Transport of 3 Field Coys started a staging march to the new area.	
	4.		17 Division was inspected by H.M. the King.	
	5		Field Coys prepared for move to new area	
HALLENCOURT	6.		C.R.E's Hd Qrs moved to Hallencourt. Field Coys entrained for new area.	
	7.		Field Coys including transport arrived in new area	
	8.		Field Coys engaged on making accommodation for the Division, erecting huts etc	
	9–14		Do. Do. Do. Do.	
	15		C.R.E. conferred with C.E. 5th Corps	
	16–20		Do. Do. Do. Do.	

A.D.S.S./Forms/C. 2118.

Army Form C. 2118

Instructions regarding War Diaries and Intelligence Summaries are contained in F. S. Regs., Part II. and the Staff Manual respectively. Title Pages will be prepared in manuscript.

WAR DIARY
or
INTELLIGENCE SUMMARY
(Erase heading not required.)

Place	Date 1918 DEC R	Hour	Summary of Events and Information	Remarks and references to Appendices
HALLENCOURT	21		Field Coys engaged in making accomodation for Division building Huts etc	[illegible]
	22		Do Do Do	[illegible]
	23		Do Do Do	[illegible]
	24		Do Do Do	[illegible]
	25		Christmas Day. C.R.E visited Field Coys	[illegible]
	26		Field Coys engaged as before making accomodation for Division	[illegible]
	27		Do Do	[illegible]
	28		Do Do	[illegible]
	29		Do Do	[illegible]
	30		do do	[illegible]
	31		do do	[illegible]

[illegible] Lieut R.E.
for CRE 17th Division.

1875 Wt. W593/826 1,000,000 4/15 J.B.C. & A. A.D.S.S./Forms/C. 2118.

77th Field Co. R.E.
78th Field Co. R.E.
93rd Field Co. R.E.
17th Division 'G' (for information)
17th Division 'Q' (" ")

Reference my Operation Order No.78 as amended by 4012 and reference 17th Divn: Administrative Instruction, all of 3.12.18.

1. Train leaves CAUDRY at 10.00 hours on the 6th inst.

2. Attention is called to para. 3 of above A.I. which must be strictly adhered to.

3. The 3 Field Coys will de-train at AMIENS on the night of the 6th and will be billeted for the night in some village West of AMIENS. A representative from my office will meet the train at AMIENS and conduct the Coys to these billets. Two lorries have been detailed to await the arrival of the Field Coys at AMIENS to convey blankets, cooking gear, etc., to final destinations of the respective Companies.

4. The Field Coys will march to their destinations, on 7th inst. viz :-

77th Field Co. R.E. to BAILLEUL
78th " " " " HALLENCOURT
93rd Field Co. R.E. to AIRAINES

5. Reference para. 3 of above Operation Order. A lorry will report to the 77th Field Co on the afternoon of the 5th inst. and after loading with tools, etc., will report to 78th Field Co for a similar purpose. Lorry will then park for the night with 78th Field Co. On following morning it will be loaded with this Coy's spare blankets, etc., and will report to 77th Field Co by 08.30 hours. After being loaded here the lorry will return to my Headquarters.

Another lorry will report to 93rd Field Co on the afternoon of the 5th inst. to be loaded in the same manner and returned to my Headquarters in the early morning of the 6th inst.

It is pointed out that each Field Co is only entitled to half of a lorry and they must not be over-loaded.

A representative from each Field Co will accompany the lorries and care must be taken that the baggage of each Company is kept separate.

6. Reference para. 4 of above Operation Order. A G.S. Wagon has been detailed to report to H.Q. of each Field Co. to take cooking gear, fuel, etc., to CAUDRY Station.

The G.S. Wagon reporting to 93rd Field Co. should report to my H.Q. after 93rd Field Co. have loaded, in order to take cooking gear, etc., of H.Q.R.E. personnel.

Captain R.E.,
for C.R.E. 17th Division.

4th Dec: 1918.

O.C. 77th Field Co. R.E.
O.C. 78th Field Co. R.E.
O.C. 93rd Field Co. R.E.
17th Division G.S.
17th Division Q.

COMMANDING ROYAL ENGINEER
No. 4912
Date.........
17th DIVISION

Reference my Operation Order No.36 of today's date.
Please make the following amendments :-

Para.2 For 4th inst: read 6th inst:
Para.4 " " " " " "
Para.5 " " " " " "
Para.6 " 4th, 5th and 6th insts: read 6th, 7th and 8th insts:

Field Coys., less Transport, will entrain at CAUDRY at 10.00 hours on the 6th inst: 17th Division 'Q' will arrange for the delivery of rations to units between 3rd and 6th insts: Captain Reid (93rd Field Co.) will assume command of personnel of Field Coys. proceeding by rail.

Sick should report to nearest Field Ambulance.

Field Companies will take part in His Majesty's Inspection on the 5th December, 1918.

[signature]
Capt: R.E.,
for C.R.E. 17th Division.

2nd Dec: 1918.

S E C R E T.

Copy No. 6

C. R. E's OPERATION ORDER No.36.

1. The three Field Coys. will move as follows on the 3rd and 4th instants :-

(a) The Transport and cyclists of three Field Coys. to proceed by road on the 3rd inst:, under the command of Major W.H.BUDGETT, O.C. 93rd Field Coy., in accordance with attached schedule.

(b) Two Officers from each Coy. will accompany the Transport.

(c) A billeting party should be sent forward each day to arrange billets.

(d) Major Budgett will issue orders direct to 77th and 78th Field Coys. as to rendezvous, time of starting, etc.

(e) A lorry will accompany the Transport with rations and forage.

2. The three Field Coys., less Transport, will proceed by rail on the 4th inst: under the command of Major J.A. WARBURTON, O.C. 78th Field Coy., who will issue orders direct to Companies.

Each man will carry a blanket.

3. Further particulars as to this move will be notified later.

4. A G.S. Wagon will report to each of the Field Coys. to take small kit and a certain proportion of cooking gear ~~to~~ & fuel to the station on the 4th inst.

Only a very limited amount of kit can be taken.

5. Two lorries will report ~~to each~~ of the Field Coys. in turn on the afternoon of the 4th inst: There will be room on these lorries for a limited supply of :-

(1) Such tools as are considered requisite for the erection of hutting.

(2) A small quantity of cooking gear.

(3) Officers' kits.

(4) Extra blankets.

Nothing more than is absolutely requisite should be loaded on these lorries.

6. Companies will entrain with rations for 4th, 5th and 6th instants. They should deal direct with their respective Train Coys. on this matter.

7. Only 10 minutes will be allowed in which to de-train.

8. ACKNOWLEDGE.

[signature]

Capt: R.E.

2nd December, 1918. for C.R.E. 17th Division.

Distribution:-

Copy No. 1 to 77th Field Co. R.E.
" " 2 " 78th " " "
" " 3 " 93rd " " "
" " 4 " 17th Division G.S.
" " 5 " " Q.
✓ " " 6 " War Diary,
" " 7 " File File.

MARCH ROUTE.

DAY & DATE	ROUTE	DESTINATION	BILLETS.
TUESDAY 3rd Dec:	Via LIGNY and ESNES	Les Rue Les VIGNES (S.W. of CREVECOEUR)	To be notified later.
WEDNESDAY 4th Dec:	Via GOUZEAUCOURT.	MANANCOURT	Arrange with Town Major.
THURSDAY 5th Dec:	Via Les MESNIL - COMBLES - MONTAUBAN and FRICOURT.	MEAULTE	Encampment (on road East of River ANCRE) midway between DERNANCOURT and ALBERT.
FRIDAY 6th Dec:	Via ALBERT - AMIENS main road.	PONT NOYELLES	Arrange with Area Commandant.
SATURDAY 7th Dec:	Via Northern outskirts of AMIENS and South bank of River SOMME through AILLY.	PICQUIGNY	Arrange with Area Commandant.
SUNDAY 8th Dec:	Via AIRAINES - HALLENCOURT.	77th Fld. Co. BAILLEUL 78th Fld. Co. HALLENCOURT 93rd Fld. Co. AIRAINES	Arrange with Area Commandant.

Army Form C. 2118.

17

WAR DIARY
or
INTELLIGENCE SUMMARY.
(Erase heading not required.)

Instructions regarding War Diaries and Intelligence Summaries are contained in F. S. Regs., Part II. and the Staff Manual respectively. Title pages will be prepared in manuscript.

CRE

40

Place	Date	Hour	Summary of Events and Information	Remarks and references to Appendices
HALLENCOURT	1		a/CRE visited works	[illegible]
	2		– do –	[illegible]
	3		– do –	[illegible]
	4		– do –	[illegible]
	5		– do –	[illegible]
	6		– do –	[illegible]
	7		– do –	[illegible]
	8		– do –	[illegible]
	9		– do –	[illegible]
	10		– do –	[illegible]
	11		– do – a/Capt J. Bone R.E. T.F. quitted Div. for DEMOBILIZATION	[illegible]
	12		– do – Lieut E. G. MORRIS DCM R.E. appointed Adjt & assumed duties	[illegible]
	13		– do –	[illegible]
	14		– do –	[illegible]
	15		– do –	[illegible]
	16		– do –	[illegible]
	17		– do –	[illegible]
	18		– do – a/Lt. Col. F.A. FERGUSON DSO R.E. rejoined unit from U.K.	[illegible]
	19		– do – Major A.C. MITCHELL R.E. T.F. – " – 77 F. Coy R.E. on handing over duties of a/CRE.	[illegible]
	20		– do –	[illegible]
	21		– do –	[illegible]
	22		– do –	[illegible]
	23		– do –	[illegible]
	24		– do –	[illegible]
	25		– do –	[illegible]
	26		– do –	[illegible]
	27		– do –	[illegible]
	28		– do –	[illegible]
	29		– do –	[illegible]
	30		– do –	[illegible]
	31		– do –	[illegible]

1/2/19

E G Morris Lieut R.E.
for Lt. Col. R.E.
C.R.E. 17 Div.

(A7092). Wt. W12839/M1293. 75,000. 1/17. H. D. & L., Ltd. Forms/C.2118/14.

Instructions regarding War Diaries and Intelligence Summaries are contained in F. S. Regs., Part II. and the Staff Manual respectively. Title pages will be prepared in manuscript.

WAR DIARY
or
INTELLIGENCE SUMMARY.
(Erase heading not required.)

Army Form C. 2118.

C.R.E. 17th Divn

Vol 41

Place	Date	Hour	Summary of Events and Information	Remarks and references to Appendices
HALLENCOURT	1st		CRE visited work in progress	[illegible]
	2nd		CRE visited ~~CRE~~ CRE 2nd Division Sunday no work.	[illegible]
	3rd		CRE visited work in progress + 93rd 78 Coy	[illegible]
	4th		— do —	[illegible]
	5th		~~CRE p~~ — do —	[illegible]
	6th		CRE proceeded to ENGLAND to attend conference on the ~~re~~formation of post bellum Army	[illegible]
	7th		a/CRE visited work	[illegible]
	8th		— do —	[illegible]
	9th		a/CRE visited C.E. Vth Corps i-open Sunday no work.	[illegible]
	10th		CRE rejoined from ENGLAND	[illegible]
	11th		CRE at HALLENCOURT.	[illegible]
	12th		— do —	[illegible]
	13th		CRE visited work in progress	[illegible]
	14th		— do —	[illegible]
	15th		— do —	[illegible]
	16th		Sunday no work.	[illegible]
	17th		CRE visited work in progress	[illegible]
	18th		— do —	[illegible]
	19		CRE visited LONGPRE CADRE Park	[illegible]
	20		— do —	[illegible]
	21		— do —	[illegible]
	22		CRE at HALLENCOURT	[illegible]
	23		Sunday no work.	[illegible]
	24		CRE visited LE QUESNOY	[illegible]
	25		CRE visited LONGPRE CADRE Park.	[illegible]
	26		— do —	[illegible]
	27		CRE visited work in progress	[illegible]
	28		— do —	[illegible]

1/3/19

[illegible] Capt. & Adjt.
17 Div Engrs.

(A7092). Wt. W12839/M1293. 75,0.0. 1/17. D. D. & L., Ltd. Forms/C.2118/14.

MARCH 1919.

Instructions regarding War Diaries and Intelligence Summaries are contained in F. S. Regs., Part II. and the Staff Manual respectively. Title pages will be prepared in manuscript.

WAR DIARY
or
INTELLIGENCE SUMMARY.
(Erase heading not required.)

CRE 17th DIVISION

Army Form C. 2118.

Vol 42

Place	Date	Hour	Summary of Events and Information	Remarks and references to Appendices
HALLENCOURT	1st		CRE visited CHOREPARK LONGPRE	[illegible]
	2nd		Sunday no work	[illegible]
	3rd		CRE visited work in progress Clearing of RE Stores from units to Central	[illegible]
	4th		– do – dump at HANGEST commenced –	[illegible]
	5th		– do –	[illegible]
	6th		– do –	[illegible]
	7th		– do –	[illegible]
	8th		– do –	[illegible]
	9th		Sunday no work	[illegible]
	10th		CRE visited work in progress	
	11th		– do –	[illegible]
	12th		– do –	[illegible]
	13th		– do – 78th Coy RE moved to HANGEST	[illegible]
	14th		– do – 93rd " " – do –	[illegible]
	15th		– do –	[illegible]
	16th		Sunday no work	[illegible]
	17th		CRE visited work in progress & inspected Coy billets at HANGEST	[illegible]
	18th		– do –	[illegible]
	19		– do –	[illegible]
	20		– do –	[illegible]
	21st		– do –	[illegible]

(A7092). Wt. W12839/M1293. 750,000. 1/17. D. D. & L., Ltd. Forms/C.2118/14.

Instructions regarding War Diaries and Intelligence Summaries are contained in F. S. Regs., Part II. and the Staff Manual respectively. Title pages will be prepared in manuscript.

MARCH 1919

WAR DIARY
or
INTELLIGENCE SUMMARY.
(Erase heading not required.)

Army Form C. 2118.

C.R.E. 17th Division

Place	Date	Hour	Summary of Events and Information	Remarks and references to Appendices
	22		C.R.E. visits Co. at HANGEST	[illegible]
	23		Sunday no work	[illegible]
	24		C.R.E. proceeds to ENGLAND on leave MAJOR A.C. MITCHELL R.E. a/C.R.E.	[illegible]
	25		a/C.R.E. visits work at LONGPRE	a.c.m
	26		a/C.R.E. visits work in progress	a.c.m
	27		— do —	a.c.m
	28		— do —	a.c.m
	29		— do —	a.c.m
	30		Sunday. a/C.R.E. visits work in progress. CAPTAIN E.G. MORRIS D.C.M. R.E. vacates appointment of Adjutant and proceeds to FLIXICOURT as Adjutant C.R.E. III Army Area Troops	a.c.m
	31.		a/C.R.E. inspects works in neighbourhood	a.c.m

(A7092). Wt W12839/M1293. 75,0.0. 1/17. D. D. & L., Ltd. Forms/C.2118/14.

Instructions regarding War Diaries and Intelligence Summaries are contained in F. S. Regs., Part II. and the Staff Manual respectively. Title pages will be prepared in manuscript.

12

WAR DIARY

~~or~~

~~INTELLIGENCE SUMMARY.~~

(Erase heading not required.)

Army Form C. 2118.

C.R.E 17 DIVISION

APRIL 1919

Vol 43

Place	Date	Hour	Summary of Events and Information	Remarks and references to Appendices
HALLENCOURT	1.4.19		MAJOR A.C. MITCHELL O.C. 77 FIELD Co. R.E. acting C.R.E. visits Companies at HANGEST and BOURDON	a.c.h.
	2.4.19		C.R.E. visits detachment of 77 FIELD Co. at BRAY-LES-MAREUILS	a.c.h.
	3.4.19		C.R.E. visits LONGPRE - 93 FIELD Co. R.E. entrains at LONGPRE and proceeds under the command of MAJOR R. St. C. REID. R.E. to join VI DIVISION.	a.c.h.
				a.c.h.
	4.4.19		C.R.E. inspects hutting sites in former 52nd BRIGADE area.	a.c.h.
	5.4.19		C.R.E. inspects hutting sites in former 50th BRIGADE area.	a.c.h.
	6.4.19		C.R.E. visits Companies in HANGEST.	a.c.h.
	7.4.19		C.R.E. inspects hutting sites in former 51st BRIGADE area.	a.c.h.
	8.4.19		C.R.E. visits work at HEUCOURT + WARLUS also inspects damage at WOIREL.	a.c.h.
	9.4.19		Work on claims in Divisional area	a.c.h.
	10.4.19		" " "	a.c.h.
	11.4.19		" " " " " C.R.E. visits companies at HANGEST.	a.c.h.
	12.4.19		" " " " " C.R.E. inspects claims.	a.c.h.
	13.4.19		" " " " "	a.c.h.
	14.4.19		" " " " "	a.c.h.
LONGPRÉ	15.4.19		D.H.Q. moves to LONGPRE + H.Q. R.E. installed there. Work on claims continued.	a.c.h.
	16.4.19		Work on claims in Divisional area.	a.c.h.
	17.4.19		" " " " " Checking stores.	a.c.h.
	18.4.19		Checking stores + clearing area.	a.c.h.
	19.4.19		Clearing area.	a.c.h.
	20.4.19		— —	a.c.h.
	21.4.19		C.R.E. visits companies at HANGEST.	a.c.h.
	22.4.19		Clearing area.	a.c.h.
	23.4.19		78 Field Co. R.E. entrains at LONGPRÉ and proceeds for England under command of Lieut. P.W. MILLER R.E.	a.c.h.
	24.4.19		77 Field Co. R.E. moves into LONGPRE	a.c.h.
	25.4.19		Clearing area.	a.c.h.
	26.4.19		C.R.E. visits LE QUESNOY.	a.c.h.
	27.4.19		— —	a.c.h.
	28.4.19		Ordnance Board checking A.F. G1098 and unserviceable stores of H.Q. R.E.	a.c.h.
	29.4.19		Clearing area	a.c.h.
	30.4.19		Clearing area	a.c.h.

A.C. Mitchell Major R.E.
a. C.R.E. 17 Div.

(A7092). Wt. W12839/M1293. 75 ,0.0. 1/17. D. D. & L., Ltd. Forms/C.2118/14.

17

Army Form C. 2118.

WAR DIARY

~~or~~

~~INTELLIGENCE SUMMARY.~~

(Erase heading not required.)

Instructions regarding War Diaries and Intelligence Summaries are contained in F. S. Regs., Part II. and the Staff Manual respectively. Title pages will be prepared in manuscript.

C.R.E. 17 DIVISION.

MAY 1919.

Place	Date	Hour	Summary of Events and Information	Remarks and references to Appendices
LONGPRÉ	1.5.19		Work on clearing of Area.	a.c.h.
SOMME	2.5.19		H.Q.R.E. entrained for England. As no officer of H.Q.R.E. proceeded with the Cadre no further War Diary is kept for C.R.E. 17 Division. The work of Acting C.R.E. is absorbed into the War Diary of 77 FIELD. Co. R.E. from this date.	a.c.h.

A. C. Mitchell Major R.E.
a C.R.E. 17 Division.

www.ingramcontent.com/pod-product-compliance
Lightning Source LLC
Chambersburg PA
CBHW080907230426
43664CB00016B/2748